Chalice Introduction
to the
Old Testament

Marti J. Steussy, editor

CHALICE
PRESS

ST. LOUIS, MISSOURI

Cover art: Detail from Sistine Chapel lunette with Ruth and Obed by Michelangelo. Photo © Nippon Television Network Corporation, Tokyo.
Cover design: Mike Foley
Interior design: Elizabeth Wright
Art direction: Michael Domínguez

Visit Chalice Press on the World Wide Web at
www.chalicepress.com

10 9 8 7 6 5 4 3   09   10   11   12   13   14

Library of Congress Cataloging–in–Publication Data

Chalice introduction to the Old Testament / edited by Marti J. Steussy.
    p. cm.
Includes bibliographical references and index.
  ISBN 978-0-827204-88-1 (alk. paper)
  1. Bible. O.T.—Introductions. I. Title: Introduction to the Old Testament. II. Steussy, Marti J., 1955-
  BS1140.3.C48 2003
  221.6'1—dc22

                                                                2003015232

Printed in the United States of America

Chalice Introduction
to the
Old Testament

Contents

List of Contributors

JON L. BERQUIST (chapter 10, Jeremiah and Ezekiel), with a Ph.D. from Vanderbilt University, is senior academic editor at Chalice Press. He is the author of several books, including *Judaism in Persia's Shadow: A Social and Historical Approach* (Fortress Press), *Incarnation* (Chalice Press), and *Controlling Corporeality: The Family and the Household in Ancient Israel* (Rutgers University Press). He is an avid dog lover and lives in rural New Jersey.

CLAUDIA V. CAMP (chapter 14, Job) holds a Ph.D. from Duke University and is professor of religion at Texas Christian University, where she has taught since 1980. Her research interests are in the areas of biblical wisdom literature, feminist interpretation, methodological issues, and canon formation. Her most recent book is *Wise, Strange and Holy: The Strange Woman and the Making of the Bible* (Sheffield Academic Press, 2000), and she is currently working on the book of Ben Sira as representative of the process of canon formation.

LISA W. DAVISON (chapter 7, Samuel and Kings) received her Ph.D. from Vanderbilt University and teaches at Lexington Theological Seminary. She has a passion for the study of women in the First Testament and is committed to educating others about the misuse of the First Testament by Christianity.

FRANK H. GORMAN, JR., (chapter 4, Exodus, Leviticus, and Numbers) holds a Ph.D. from Emory University and occupies the T. W. Phillips Chair of Religious Studies at Bethany College in West Virginia. His academic interests include creation theology, ritual studies, the Bible and culture, and Pentateuchal theology.

LOWELL K. HANDY (chapter 2, Geographical and Historical Background; chapter 15, Other Writings) holds a Ph.D. from the Divinity School at the University of Chicago and works for the American Theological Library Association. His research interests are historical and include the religion of ancient Judah and Israel, biblical historiography, and Josiah studies.

WALTER HARRELSON (chapter 16, the Apocrypha) is Professor Emeritus of the Vanderbilt University Divinity School and an adjunct professor at Wake Forest University Divinity School. He did his Th.D. work at Union Theological Seminary in New York City under the direction of James Muilenburg. He is particularly interested in the life, thought, and worship of Second Temple Judaism and of early Christianity. He is also a long-time member of the Christian Scholars Group on Jewish-Christian Relations (Boston College) and of the Church Relations Committee of the U.S. Holocaust Memorial Museum.

CAROLYN HIGGINBOTHAM (chapter 6, Joshua and Judges) holds a Ph.D. from Johns Hopkins and is now academic dean and professor of Hebrew Bible at Christian Theological Seminary in Indianapolis. She has conducted archaeological field work in the Middle East and has a special interest in the relationships of Egypt and Palestine in ancient times.

RICHARD H. LOWERY (chapter 3, Genesis) received his Ph.D. from Yale and teaches at Phillips Theological Seminary in Tulsa, Oklahoma. He is particularly interested in the interface between the Bible and contemporary justice and human rights issues.

SAMUEL PAGÁN (chapter 8, Ezra, Nehemiah, and Chronicles) holds doctorates from Jewish Theological Seminary in New York and the South Florida Center for Theological Studies. He is currently president and professor of Bible at the Evangelical Seminary of Puerto Rico. He is particularly interested in educating pastors and scholars whose theology will be sensitive to both local context and global issues.

DALE PATRICK (chapter 5, Deuteronomy) holds a Th.D. from the San Francisco Theological Seminary/Graduate Theological Union and teaches at Drake University. His research and writing have focused especially on the topics of Job, biblical law, and biblical theology.

LEO G. PERDUE (chapter 13, Proverbs and Ecclesiastes) holds a Ph.D. from Vanderbilt University and is currently professor of Hebrew Bible at Brite Divinity School, Texas Christian University. A well-known scholar of the Hebrew Bible's wisdom literature, Dr. Perdue is also deeply engaged with the enterprise of biblical theology and will be active as both editor and author in Abingdon's Library of Biblical Theology series.

RAYMOND F. PERSON, JR. (chapter 11, The Book of the Twelve) received his Ph.D. in Hebrew Bible and Semitic Studies from Duke University and teaches at Ohio Northern University. His research focuses on ways in which conversation analysis and the study of oral traditions can inform our study of the Bible and especially its prophetic literature.

MARTI J. STEUSSY (chapter 1, Introduction; chapter 7, Samuel and Kings; chapter 12, Psalms) holds a Ph.D. from Vanderbilt University and is MacAllister-Petticrew Professor of Biblical Interpretation at Christian Theological Seminary in Indianapolis. Her biblical areas of interest include the David stories, Psalms, Job, and creation traditions. Her theological interests include religion/science dialogue, animal issues, environmental ethics, and storytelling.

MARY DONOVAN TURNER (chapter 9, Isaiah) received her Ph.D. from Emory University and is now Carl Patton Associate Professor of Preaching at the Pacific School of Religion in Berkeley, California. Within her general fields of Hebrew Bible and preaching, she is particularly interested in the issue of women's voice and proclamation. She recently served one year as interim minister in a northern California congregation, an experience that raised new and challenging questions about the varied and complex dimensions of ministry.

Introduction

MARTI J. STEUSSY

Why Study the Old Testament?

Welcome to the study of the Old Testament! But why? Why study a complex collection of books written more than two thousand years ago?

To most Jews and Christians, the answer is obvious: because these books are, according to Judaism and Christianity, "Holy Scripture." Persons who hold this view of the Bible naturally approach it with a particular interest in what it says about God and God's relationships with and expectations of human worshipers. We should note, however, that such persons may vary a good deal in exactly how they understand God's role in the development of the scriptures—some assume that God chose each individual word, whereas others think more in terms of testimonies, from persons belonging to particular times and cultures, about their encounters with God. In addition, believers read the Bible under the influence of centuries of religious tradition and reflection. For example, most take it as given that God knows everything, including the future, and they interpret God's actions in biblical narratives with this assumption in mind, although such details as the comment, after Abraham's near-sacrifice of Isaac, that "*now I know* that you fear God" (Gen. 22:12, italics added) might suggest that God was not sure what Abraham would do. As another example, Jewish readers typically interpret God's deliverance of the Hebrews from Egypt as an act of faithfulness toward the descendants of Abraham, Isaac, and Jacob, whereas Christian readers more often categorize it as an instance of God's care for the oppressed (for more on Jewish and Christian interpretation, see the book by Greeley and Neusner in the Resources section at the end of this chapter). Because of their varying assumptions and traditions, religious readers come to a variety of conclusions about what the Bible teaches.

Whether or not one acknowledges the Bible as an authoritative religious document, one might be interested in it as a classic of world literature, testifying to *human* nature's better and worse potentials. Believers and nonbelievers alike have been fascinated by the family relationships portrayed in Genesis and poetic visions of swords beaten into plowshares (Isa. 2:4 and Mic. 4:3). King David's crimes of adultery and murder (2 Sam. 11) resonate all too clearly with our own experiences of loved and trusted leaders who succumb to the temptations of power. Biblical psalms reflect the depths of anger, bitterness, and alienation (see Psalm 88) and also moments of deep peace (see Psalms 23 and 131) and exuberant awe (see Psalm 8). Literary readers typically experience the Bible less as a voice from long ago and far away than as an encounter with characters whose yearnings and fears resonate with our own.

Still others study the Old Testament for historical reasons. Some focus on the history and culture that it tells about and arises from, the ancient Near East in the thousand years preceding imperial Rome. Others are more interested in its influence on subsequent centuries of Jewish, Christian, and Muslim history. Medieval European paintings and Shakespeare's plays, for instance, are rife with First Testament motifs. Although study of the Bible's later impact is relatively noncontroversial, examination of its relationship to ancient Near Eastern history and culture has prompted a great deal of argument. Those who assume that biblical religion was utterly unlike the ancient world's pagan religions seldom want to hear about the parallels between Israel's culture (including religion) and that of Israel's neighbors, and those who take biblical narratives as straightforward historical reports find it quite alarming when scholars question the historical accuracy of beloved stories such as those of the first couple in Eden, Abraham's family, the exodus, Joshua's conquest of Jericho, David's empire, or Jonah's adventures with the big fish and the evil city of Nineveh.

Are religious, literary, and historical approaches to the Hebrew Bible simply incompatible, then? Let us begin with the two "secular" approaches, literary and historical. These approaches do differ in the kinds of observations they yield about the Bible. Literary readers usually interpret the story *as told* (taking, for instance, Exodus 2's story of baby Moses in the basket as a "given" for understanding what follows). Historical inquirers, meanwhile, often separate layers within the text and ask what traditions and events might account for the observed layering (noting, for instance, the impracticality of Pharaoh's behavior in Exodus 1 and 2 and the appearance of the basket motif elsewhere in the ancient world and concluding that the basket story is probably a folk motif that became attached to Moses' story long after Moses' own lifetime). Also, literary readings often emphasize features compatible with our own experiences and understandings (for instance, the assumption that God should be praised when good things happen), whereas historical approaches tend to highlight what is different and strange (the expression of praise by blood sacrifice). But in principle the approaches do not conflict: There is no reason why the books cannot be understood as at once arising out of and illustrating their particular cultures and also artfully portraying enduring impulses of human nature. Furthermore, because religion is part of history and a deep-seated feature of human existence, both literary and historical scholars may be quite interested in what the Bible says about God.

From the religious side, responses to literary and historical studies have been varied. Some believers find it offensive to speak of reading the Bible as literature, because this seems to put the Bible on a level with other literary classics and may also be taken to suggest that it is fiction. Also, religious readers usually expect God's character to be consistent throughout the Bible (or at least within each testament), whereas many literary readers feel that different passages offer different characterizations of God. On the positive side, the literary critic's emphasis on exact wording and interpretation of the story as told (not as historically reconstructed) dovetails well with types of religious approaches that emphasize the Bible's exact wording.

For those religious readers who look for God's involvement more in actual events than in the words used to tell about them (in other words, for religious readers who think more in terms of events than words), the tensions may be greater. Literary focus on details of wording may seem picayune, and historians' arguments about divergences between events and biblical assertions may seem to strike at the very validity of faith. Yet other history-oriented religious readers are not bothered by the idea that the accounts of biblical events may show evidence of the same interpretive embroidering and intermixing of legend that we find in other histories from the ancient world. They ask, Why can't God work through storytellers as surely as through floods and earthquakes?

What to Expect in the Chapters of This Book

One of the difficulties of writing an introductory Bible textbook is that massive scholarly discussion surrounds each portion of the biblical writings. No one scholar can be up-to-date on all the discussions even within a single testament. This book therefore incorporates contributions from a number of scholars, each having a special interest in the books about which he or she is writing. All the contributors are academically trained biblical scholars associated with the Christian Church (Disciples of Christ), an ecumenically oriented Protestant denomination that has historically welcomed the application of scholarly tools to the biblical text. As participants in a Christian tradition, all contributors have an interest in what the Bible says about God and how it is appropriated by faith communities, although they do *not* assume that every reader of this book belongs to such a faith community. All seek to honor the validity of Judaism's relationship to the Hebrew Bible, while also claiming the books as spiritually relevant for Christians. Each, as a historically trained scholar, is committed to reading the Bible in a way that takes account of the texts' ancient contexts. Each also has an interest in the literary qualities of the completed biblical books that he or she writes about. Thus, each writer seeks to be sensitive to religious, literary, *and* historical interests.

Within this broad framework of similarity, individual authors vary in their emphases. These differences of approach are dictated in part by the character of the biblical materials and in part by the particular interests of the modern authors. So, for instance, the chapter on Joshua and Judges attends rather strongly to historical questions, partly because such questions have dominated scholarly discussion about these two books and partly because the author is an archaeologist with particular interest in historical issues. By contrast, the Isaiah chapter focuses on literary themes and motifs uniting the three major portions of Isaiah (which are generally thought to have come from at least three different authors). This again reflects both the character of current scholarly conversation about the book and particular interests of the writer, who is a preaching professor and theologian as well as a biblical scholar. Chapter 11, on the Book of the Twelve (that is, the collection of twelve short prophetic books running from Hosea to Malachi), takes yet a different direction. It focuses not so much on the events of which the text speaks, nor on the present forms of individual books, but on the process of growth that these prophetic writings seem to have undergone within the individual books and in their ordering as a unified, twelve-part work.

Because of these different concerns and emphases, not every chapter follows exactly the same outline. In each chapter, however, you can expect to find information about prevailing scholarly opinion on the date, authorship, and historical context of the book or books being discussed, the literary contours of the material, and key theological ideas. At the end of each chapter you will find a short list of English-language sources for further reading. Within the chapters, these additional resources are referred to by the author's name and, where appropriate, specific page numbers.

Ordering the Books of the Hebrew Bible

To explain why this book is arranged as it is, I need to say a word about an issue of special concern to biblical scholars: the relationship of biblical materials to the historical contexts in which they were *written* (or edited). Without thinking, we often assume that books describing very ancient events (such as Genesis, which tells about events from creation through the time of Abraham's great-grandson Joseph) must be older than those that describe later events (such as 1 and 2 Samuel, which tell about the establishment of kingship in Israel several centuries after Joseph's time). But a moment's thought will show that this is not necessarily true. A book about dinosaurs is not necessarily older than one about the Roman Empire. The situation gets even more complicated because some biblical books appear to have been assembled over long periods (centuries), so a single book such as Isaiah may be related to multiple historical contexts.

Why should we care about when a book was written? We should care because it often illuminates the themes and concerns of the book. Again, we can draw a modern comparison. A biography of George Washington written during the U.S. bombing of Iraq might well emphasize Washington's opinion that the United States should stay out of conflicts on other continents. Another author writing at the same time on the subject of George Washington might argue that without assistance from other nations such as France, Americans would never have been able to throw off the perceived tyranny of Great Britain. In each case, the author's telling of Washington's story would likely reflect something of the author's view on American military action in the Middle East in the author's own time. In a similar way, the recurrent themes of exile and God's promise of land in Genesis probably reflect the importance of those themes for the community that gave Genesis its present form.

This means that most of our chapter authors refer not only to the periods about which their books tell but also to the issues of the periods in which the books took shape—sometimes centuries removed! This can be confusing to students as they try to figure out the relationships between the order in which events are supposed to have actually happened, the order in which various writings were composed, and the order in which books appear in printed Bibles.

The events being *told about* begin with creation. Next come family stories of Israel's ancestors, then God's deliverance of Israel from Egypt (in the 1200s B.C.E.) and the making of a covenant between God and the people in the wilderness. After a period of wilderness wandering, the Israelite tribes settle in Canaan and eventually (around 1000) decide that they need a king. Three generations later, the kingdom splits into two parts. The larger, richer northern part, named Israel, is conquered in 722 or 721 by Assyria, an ancient superpower with its capital in Mesopotamia (the area between the Tigris and Euphrates rivers, where modern Iraq lies). The smaller Southern Kingdom, Judah, with Jerusalem as its capital and descendants of David as its kings, lasts about a century and a half beyond the fall of Israel, but eventually falls (in 587 or 586) to a new Mesopotamian superpower headquartered in Babylon. The Babylonians carry Judah's political and religious leaders off into exile. About fifty years later, a Persian king defeats Babylon and sends some of the exiled Judean leaders back to Jerusalem to head up a temple-centered colonial government. Alexander the Great eventually absorbs this territory into a new Greek-dominated empire (331). In the second and first centuries before Christ, Judea enjoys a period of independence (167–37 B.C.E.) from Alexander's successors. Then it becomes part of the Roman Empire.

The story of *composition* begins at the time of the exodus or even earlier, with poems and legends handed down by word of mouth. In the period of the kings, court records, speeches of prophets, temple prayers, poems, stories, and perhaps some legal codes are written down. In the last decades of the Southern Kingdom (Judah) and after its fall, these pieces are assembled into something like the present form of Genesis through 2 Kings. During the period of temple-centered colonial government following the exile, the books of the Torah ("teaching," Genesis through Deuteronomy) come to be recognized as having a very special religious importance, but a clearly defined "canon" (collection of authoritative writings) has not yet emerged. Religious books are still being written up to and beyond the time of Jesus. There is disagreement between Jews and Christians, and between different groups of Christians, about which of these later writings (many of which are discussed in chapter 16 of this book) should be regarded as authoritative.

To the extent that various parts of the First Testament reflect concerns and beliefs of their *writers'* times as much as or more than the concerns of the times being written *about,* one might conceivably want to study them in the order in which they were *written.* Some introductory Bible textbooks do adopt this approach (one example is the textbook by Humphreys, listed in the bibliography at the end of this chapter). There are two problems with this approach. First, there is lively debate over the dating of many biblical writings—we can make well-educated guesses, but we aren't absolutely certain that these are correct. (In the chapters of this book, you will be given the reasons why scholars date the various books as they do and also be told about some of the more important controversies.) Second, jumping from text to text according to the estimated dates of *telling* makes it hard to get a sense of the time line of the story being *told,* especially in books such as Genesis through Numbers, where story threads from several different tellers at different dates seem to be intertwined, sometimes within individual chapters.

So why not arrange the materials according to the time line of the events that they tell *about?* Part of the traditional Jewish ordering of the books (shown in the left column of the table below) does this. Together, the books of the Torah and Former Prophets tell a sequential story running from creation to Babylonian exile. The Major Prophets (Isaiah, Jeremiah, and Ezekiel) are also arranged in roughly historical sequence, except that this sequence overlaps the one in Genesis through 2 Kings. The short books

Jewish and Western Christian Canon Arrangements

JEWISH CANON	CHRISTIAN CANONS*
Torah ("Law" or Teaching) Genesis, Exodus, Leviticus, Numbers, Deuteronomy	**Historical Books** Genesis, Exodus, Leviticus, Numbers, Deuteronomy
Prophets **Former Prophets** Joshua, Judges, 1 & 2 Samuel, 1 & 2 Kings **Latter Prophets** *Major Prophets* Isaiah, Jeremiah, Ezekiel *Minor Prophets* Hosea, Joel, Amos, Obadiah, Jonah, Micah, Nahum, Habakkuk, Zephaniah, Haggai, Zechariah, Malachi	Joshua, Judges, Ruth, 1 & 2 Samuel, 1 & 2 Kings, 1 & 2 Chronicles (*1 Esdras*), Ezra, Nehemiah, Esther (or longer version of Esther, Judith, Tobit, 1 & 2 Maccabees, *3 Maccabees*) **Poetic Books** Job, Psalms (*with Psalm 151, Prayer of Manasseh*), Proverbs, Ecclesiastes, Song of Solomon (Wisdom of Solomon, Sirach)
Writings Psalms, Job, Proverbs, Ruth, Song of Solomon, Ecclesiastes, Lamentations, Esther, Daniel, Ezra, Nehemiah, Chronicles	**Prophetic Books** Isaiah, Jeremiah, Lamentations (Baruch, Letter of Jeremiah), Ezekiel, Daniel (or longer version of Daniel including the Prayer of Azariah and the Song of the Three Jews, Susanna, and Bel and the Dragon) Hosea, Joel, Amos, Obadiah, Jonah, Micah, Nahum, Habakkuk, Zephaniah, Haggai, Zechariah, Malachi

*Parenthetical, nonitalicized items appear in Roman Catholic and Orthodox canons but not the Protestant canon. Italicized items appear only in the Orthodox canons. The Greek Orthodox canon places the twelve Minor Prophets before the Major ones and adds 4 Maccabees as an appendix; Slavonic Bibles contain an additional book of Esdras.

of the Minor Prophets (Hosea through Malachi) do not appear in historical order, nor do the books of the Writings. The books in this latter category seem in general to have been completed later than books in the first two divisions. So the Jewish canon places some books (Torah and Former Prophets) in order of what they tell about, but groups others by type (for instance, the Former and Latter Prophets), length (the Major and Minor Prophets), or date of completion (the Writings).

The ancient Greek translation of the Hebrew Bible rearranged its books, as shown in the right-hand column of the table on page 7 and also added some additional ones. (The extra books appear in parentheses in the table and are discussed in chapter 16 of this volume.) Early Christians adopted this expanded and rearranged collection as their Old Testament. Many centuries later, Protestant reformers denied the doctrinal authority of the Old Testament books that were not in the Hebrew Bible. This left Protestants with an Old Testament containing the same books as the Hebrew Bible but ordered according to Christian tradition derived from the Bible of ancient Greek-speaking Jews.

The Christian arrangement of books resembles the Jewish arrangement in two important ways: It begins with a cluster of books telling a more or less sequential historical story, and it groups prophetic books together (although at the end rather than in the middle). However, many of the books categorized as "Writings" in the Jewish canon are treated as historical or prophetic in the Christian canon. Ruth appears between Judges and 1 Samuel. In the Protestant canon, 1 and 2 Chronicles, Ezra, Nehemiah, and Esther appear after 2 Kings to extend the historical sequence into the Persian period. The Roman Catholic canon extends the sequence further by including an additional Ezra book, Judith, Tobit, and 1 and 2 Maccabees; the Orthodox canon contains these plus 3 Maccabees and, in an appendix, 4 Maccabees. Christian canons place Lamentations with Jeremiah (because of an almost certainly false tradition that Jeremiah wrote Lamentations) and classify Daniel as a prophetic book. The Christian sequence thus comes closer than the Jewish sequence to arranging books in order of what they tell *about,* but it too arranges some books by type (for instance, the poetic books) or length (for instance, the twelve Minor Prophets) rather than story order.

To help you keep the story straight, this book gives you a chapter of historical overview (chapter 2) before we turn to direct discussion of biblical materials. This overview will give you information about the history and culture of Israel's ancient Near Eastern neighbors, as well as the history directly addressed in the biblical story. It contains a chart (pp. 18–19) with side-by-side comparisons of what was happening in Egypt, Mesopotamia, and Palestine at various times and another chart (p. 23) showing the kings of Judah and Israel. You may want to refer back to this material as you are reading later chapters.

In subsequent chapters, biblical books are discussed in more or less the order of their appearance in the Jewish canon. This has the advantage of grouping together books that are similar in literary type and (very roughly) date of writing. So, for instance, it places Daniel in the company of other Second Temple period literary works rather than treating Daniel as a prophetic book. However, we have followed the Christian ordering in discussing Chronicles, Ezra, and Nehemiah immediately after Genesis–Kings, because the Chronicles and Ezra–Nehemiah chapter gives an introduction to the Persian period that will make the subsequent discussions of Isaiah and the Writings more understandable. The chapters on the Writings discuss Proverbs and Ecclesiastes together because of their similarity in genre. The additional Old Testament books that appear in Roman Catholic, Anglican, and Orthodox canons are discussed in chapter 16.

Matters of Terminology

Old Testament, Hebrew Bible, or First Testament?

The existence of several different canons calls our attention to an important issue: The material we will be studying is sacred to a variety of religious communities. Many of the terms used in connection with it have roots in conflict between those communities. For instance, the term *Old Testament* was coined by a second-century Christian named Marcion. Marcion advocated dropping the Old Testament from the Christian Bible entirely because he felt that it called for the worship of an evil deity, a malicious and destructive one, who was not the same as the loving God revealed by Jesus. To this day, many Christians continue to think of the Old Testament's God as wrathful and the New Testament's God as loving, and many share Marcion's view that the "old" covenant with the Jewish people was somehow faulty or misguided and that whatever validity it did have has been superseded by the "new" Christian covenant. The term *Old Testament* is thus troublesome because of both its association with Christian anti-Judaism and its implication that the testament in question is no longer valid or important for Christians.

But what to call it instead? Many scholars use the term *Hebrew Bible.* That is not quite accurate, because some of the so-called Hebrew Bible (parts of Ezra–Nehemiah and Daniel, plus a few scattered phrases elsewhere) is written in Aramaic rather than Hebrew. Furthermore, we have noted that the Old Testament of non-Protestant Christians includes books from the ancient *Greek* Jewish Bible that are not part of the present *Hebrew* Jewish Bible. Finally, for Christians who hear "Hebrew" as an ethnic/religious adjective rather than a linguistic one, the term *Hebrew Bible* may suggest something that is really somebody else's concern and not properly part of the Christian Bible at all. This has led to yet another proposal that the two parts of the Christian Bible be referred to as the First Testament and Second Testament, a terminology intended to underscore the primary and irreplaceable role of the First Testament. Without denying the legitimacy and importance of the Second Testament, this terminology insists that the Second can be properly understood only as an outgrowth of and in conjunction with the First.

Of these various options, *Old Testament* is the most familiar, and for that reason we have used that term in the title of this book. Within the book, however, you will more often find the terms *Hebrew Bible* and *First Testament.* In using these terms, the writers attempt to honor the First Testament's ongoing relevance for both Jews and Christians.

B.C. or B.C.E.?

Questions of the relationship between Christians and non-Christians arise again in connection with the terminology used for dates. You are probably accustomed to the use of the abbreviations B.C. and A.D. (short for "before Christ" and "*Anno Domini,*" or "the year of our Lord") in citing ancient dates. This customary usage has two problems. First, it is inaccurate: Our best scholarship suggests that Jesus was probably born a few years "B.C." Second, many non-Christians feel uncomfortable using a dating system that incorporates a confession of Jesus' lordship ("our Lord"). Yet this Christian system of year numbering is the present international standard— if Jewish scholars were to substitute Jewish year numbers (starting from a computed date of creation in what Christians would call the 4000s B.C.), most readers would not know what they were talking about! The solution adopted by most archaeologists and historians of the ancient Near East is to keep the numbering associated with the widely adopted Christian system but to qualify the numbers with the abbreviations B.C.E. and C.E. ("before the Common Era" and "Common Era") rather than B.C. and A.D. We use B.C.E. and C.E. in this book. (Assume B.C.E. for dates given without qualifiers.)

Note, by the way, that just as the term *twentieth century* C.E. refers to the 1900s (not the 2000s), the term *sixth century* B.C.E. refers to the 500s (not the 600s). Also remember that in the B.C.E. period, the sixth century comes *before* the fifth! To avoid confusion, century references in this book are usually given in the form "500s B.C.E." rather than "sixth century B.C.E."

God, the LORD, *Jehovah, Yahweh, or YHWH?*

The First Testament uses a variety of terms to refer to God. One of the most common terms is *elohim*. This word, which is plural in form, can refer to "gods" (deities in general) or, with singular meaning, to "God" (*the* one deity who covenants with Israel). In English we can usually tell how the word *god* is used by whether it is capitalized. Hebrew does not use capital letters (capitalization in English Bibles comes from the translators), but it is usually clear which meaning is at stake. The first verse of Psalm 82 says, "*Elohim* has taken his place in the divine council." Here, *elohim* has a singular verb and clearly refers to God. But in verse 6 of the psalm, God says to the other members of the council, "You [plural] are *elohim*." Here, *elohim* has to mean gods. In a few places, the meaning is unclear. In Genesis 3:5, the snake tells the woman that when she and her man eat the fruit of the forbidden tree, "you [plural] will be like *elohim*." Will they be "like God" *(New Revised Standard Version)* or like "gods" *(King James Version)*? We cannot say for certain.

There is another Hebrew word used for God that has none of this ambiguity, because it is a proper name (like Susan or Thomas) rather than an ordinary noun (like god). In ancient Hebrew, which used only consonants, this name was spelled *YHWH* (or, using an older system of Hebrew-to-English equivalences, *JHVH*). From the spelling in some Greek-language Jewish writings, it appears that the name was probably pronounced "Yahweh." In the time before the fall of Jerusalem, this name appears to have been used as freely as we use the name God. In the final centuries B.C.E., however, Jews began to use the substitute title "my Lord" (*adonai*) instead of saying the divine name aloud. There were probably several reasons for this, including a desire to avoid wrongful use of the name (Ex. 20:7) and to communicate with potential converts who were used to addressing their high god by noble title. Centuries later, when medieval Jewish scholars added vowels to the Hebrew text, they took the consonants of *YHWH* (still present in the Hebrew to this day) and added the vowels of *adonai* to remind readers to make the substitution. Still later, a medieval English clergyman produced the word *Jehovah* when he tried to write out the divine name as it appeared in the text, with the consonants of *YHWH* (*JHVH* in medieval spelling) and the vowels of *adonai*.

Most modern English translations of the Hebrew Bible follow the ancient Jewish custom of substituting a title for the divine name. When they do this, however, they write the title in small capital letters "the LORD" to show that in this place, the Hebrew text actually reads *YHWH*. So, for instance, in Deuteronomy 10:17, the Hebrew text says that "*YHWH* your *elohim* is *elohim* of *elohim*." The *New Revised Standard Version* (NRSV) reads, "the LORD your God is God of gods," with the small caps showing that "the LORD" is actually being substituted for "*YHWH.*" (Later in the verse, in the phrase *adone ha'adonim,* "Lord of lords," the divine name is not being used and so "Lord" is not written in small capital letters.) The advantage of this system is that it respects Jewish concerns about use of the divine name. The disadvantage is that we lose track of the fact that this biblical God actually has a *name.* When you think about it, Isaiah 47:4's proclamation that "the LORD of hosts is his name" doesn't make a great deal of sense—there is, in English, no actual *name* in that verse. It makes more sense when we notice the capital letters and realize that in the Hebrew text, the verse says, "*YHWH* of hosts is his name."

How then shall we translate God's name? "The LORD" doesn't give the same effect as an actual name. Speaking of "the One" or "the Eternal" or "*HaShem*" (Hebrew for "the name"), as some Jewish readers do, likewise loses the effect of a proper name. "Jehovah" looks like a name and is familiar to many readers in the English-speaking world but is historically incorrect. In this book, we will simply use the consonants YHWH. Their distinctiveness will, we hope, remind you that this is really a name, not a title. The unpronounceability of the consonants-only form will, we hope, serve as a reminder that tradition does not speak this name lightly.

He, She, or It?

Yet another controversy about language arises less out of historical conflicts than out of contemporary theological conversation. Many believers today are uncomfortable calling God "he" because they believe that God the creator transcends human gender distinctions. At the same time, it seems clear that the ancient writers thought of God as masculine, even though they often use feminine images for God (for instance, Deut. 32:18, "You were unmindful of the Rock that bore you; you forgot the God who gave you birth") and in one case a feminine pronoun is used for God (Num. 11:12–15, "Did I conceive all this people?...If this is the way you [feminine] are going to treat me, put me to death at once"). In speaking of God in a general way, this volume avoids pronouns that assign a gender to God. When quoting ancient writers, however, or speaking of how ancient people understood God, masculine pronouns may be used.

Study Helps

Within this volume, we have provided several study helps for you. I have already mentioned that chapter 2 provides an overview of ancient Near Eastern history, geography, and culture, with two summary charts (pp. 18–19 and 23). I have also noted that each chapter ends with a bibliography of resources for further study. On pages 267–70 you will find a glossary of important terms and historical periods; please refer to it when you encounter a word you don't recognize.

By itself, however, this book will not suffice to acquaint you with the writings of the First Testament. You need to read those writings yourself, and so you will need a Bible. Quotations within this book come, unless otherwise indicated, from a particular English translation called the *New Revised Standard Version* (NRSV) with one modification: Where NRSV reads "the LORD," this book substitutes "YHWH." Although an NRSV Bible would be the least confusing companion to this text, any good modern translation should suffice. Whichever translation you choose, look for one that includes the books of the Apocrypha and not just the books of the more limited Jewish or Protestant canons. The chapter and verse numbers given in this text follow the Christian numbering system used in most English translations (this system occasionally varies by a few verse numbers from the numbering used in the Hebrew text).

Bible translations are often published in study editions that contain maps, notes, and explanatory articles in addition to the actual biblical texts. Some study Bibles are primarily concerned with helping believers connect biblical teachings to particular doctrines and to daily life today (that is, they take a strictly religious approach to the Bible). Others present insights drawn from historical and literary approaches. The second type—the study Bible that gives historical and literary, as well as religious, observations—will be the most helpful for use in conjunction with this textbook. Two such study Bibles, the *HarperCollins Study Bible* and the *New Oxford Annotated Bible* (both containing the NRSV translation), are listed in the bibliography at the end of this chapter. These study Bibles include maps of Palestine and the ancient Near East at various times. You will find that the history of Israel's life in the ancient Near East is easier to follow if you make a point of looking up the locations under discussion. You can find additional information on people, places, biblical books, and other matters in the *HarperCollins Bible Dictionary;* for more detail, see the multivolume *Anchor Bible Dictionary.*

Resources

Paul J. Achtemeier, ed. *The HarperCollins Bible Dictionary.* Rev. ed. New York: Harper San Francisco, 1996.

Michael D. Coogan, Marc Z. Brettler, and Carol A. Newsom, eds. *The New Oxford Annotated Bible: New Revised Standard Version with the Apocrypha.* 3d ed. Oxford and New York: Oxford University Press, 2001.

David Noel Freedman and Gary A. Herion, eds. *The Anchor Bible Dictionary.* 6 vol. New York: Doubleday, 1992.

Andrew M. Greeley and Jacob Neusner. *Common Ground: A Priest and a Rabbi Read Scripture Together.* Rev. ed. Philadelphia: Pilgrim Press, 1996.

W. Lee Humphreys. *Crisis and Story: An Introduction to the Old Testament.* Mountain View, Calif.: Mayfield, 1990.

Wayne A. Meeks, ed. *The HarperCollins Study Bible: New Revised Standard Version with the Apocryphal/Deuterocanonical Books.* New York: HarperCollins, 1993.

2

Geographical and Historical Background for Understanding Ancient Israel

LOWELL K. HANDY

Pre-Israelite Palestine

Ancient stone tools found in Palestine show us that humans have lived in the region for at least 1.4 million years. These tools and the animal bones found with them link Palestine's culture and ecology to northeast Africa, a relationship that continues through subsequent ages.

Modern humans first moved into Palestine from Africa about 250,000 B.C.E. At that time, the terrain from the North African Atlantic coast to the Iranian highlands was wet, with large populations of prairie and river animals. Then, about 47,000 years ago, the climate began to dry, resulting in a reduction of game and an increase in the amount of vegetation in the human diet. By the Natufian Period (approximately 10,000–8500 B.C.E.), several small settlements had been built around natural stands of grain and other consumable vegetation. Formerly wandering hunters and gatherers became villagers, and their social roles diversified.

The revolution in human society came in the Neolithic Period (approximately 8500–3700 B.C.E.): farming. Controlled planting and harvesting of wheat and barley meant a relatively secure food source and a certain amount of choice in locations to settle. With farming came domestication of animals—especially sheep, goats, pigs, and donkeys—for food and labor. Numerous towns developed from the arid Negev to the fertile Galilee, each surrounded with agricultural fields and containing specialized labor. A population explosion in the Syrian towns continued even as, for unknown reasons, many of the southern settlements were suddenly abandoned in approximately 5500 B.C.E.

Long-distance trading with Egypt and Mesopotamia in grains, oils, and wine developed throughout the third millennium (2000s B.C.E.), and by the beginning of the second millennium (1000s B.C.E.) larger towns included industrial buildings, fortifications, and palace-temple complexes along with housing units. Many of these sites would later be incorporated into Judah and Israel, but early in the second millennium their cultural and political ties were with Egypt. Hazor in the north and Lachish in the south became the largest urban centers, but even they were often subject to direct Egyptian rule, a control that Egypt exerted from the Mediterranean coast to the eastern highlands as far north as modern Lebanon. Egypt's influence on Canaan included both political control and cultural interaction, with Egyptian forts maintained as far north as Hazor and Megiddo. Through the second millennium, Egyptian deities were found throughout Canaan. The goddess Hathor and the god Bes remained popular in the area through biblical times.

Egypt

Egypt itself had developed from Nubia, spreading northward along the Nile beginning in the fourth millennium (3000s B.C.E.). Nubian art, architecture, and religion formed the basis for Egyptian culture. Although Egyptians saw themselves as an ethnic unit, there were two areas, designated as Upper and Lower Egypt, that kept their independence from each other. Not all rulers governed both.

Ancient Egyptian history is usually divided into three kingdoms and three intermediate periods. During the kingdoms, Egyptian culture and trade flourished and Egypt directly controlled the neighboring regions of Nubia, Libya, and Canaan. During the intermediate periods, Egypt fell to foreign rulers or collapsed into civil war.

The Old Kingdom (2686–2181) created much of what is thought of as ancient Egypt. Its literature included wisdom texts in the form of advice from parents to children, hymns in praise of many deities, and advice recorded for the deceased in numerous copies of the Book of the Dead. Because life was perceived to be good, Egyptians developed an elaborate ritual for the dead to allow the soul to reach a wonderful kingdom in the west where the good life continued. The pyramids were constructed as elaborate royal tombs. Numerous deities helped the sun god recreate the world each day and aided in saving the righteous. Their temples became enormous complexes serving not only for worship but also for communication, trade, and the banking system; these were run by both hereditary priestly families and ordinary Egyptians who served as priests for specified terms.

A series of civil wars brought the first of the intermediary periods. Asian peoples took up residence in the Nile Delta even as Egypt lost control over Canaan. However, during the Middle Kingdom, Egypt restored its power over Canaan. Egypt henceforth thought of Canaan as a territory belonging to Egypt. Then, from 1730 to 1550, invaders from Canaan and Crete, called Hyksos, overran much of Egypt; this is known as the Second Intermediate Period.

In 1570 Ahmose I successfully revolted against the Hyksos and in twenty years drove them from power, ushering in the New Kingdom. New Kingdom Egypt was an empire. It controlled Nubia, Libya, Sinai, Canaan, and the Eastern Mediterranean coast as far north as modern Lebanon. To the north, the equally powerful Hittite Empire, centered in Asia Minor, controlled the Phoenician cities with which Egypt traded. Militarily the Hittites appear to have been superior to the Egyptians, but in commerce, the Egyptians had no peers. Regular sea trade extended almost around Africa, bringing in silver, gold, gem stones, foodstuffs, diverse animals, woods, and ivory. Land trade with Sinai and Canaan brought copper, bronze, gold, salt, grain, wine, and oil. From farther afield came art and luxury goods from Mesopotamia, Crete, Cyprus, and the Aegean, with trade items from as far as Central Europe. In exchange, Egypt sent out cloth, glass, metalwork, carved stone, and especially food.

Under Ramesses II, Egypt reached its pinnacle of power but could not maintain it. His son Merneptah made an extensive military campaign into Canaan, quelling local towns. Merneptah's boast that he had destroyed a people called "Israel" is the earliest written reference to Israel. Libya invaded Egypt during Merneptah's reign, eventually taking the Delta. Libya in turn was routed by the Sea Peoples, Aegean invaders who, having already damaged or destroyed the Hittite Empire and several Phoenician cities, swarmed from sea and land into the Delta. The Egyptians managed to push them into southeastern Canaan, where they became known as the Philistines. This so weakened Egypt that Libya had no trouble recapturing Egypt, instigating the Third Intermediate Period. In 1030 Egypt gave up control of Canaan and settled into a series of internal wars.

Phoenician cities took up the trade Egypt had abandoned when it fell into a defensive posture. Never united, these independent cities traded in all directions, becoming *the* cosmopolitan cultural centers of the early first millennium. Not only did they transfer goods from other places, but their own cedar and purple cloth were desired everywhere. To their south the

Time Line

Dates	Egypt	Canaan	Mesopotamia
2000 B.C.E.	Middle Kingdom to 1730	Fortified cities with Egyptian cultural and political ties	Civil wars to 1794
	Hyksos rule 1730–1550		Dynasty of Babylon 1894–1595 *Hammurabi* 1792–1750
1500	New Kingdom 1550–1080	Egyptian control	Kassite rule ±1530–1155
	Ramesses II 1279–1212 *Merneptah* 1212–1202	Phoenician trading cities independent of Egypt	
		Five central Philistine cities founded	
	Third Intermediate 1079–525	Egypt cedes Canaan's independence 1030	
		Rise of numerous small independent states	
1000	Libyan rule 945–715	United monarchy ±1020–930	Neo–Assyrian Empire 934–609

Dates	Egypt	Canaan						Mesopotamia
		Judah	Israel	Edom	Moab	Ammon	Aram	
	Sheshonq I 945–924							
	Nubian rule 727–664		Assyria			Assyria	Assyria	Shalmaneser V 726–722
	Saite rule 664–525							Sennacherib 704–681
	Necho 610–595	Babylon	Babylon	Babylon	Babylon	Babylon	Babylon	Neo-Babylonian Empire 626–539 Nebuchadnezzar II 604–562
500	Persia 525–332	Persia	Persia	Persia	Persia	Persia	Persia	Persian Empire 550–330 Cyrus the Great 559–530 Darius I 522–486
	Alexander the Great 332–330							Alexander the Great 330–323
	Ptolemaic Empire 305–30	Ptolemy	Ptolemy	Ptolemy	Ptolemy	Ptolemy	Seleucid	Seleucid rule 323–238
		Seleucid Judah	Seleucid Judah	Seleucid	Seleucid	Seleucid	Rome→	Parthian Empire 238→
1	Cleopatra VII 51–30 Rome 30→	Rome→	Rome→	Rome→	Rome→	Rome→		

Philistine cities, also independent towns, quickly picked up the culture and religion of the local territory but continued to produce pottery in the fashion of their Aegean origins. Beer mugs, it is often pointed out, define their settlements. Canaanite territory released from Egyptian control fell into numerous conflicting mini-powers that would, over a century and a half, slowly develop into the petty states of Edom, Moab, Ammon, Judah, Israel, and Aram. However, many of the important centers, including Hazor and Lachish, would be destroyed in the process.

Mesopotamia

To the east, the Tigris and Euphrates river valley, known to the Greeks as Mesopotamia, had developed on its own. Sumerian culture on the Persian Gulf consisted of a series of feuding cities with distinctive temples and human-built holy mountains. Each city had its own ruler, its own deities, and its own army. These fought each other almost without break through the fourth and third millenniums until Sargon of Akkad invaded from the north, forging the first empire in the region in approximately 2300 B.C.E. At its height, the Akkadian Empire reached from Syria to the Iranian highlands, producing epic literature, hymns, and the first known law codes. The empire did not last long, and the Mesopotamian civil wars resumed until the reign of Hammurabi (1792–1750 B.C.E.).

To the north of Sumer arose two cities that would be the power bases in Mesopotamia for the next one-and-a-half millennia: Babylon to the south and Ashur to the north. The Old Babylonian Empire began in 1894 and slowly expanded outward, taking in all territory of the Akkadian Empire and then expanding northward. Under Hammurabi, Babylon exploded in all directions, creating an empire that, although steadily contracting after his death, would last until the Hittites overran Babylon in 1595. The religious veneration of Marduk, patron deity of Babylon, and the rituals developed for him became the religious legacy of the Babylonian Empire, heavily influencing the Assyrians and their god Ashur. More impressive was the compilation of a lengthy law code under Hammurabi, so valued that in later times Elamites would haul the code off as booty.

After 1595 Babylon was controlled by the Kassites, who prided themselves on maintaining Babylon's traditional culture. Mesopotamian art and literature were actively traded to Canaan, Syria, Egypt, and Asia Minor. In the north, the Assyrians made a peace treaty with Babylon and then moved troops westward as far as the Phoenician cities during Egypt's retreat from its Asian territories. However, by 1030 Assyria had returned to its home region, perhaps in reaction to the disturbances of the Sea Peoples coming through Syria and Canaan.

Israel and Judah

Israel and Judah arose during this interlude from Egyptian control over Canaan. Philistine cities were established along the coast to the west, and Aram, to the north, was free of both Egyptian and Assyrian pressure. The hill country west and north of the Jordan River became a target for expansion by both these minor powers. In response to military and immigrant incursions, the varied peoples of the area decided to unite for mutual defense. From Galilee southward to the north end of the Dead Sea, a loose confederation formed under a selected ruler, Saul, and an agreed-upon deity, YHWH. Saul appears to have been a petty ruler among the Benjaminites. The origins of the worship of YHWH elude us. This king and his deity became the uniting figures of a political entity called Israel.

Most of Israel's population was involved in farming. Barley, wheat, flax, olives, grapes, legumes, dates, and other fruits were grown over large expanses of the country. Sheep, goats, cows, donkeys, and pigs were common livestock. A limited amount of fishing took place on the Sea of Galilee and the Jordan River. Urban areas continued the same production they had engaged in for more than a millennium: oil, wine, cloth, and pottery, with some metalworking along the Jordan. Once united, Israel controlled three major trade routes, one connecting the Philistine and Phoenician cities, a second running beside the Jordan River, and a third through the Jezreel Valley connecting the eastern highlands with the Mediterranean coast.

The indigenous Canaanite religion continued through the reign of Saul and for the duration of an independent Israel. A pantheon of deities served in a hierarchy under the divine rulers of the universe: El and Asherah. The deities were believed to have responsibility for every aspect of the agricultural, political, and personal lives of the population. A level of important but cantankerous divinities, including Baal, Anat, Mot, Yam, Yareah and Shemesh, were responsible for seeing that the world functioned smoothly and were the divine rulers of political states. Specialist deities, such as Baal-zebub, were experts at specific chores, and all these deities communicated with one another and with humans via their messengers, or *angels* (a word that in Hebrew and Greek means simply "messenger"). These deities continued to be worshiped in sacrificial rites at temples and shrines throughout the existence of Israel, with El being understood as another name for YHWH, divine owner of the land of Israel.

Judah was organized some time after the development of Israel to its north. Judah consisted of pasturage suitable for sheep and goat herding, as well as farmland for barley, olives, dates, and grapes. Major cities with agricultural processing facilities fell within this new state, including the rebuilt Lachish. Judah lacked any major trade routes and for most of its existence lacked any access to the sea. With a much less strategic location, Judah came under less external pressure from major powers than did Israel. However, the relation between Israel and Judah was seldom peaceful.

The uniting of Israel and then of Israel to Judah is often referred to as the United Monarchy. The Bible records that under David this entity expanded to include the neighboring areas of Edom, Moab, Ammon, and Aram. Such an extended state required the expertise of a bureaucracy and the force of a collection agency. The structure that developed owed much to the Egyptian government that had long controlled Canaan. The United Monarchy began its collapse during David's reign in the form of a civil war between Judah and Israel. By the time Solomon's reign came to an end, Israel was virtually a conquered state under Judah's control. Solomon's royal projects, including his palace and temple construction, cost Israel greatly and were resented because they were used to centralize power in the Davidic dynasty of Judah. When Rehoboam rose to Judah's throne, Israel successfully broke away, selecting as leader a minor government functionary named Jeroboam, who had led a failed revolt against Solomon before fleeing to Egypt.

Just before the breakup of the United Monarchy, much of Egypt was overrun by Libya. In accord with the notion of Canaan as Egyptian territory, Sheshonq I (biblical Shishak) attacked Judah and Israel in 925, inflicting heavy damage. Upon being paid a large tribute by Judah, Sheshonq left the two countries alone to fight each other. The embattled Jeroboam had to fight Judah while building political and religious establishments, including temples at Dan and Bethel, to rival those of Jerusalem. Upon Jeroboam's death, Israel collapsed into civil war.

The civil wars in Israel ended with Omri seizing the throne. He and his son Ahab built a permanent capital at Samaria, using the best in contemporary architecture and decor. Omri allied himself closely with the Phoenician cities, marrying his heir apparent (Ahab) to Jezebel, a princess of Sidon. Jezebel brought with her the cosmopolitan culture into which she had been raised. The amount of power she understood to be invested in the ruler was foreign to pastoral Israel, and her preference for the worship of the god Baal scandalized some. Politically the Phoenician connection aligned Israel with the minor states to the west of Assyria against Assyria's expanding power. This confederation of states included Judah. King Jehoshaphat of Judah married his son Jehoram to Athaliah, daughter of Ahab and Jezebel. This brought a period of peace between the two nations. It also brought Phoenician culture and deities into Jerusalem. During this period of alliance under Ahab, Israel expanded, conquering Moab and leading a coalition of petty states, with Egyptian support, in a rout of the Assyrian army in 853.

Table of Rulers of Judah and Israel

JUDAH		ISRAEL	
		Saul?	−1000?
David	1000?–970?	Eshbaal*	1000?–998?
Solomon	970?–930?		
Rehoboam	930?–914	Jeroboam I	930?–909
Abijah	914–911		
Asa	911–870	Nabat*	909–908
		Baasha	908–885
		Elah*	885–884
		Zimri*	884
		Tibni*	884–880
		Omri	884–873
Jehoshaphat	870–845	Ahab	873–852
		Ahaziah	852–851
		Joram*	851–842
Jehoram	845–842		
Ahaziah*	842		
Athaliah*	842–835	Jehu	842–815
Jehoash*	835–802	Jehoahaz	815–804
Amaziah*	802–776?	Joash	804–790
		Jeroboam II	790–750
Uzziah	776?–742?	Zechariah*	750–749
		Shallum*	749
		Menahem	749–738
		Pekahiah*	738–736
Jotam	742?–735?		
Ahaz	735?–726	Pekah*	736–732
		Hoshea	732–722
Hezekiah	726–697		
Manasseh	697–642		
Amon*	642–640		
Josiah	640–609		
Jehoahaz	609		
Jehoiakim	609–598		
Jehoiachin	598–597		
Zedekiah	597–586		
Gedaliah*	586–582		
Judas	165–160		
Jonathan	160–142		
Simon	142–135		
John Hyrcanus	l135–104		
Judah Aristobulus	l104–103		
Alexander Jannaeus	103–76		
Salome Alexander	76–67		
Aristobulus II	67–63		
Hyrcanus II	63–43	? = very uncertain date	
Matthias Antigonus	40–37	* = assassinated	

Ahab's sons could not hold the land and not only lost Moab but were invaded by Aram, losing the northern third of Israel proper.

In 842 Jehu, Joram's field general, revolted, killing the kings of both Israel and Judah. A massacre of the entire family of Omri removed all vestiges of the dynasty in Israel, but in Judah, Athaliah seized the throne from her grandson and ruled for seven years in a very hostile environment. She was assassinated and replaced by Jehoash, a child whom supporters claimed was her sole surviving descendant. In Israel, Jehu sought the support of Assyrian King Shalmaneser III, paid tribute, and accepted vassalship for Israel in return for the throne. The alliance of western petty states collapsed as Israel's ties with Phoenicia and Judah were severed. Jehu's dynasty ruled in Israel for almost a century, almost constantly at war with Aram and often at war with Judah.

Judah, militarized under Jehoash's successor, Amaziah, attempted to expand by annexing Edom and invading Israel, but Edom quickly regained its independence and Israel defeated the invading army. The double disaster ended in the assassination of the Judean king at Lachish, the largest city in his kingdom. His son Uzziah and King Jeroboam II of Israel allied themselves and ruled over extended periods of peace in both realms. Jeroboam II restored Israel's boundaries at the expense of Aram in the wake of Assyrian attacks on Aram's eastern border. Trade with the Phoenician cities resumed. Both the Bible and archaeological excavations suggest that this was a period of general prosperity in Israel.

Peace for Israel would not outlast Jeroboam II; his son was assassinated and a short civil war ended just as a new Assyrian king rose. Tiglath-pileser III (744–727 B.C.E.) had big plans. He reorganized the Assyrian bureaucracy and then broke a long-observed treaty with Babylon, which Assyria annexed. The Mediterranean Sea, with its commerce and lumber, was now a major goal of Assyrian expansion. Tiglath-pileser III began a series of summer marches to the west, into Aram. The squabbles between Aram and Israel suddenly disappeared as the two states hastened to recreate the old coalition of petty states to face Assyrian troop movements.

Judah, under Ahaz, refused to join the coalition, leaving a potential enemy at Israel's rear. Aram's King Rezin and Israel's King Pekah besieged Jerusalem in an attempt to coerce Ahaz to reconsider. Instead, Ahaz requested help from Tiglath-pileser III. The Assyrian's response was rapid and effective: Aram, northern Israel, and the Philistine cities were overrun and incorporated into Assyria. It was only a matter of time before the rest of Israel was overrun. Shalmaneser V besieged Samaria. The city fell to Sargon II in 721, and the upper class of its population was redistributed throughout the empire. Israel became a region within Assyria, named after its capital Samaria, and peoples from other conquered lands were resettled there, bringing their own religions and deities.

In Judah, Hezekiah became king in time to witness the destruction of Israel. Unlike his father, he attempted to confront the Assyrian expansion. The Nubians, who had recently overrun Egypt, promised him military aid, so Hezekiah switched allegiance from Assyria to Nubia. The political foolishness of this move became apparent in 701 when Sennacherib invaded Judah. He leveled the major cities, including Lachish, then laid siege to Jerusalem itself. Due to internal problems in Egypt, the Nubian forces were slow to respond. Sennacherib was ready for them when they arrived. Assyria would henceforth support native Egyptian insurrection groups against the Nubian kings. Jerusalem survived because a revolt within the Assyrian royal family required Sennacherib to return to Assyria. Nonetheless, Hezekiah had a huge tribute to pay to Assyria. The western third of Judah was given to the Philistine cities, which had remained loyal to Assyria.

When Manasseh came to the throne, massive reconstruction needed to be done. Apparently aware of the political situation, Manasseh remained loyal to Assyria. He worked hard to rebuild Judah's cities. Because Judah stayed loyal and did not get involved with battles between Nubia and Assyria over the Philistine cities, its western territory was returned to it.

Assyria's King Esarhaddon (680–669) finally defeated the Nubians, taking Assyrian troops far into Egypt and leaving all of Canaan in Assyrian control. The last major Assyrian King, Ashurbanipal, removed the Nubians from Egyptian rule and placed his own choice on the Egyptian throne. In 653 Psamtik I declared Egypt independent of Assyria, apparently with Ashurbanipal's assent. To the bitter end Egypt would remain loyal to the Assyrians who had helped them throw off Nubian rule.

When Manasseh died, his son was assassinated and his grandson, at the age of eight, came to the throne. Josiah initially remained loyal to Assyria, but when Ashurbanipal died the empire fell into civil war. Babylon declared independence. Under Nabopolasser (626–605), the Medes and the Babylonians allied and violently destroyed Assyria. They tried to include southern Canaan in the Neo-Babylonian Empire, but Psamtik I defeated the Babylonian army as soon as it entered Philistine territory. This left Josiah, whose country was still formally part of the dissolving Assyrian empire, facing a resurgent Egypt and an angry Babylonian empire. Actual independence was not a real option, but a major cultic (worship) reform was. Whatever his relation to the neighboring states, Josiah lost his life attempting to reach King Necho of Egypt, who was leading an army north to aid the remnant of the Assyrian royalty. The Egyptian help came too late as Assyria ceased to exist at one last battle in Syria.

The last three kings of independent Judah had no functional power. Josiah's son Jehoahaz was removed by Necho as the Egyptians returned from fighting in the north. Jehoiakim, placed on the throne by Necho, was on the wrong side as the Babylonians moved into the territory. Jehoiachin came to the throne just in time to have the Babylonians overrun Jerusalem. In 601 Nebuchadnezzar's Babylonian army marched up the Nile valley, cutting off Egyptian aid for Canaan. In 597 the Babylonian army captured Jerusalem and set Zedekiah, of the Jerusalem royal family, on the throne. He revolted on the advice that Egypt would help him. The Babylonians established Gedaliah as governor; he revolted on the same advice. Babylonia crushed both revolts and took over direct control of Judah after the latter.

The Exile and the Persian Period

Three series of deportations decimated the elite of Jerusalem, though the rural agricultural community probably went about its business on a fairly normal basis. How Babylon ruled Judah is unknown, but in Mesopotamia the deported Judeans settled down for a long stay. They opened businesses, set up community groups, and perhaps even began religious and educational institutions. Less competent Neo-Babylonian rulers followed Nebuchadnezzar, and the empire fell in a coup to Nabonidus in 555. Nabonidus was less than beloved by the populace, probably due to his decision to live for a decade in Arabia. During this time, his son Belshazzar acted as regent in Babylon.

King Cyrus II (the Great) of Persia, declaring that Marduk had selected him to take over Babylon and restore its proper religion, overran the Babylonian Empire in 539. Cyrus swiftly replaced priests and bureaucrats with his faithful followers and got rave reviews from these newly appointed subordinates. He also decreed that the Jews (that is, Judah's exiles and their descendants) could, with Persian backing, blessing, and funding, return to Judah, because (Cyrus said) YHWH had selected him to restore the proper religion in Judah. Only a small fraction of the Jews living in Mesopotamia accepted the offer, but the royal heir to the Judean throne, Zerubbabel, and the high priest, Joshua, among others, made their way to Jerusalem. Zerubbabel did not become a new king. Instead, the Persians appointed governors. High priests became the leading figures in the Jewish community throughout the Persian Period.

Although the Persian government spoke of indigenous control, its official "Judeans" were the Jews who had been in exile. Those whose families had never left Judah had to adapt to the rules proposed by these official Judeans. Tradition credits Ezra, a Jewish scribe working for the Persian government, with bringing to Jerusalem the Torah that became normative for both the Jews in Judah and the Samaritans, who lived in the area formerly known as Israel.

The Persians did help rebuild Jerusalem's temple, which was dedicated in 515. Meanwhile, Samaria and Judah vied, sometimes violently, for political recognition. Nehemiah, governor in the midst of this conflict, succeeded in building Jerusalem's defenses and obtaining official recognition for Jerusalem. With Persia in control of an empire stretching from India to Nubia, Judah was no longer on the edge of battling powers. It appears to have settled in for a relatively peaceful time of priestly rule under Persian domination.

The Hellenistic (Greek) Period

In 333 Alexander II (the Great) of Macedonia raised an army to fight one battle against King Darius III of Persia in Asia Minor. Darius was no general and the battle was too easily won, so Alexander began a ten-year march through the Persian Empire. In 331 Judah passed from Persian to Hellenistic control apparently without much change in the region. When Alexander died in 323, his generals divided what was left of the Persian Empire among them. The Seleucids accepted Mesopotamia, Syria, and eastern Asia Minor, Mesopotamia being lost within a century to Parthia (the renewed Persian Empire). The Ptolemies received Egypt and its traditional territories in Asia, including Judah. Greek customs, literature, and philosophy came with the Ptolemies. Many in Judah avidly took up the new lifestyle, some even moving to Alexandria and other cities in Egypt, but the Ptolemies took little interest in Judah.

Farther west, Rome had been expanding around the Mediterranean. Thrusting eastward from Greece and Macedonia, Rome slowly pushed the Seleucids out of Asia Minor and restricted their territory in Syria. Early in the second century (198 B.C.E.), the Seleucids did manage to capture Judah, but further attempts to annex Ptolemaic territory were thwarted by Rome, which depended on Egypt for grain. In 168 the Seleucid King Antiochus IV (Epiphanes), goaded partly by frustration over Roman interventions, suppressed Jewish religious practices and desecrated Jerusalem's temple. This led to a revolt by the Hasmonean family, which succeeded in reclaiming the land and resanctifying the temple in 164.

One of the revolt leaders, Judas, became the ruler of an independent Judah when Rome granted recognition in 161. However, Judah continued to suffer factional strife. Hostility against the Hasmoneans increased when a later leader, Simon, accepted both the crown and the priesthood (in violation of Torah). When civil war broke out between claimants to the throne in 69–63 B.C.E., Rome restored order but did not leave. In the Roman civil war, fought off Judah's coast, the Idumean King Herod sided first with

Anthony and Cleopatra VII (last Ptolemaic ruler of independent Egypt) until it was clear that they would lose, then switched sides and was rewarded by Rome with Judah's kingship in 37 B.C.E. With this, Judah entered the Roman Empire.

Resources

Jon L. Berquist. *Judaism in Persia's Shadow: A Social and Historical Approach.* Minneapolis: Fortress Press, 1995.

Amélie Kuhrt. *The Ancient Near East, c. 3000–330 BC.* 2 vols. London: Routledge, 1995.

Amihai Mazar. *Archaeology of the Land of the Bible, 10,000–586 B.C.E.* New York: Doubleday, 1990.

J. Maxwell Miller and John H. Hayes. *A History of Ancient Israel and Judah.* Louisville, Ky.: Westminster/John Knox Press, 1986.

Donald B. Redford. *Egypt, Canaan, and Israel in Ancient Times.* Princeton, N.J.: Princeton University Press, 1992.

Jack M. Sasson, ed. *Civilizations of the Ancient Near East.* 4 vols. New York: Charles Scribner's Sons, 1995.

3

Genesis

RICHARD H. LOWERY

Creation and global destruction, prosperity and famine, sexual and political intrigue, rivalry, trickery, betrayal, and murder: Genesis is a nonstop, action-packed series of adventures, a multigenerational road story about struggle, grace, forgiveness, and the companionship of God.

The intriguing cast of characters includes good people who do bad things, bad people who do good things in spite of their bad intentions, people of courage, cowardice, and mind-numbing stupidity. One of the most interesting characters is the ever-present though largely hidden deity whose motivations are obscure and whose actions are often unpredictable. Known by various names, God in Genesis is at times informed and decisive, utterly in control, like an ancient Near Eastern monarch whose decrees are absolute, whose word is law, whose favor is sweet, and whose wrath is deadly. At other times, God seems unaware and reluctant to act, surprisingly patient, astoundingly open to suggestion, unsure about how things might play out, and willing to "go with the flow" set by the free choices of human partners. The constant in the ever-twisting narrative that emerges is God's unfailing presence with the occasionally heroic and always dysfunctional family through whose story God intends to bless the whole earth. From exile to exile, through their never-ending journey, God is with them.

Authorship and Social Setting

Genesis, like most other biblical books, does not tell us who wrote it. By the time of Jesus, the first five books of the Bible were ascribed to Moses, the hero of Exodus. In Hebrew, these five books are called the *Torah,* which means "teaching," although it is often translated "law." Scholars sometimes refer to the collection as the *Pentateuch,* which is Latin for "five books." Because the Torah includes a report of Moses' death, it is quite unlikely that Moses actually wrote these books, at least in the form we now have them. The ancient claim of Mosaic authorship had more to do with religious authority than literary authorship. Associating the Torah with Moses connects it with the exodus from Egypt and the gift of God's law at Mount Sinai and signals that these books preserve foundational stories for biblical faith.

Though we may never know the names of the writers of Genesis, we can draw broad conclusions about how and why the book was written. From the outset, it confronts the careful reader with inconsistencies and contradictions. For example, Genesis 1 and 2 tell two different stories about the creation of life on earth, using different names for God: *Elohim* ("God") in Genesis 1 and *YHWH Elohim* (usually translated "the LORD God") in Genesis 2. This curious inconsistency continues throughout the book, often corresponding to double versions of the same stories.

For example, Genesis 16:1–14 tells about Hagar, an Egyptian slave in the household of Abram. Abram's wife Sarai gives Hagar to Abram as a sexual partner, because Sarai is unable to conceive. When Hagar becomes pregnant, Sarai becomes jealous and abuses her slave so severely that Hagar flees into the desert. By a spring of water, Hagar encounters "an angel of YHWH" who urges her to return to her mistress and, in words that echo God's earlier covenant with Abram, promises Hagar countless descendants through the son she is carrying. In the astounding verse 13, this African slave becomes the only character in the Bible to name God: "She named YHWH who spoke to her. 'You are 'El-roi ("God of seeing"),' for she said, 'Have I really seen God and lived after seeing?'" (Translations in this chapter are by the author.)

A similar story is told in Genesis 21:8–21, after Sarah miraculously gives birth. In this version, Sarah flies into a jealous rage when she sees Hagar's son Ishmael playing with Sarah's son Isaac. She demands that Abraham drive Hagar and Ishmael into the desert alone, a certain death sentence. At God's urging, Abraham agrees to Sarah's demand, banishing Hagar and Ishmael to the desert. When their water is depleted and they are on the verge of death, "an angel of God (*Elohim*)" calls to Hagar from heaven, promising her that God will "make a great nation" of Ishmael. God shows her a water well, and she and the boy are saved.

Besides these and other apparent "doublets" (multiple versions), Genesis contains several inconsistencies and curious sequences of events. For example, in Genesis 20, Sarah successfully masquerades as a marriageable virgin (that is, a pubescent girl in her early teens), though earlier chapters portray her as a postmenopausal woman, ninety years old. When Abraham drives Hagar and Ishmael into the desert in chapter 21, he puts Ishmael on Hagar's shoulder, though earlier chapters indicate that Ishmael is at least sixteen or seventeen years old. Such logical inconsistencies suggest that these and other stories in Genesis may have circulated independently, probably orally, before they were strung together in our current written narrative.

Nineteenth-century biblical scholars saw these peculiarities as evidence of a long process of development, with duplicated stories coming from different sources or documents written at different times in different places, by different authors with different interests. The German scholar Julius Wellhausen gave the definitive statement of this "documentary hypothesis," establishing a scholarly consensus that held largely firm for a century.

As refined and revised over the years, the documentary hypothesis argues that the Pentateuch was compiled from four originally independent literary sources. The oldest source, associated with the garden of Eden story and stories in Genesis that use the divine name YHWH, originated in Judah. Usually dated to the 900s or 800s B.C.E., this Yahwistic source (abbreviated J, according to the German spelling) was associated with the royal court in Jerusalem. J had a literary counterpart in the Northern Kingdom, preserved in the Pentateuch in highly fragmented form. This Elohistic source (E) is usually dated to the 800s or 700s and was added to J sometime after the fall of the Northern Kingdom in 722 B.C.E. The evidence for E has always been slight, and some scholars who otherwise subscribe to the documentary hypothesis doubt the existence of a coherent independent source E. Around the end of Babylonian exile, J or JE was revised and supplemented by a Priestly source or editor (P, around 538 B.C.E.) interested in restoring temple worship as the center of religious-political life for the community of returning exiles in Jerusalem. In contrast to J, whose characters use the divine name YHWH from Adam and Eve on, P says that this name was first revealed to Moses at Mount Sinai (Ex. 3:14–16; 6:2–3). So throughout Genesis, P refers to God by the generic terms *Elohim* and *El* ("God"). P does not, however, edit J's use of the proper name YHWH out of Genesis. In addition to these two major sources (J and P) and one minor source (E), scholars identify a fourth source, the Deuteronomist (D), which is almost exclusively confined to the book of Deuteronomy. Connected in style and outlook with the historical books Joshua–Kings, D is associated with the cultic-political reform of King Josiah (621 B.C.E.) reported in 2 Kings 22—23.

Since the late 1970s, the documentary hypothesis has come under serious challenge. Some have questioned the literary coherence of the major sources. Others have proposed later dates for the earliest coherent sources, dating J to the Babylonian exile and P to the Persian period (539–331 B.C.E.). Some have suggested that the Pentateuch and the histories (Joshua–Kings and Chronicles) were written entirely in the Persian or Hellenistic (331–164 B.C.E.) periods as political propaganda. Philip R. Davies, for example, suggests they were written to bolster the political claims of Mesopotamian bureaucrats sent by the Persians to administer the province of "Yehud" in and around Jerusalem. These immigrants grounded their right to rule in fictional promises made in the ancient past by the local deity YHWH to their fictional ancestors Abraham, Jacob, Joseph, Moses, Joshua, and David. Apart from these specific literary and historical challenges to the documentary hypothesis, the more general impact of redaction criticism, canonical method, and various narrative and reader response approaches in the closing decades of the twentieth century has focused scholarly attention on the final form of the text and reduced interest in sources.

Even though current scholarly opinion about the authorship, dating, and literary development of Genesis is unsettled, each of the approaches outlined above offers important insights for a theological interpretation of Genesis. From the precritical notion that Moses authored Genesis, theologically attuned interpreters can appreciate the revelatory character of these stories. When celebrated and analyzed with eyes of faith, they help readers touch the deep sources of faith and connect with others who have drawn inspiration and identity from these narratives. Critical methods highlight multiple voices that are not easily harmonized or dismissed. The truths of Genesis grow out of various perspectives brought to bear on matters of common interest, as human communities struggle to name their experiences of divine grace. Good interpretation thus requires attention to the book's inconsistencies and its contexts of human struggle.

Recent scholarship has focused on the Persian Period as the social-historical context for Genesis in its present form. As returning exiles, outsiders sent by imperial decree to rebuild and govern Jerusalem, the ancient writers, readers, and hearers of Genesis were shaped to the core by the ambiguities of life lived between deprivation and power, between privilege and impotence in the face of foreign rule. This social-political setting makes sense of the themes of exile and return that wind through Genesis like a double thread, weaving the stories and fragmentary traditions into a diverse narrative whole that promises abundant life in a homeland but finally leaves the promise unfulfilled. Poignantly, the book ends with Joseph, the Hebrew governor of Egypt, dead, his corpse embalmed for burial someday in the promised land.

Reading through Genesis

Genesis may be divided into four major sections: the Primeval History (chaps. 1—11), the Abraham and Sarah Narratives (12—25), the Jacob

Narratives (25—36), and the Joseph Novella (37—50). Throughout, themes of exile and return and God's abiding presence figure prominently.

The Primeval History (Genesis 1—11)

The first eleven chapters of Genesis contain stories and genealogies that describe the origins and early development of human society and culture. After an introductory creation narrative, the Primeval History features two major stories (the garden of Eden and Noah's ark), two short tales (Cain and Abel and the tower of Babel), and a mythological fragment. The narratives are tied together by a series of genealogies, the last of which provides a transition to the Abraham and Sarah Narratives.

The Priestly creation narrative (1:1—2:4a) introduces Genesis, asserting the fundamental goodness of the created world and presenting a very high view of humans' place in the universe. Uniquely among the creatures, women and men are created "in the image of God" so they may "rule the earth" as God rules the universe. The world of Genesis 1 is a benevolent vegetarian utopia, where no living creature must die that another may live. Unlike the harsh, uncertain life of unceasing toil and political domination faced by most peasant households in ancient Israel, the world of Priestly creation is exuberantly productive, yielding seven days of wealth for six days of work. Seventh day rest is the crown of creation, the fulfillment of God's creative activity and the model for human life in this abundant world. Sabbath, the untroubled leisure of a sovereign ruler secure in power, is the royal birthright of every human being created in God's image.

If Genesis 1 celebrates the wondrous potential of humans, the remaining stories in the Primeval History remind us of human limits. The first of these describes the creation of a solitary human (*adam*) from the muddy humus (*adamah*). The human comes alive when YHWH breathes into its nostrils. YHWH plants a garden in Eden, an oasis in the midst of the universal desert, and puts *adam* in the garden to farm it.

The geographically impossible coordinates of the garden (2:10–14) suggest that Eden is not a specific place. The "four rivers" that flow out of Eden do not all occupy the same continent in the real world, much less share a common source. They do, however, define the boundaries of the inhabited world as ancient Israel knew it. Standing at the "source" of the whole human world, Eden is everywhere—and therefore nowhere in particular. The story of Adam and Eve is the story of every man and woman, a meditation on the human condition.

YHWH worries that the human is alone and, in a trial-and-error attempt to find *adam* a suitable mate, creates all the animals. Finally YHWH puts *adam* into a deep sleep, takes one of its ribs or sides, and fashions a companion. Now for the first time, the story uses gender-specific words, "man" and "woman." "This at last is bone from my bone and flesh from my flesh!" the human exclaims. "This one will be called 'woman' (*'ishshah*) because she was taken from man (*'ish*)." Here, the creation of the first human precedes the creation of all other animals and of sexually differentiated humanity, in contrast to Genesis 1:26–27, where humans are created male and female simultaneously after all other creatures are made.

The second Eden episode (Gen. 3) is set up in 2:16–17, where YHWH forbids the human to eat from "the tree of knowing good and evil." YHWH's reluctance to give humans the power of moral discernment stands in stark contrast to portrayals in biblical wisdom literature (Proverbs, for example) that celebrate human knowledge of right and wrong and characterize the pursuit of such wisdom as the epitome of faithfulness to God.

Genesis 3:1 introduces a common ancient Near Eastern wisdom figure, the serpent, to lead humans to the knowledge of right and wrong. (Because snakes shed their skins and appear to rejuvenate themselves, they were associated with healing, longevity, and wisdom.) Although 3:6 says her husband is "with her" during the conversation with the serpent, the woman speaks for the couple, a striking reversal of the ancient social norm. The snake assures them that they will not die for eating the fruit of wisdom. Instead, "God knows that on the day you eat from it, your eyes will be opened and you will be like God(s), knowing good and evil" (v. 5). They eat. Then "their eyes were opened, and they knew that they were naked." When God later interrogates them, the man accuses the woman and blames YHWH for creating her. The woman accuses their teacher the snake. Like Prometheus in Greek myth, the serpent pays a heavy price for sharing heavenly knowledge with mortals: YHWH condemns it forever to crawl on its belly and eat dust.

God punishes the human couple, making their labor more difficult and binding them more closely to their work. God increases the pain of childbirth, yet gives the woman an irresistible desire to produce children. Her desire has social consequences: "Your husband will rule you" (3:16). God punishes the man by making agriculture less productive, cursing the earth to yield thorns and thistles. "In toil, you will eat from it all the days of your life...By the sweat of your face you will eat bread" (3:17, 19). The price of human wisdom is the irresistible urge to produce and reproduce life, a desire that inevitably meets with failure, struggle, pain, and death.

The "curses" God places on the first couple describe socioeconomic realities in ancient Israel. Subsistence agriculture was precarious and difficult. Ancient families ate "by the sweat of their face," when they managed to eat at all. For a variety of economic and cultural reasons, women lived under the social and political authority of fathers and husbands who controlled household property. Women's fertility served a key economic function, because children provided essential household labor. So the ability to produce children determined women's social value and deeply shaped their personal identities. The "curses" of Genesis 3, so closely tied to the specific social realities of ancient agriculture, are not easily applied to postindustrial societies, where agriculture is more productive, food is more plentiful, child labor is less necessary, childbirth is safer, and women are freer to make their own sexual and political choices. Today, women are no more "cursed" to be ruled by their husbands than men are "cursed" to battle thorns and thistles for each day's meager meal.

At story's end, YHWH confirms what the serpent told the man and woman at the beginning: "The human has become like one of us, knowing right and wrong. Now he might reach out and also take from the tree of life, eat, and live forever" (3:22). To preserve a distinction between human and divine, God expels humans from Eden, reiterating their original mandate to work the earth (cf. 2:15). The story now comes full circle: When YHWH began to create, "no plant of the field was yet in the earth and no herb of the field had yet sprung up...because there was no human to work the ground" (2:5). Now, at the end of chapter 3, exiled from Eden and newly wise, Adam and Eve bring agriculture and life to the desolate world outside utopia.

Though traditionally described as a "fall," the garden of Eden story portrays a fall upward. Humans trade paradise for wisdom and, in the process, cause the universal desert to bloom. They forfeit blissful innocence for the godly power of moral discernment, the ability to know right and wrong and to choose. The world prospers as a result. The "fall" in this story is the painful process of growing up, maturing into moral beings, becoming fully human and thus "like God."

The other stories in the Primeval History are variations on the theme of humans' likeness to and distinction from God. In the Cain and Abel story, Cain, the farmer, murders his brother Abel, the shepherd, usurping God's role of giving and taking life. YHWH curses Cain "from the ground" and condemns him to a life of wandering. Exiled from the farm, Cain builds the first city. His descendants create the arts and crafts of urban culture.

Noah's story closely parallels an ancient Mesopotamian story about the gods' failed attempt to destroy humanity with a universal flood. Humans survive because the wisdom god secretly warns a favored human, instructing him to build a giant boat and stock it with animals. The floating zoo survives the flood and repopulates the earth.

The biblical story combines two slightly different versions. J's flood lasts forty days. YHWH decides to destroy humans because "every thought they have is only evil all day long" (6:5–6), but finally saves them, telling Noah to build a boat and rescue *seven pairs* of every "clean" animal and one pair of every "unclean" (7:2–3). In P's version, God floods the earth because it is "corrupt and full of violence" (6:11–13), but makes a "covenant" with Noah (6:18), instructing him to build an ark and bring *a single pair* of every animal, clean and unclean (6:19; 7:8–9). The flood lasts 150 days (7:24; 8:3) and is described in terms that recall P's creation story in Genesis 1. Except for the ark, a tiny box of ordered creation, the world returns to the watery chaos that filled the universe before God began to create heaven and earth (1:1–2).

The merging of the two versions confuses the details somewhat, but the basic idea is clear: God's compassion finally overcomes God's wrath. Like the Mesopotamians' loose-lipped wisdom deity, God undermines God's own plan, saving humanity by warning Noah and showing him how to survive. Although "sorry," "grieved," and perhaps even furious with the violence and corruption of the earth, God finally saves the world, making a covenant with Noah and all flesh never again to undo creation (9:8–11) and putting the rainbow in the sky to signal this everlasting nonaggression treaty (9:12–17). God also underlines the value of human life by formalizing the implicit prohibition of murder in the Cain and Abel story. Human blood must not be shed because God made humans "in the image of God" (9:6).

The tower of Babel story (11:1–9) echoes the garden of Eden. In this utopian world, "all the earth had a single language" (v. 1). Humans develop a process for firing bricks and decide to build a city with a tower whose top will reach into the sky, where divine beings dwell. YHWH worries that "now nothing they set their mind to do will be impossible for them!" (v. 6). In Eden, humans had become "like God(s)" by knowing right and wrong (3:22). Now human technology threatens once again to bridge the gap between heaven and earth. To preserve the boundary, God confuses the universal language and disperses the people. They leave Babel in the plain of Shinar (an ancient name for Babylon) and scatter throughout the earth, ironically fulfilling their mandate from God at creation to "fill the earth" (1:28).

The genealogy that follows leads to Abraham, the progenitor of Israel whose emigration from Babylonia to Canaan foreshadows the path taken in the 500s and 400s B.C.E. by returning exiles, who were the likely authors and original audience of Genesis as we know it.

The Abraham and Sarah Narratives (Genesis 12—25)

The second section of Genesis consists of stories about the original ancestors of Israel, Mesopotamian immigrants: Abram/Abraham, Sarai/Sarah, and their son Isaac. Isaac is a minor, generally passive character whose few appearances largely function to move the plot from Abraham to Jacob/Israel. These stories feature God's promise that Abraham's lineage will produce countless descendants and possess a permanent homeland in the already occupied land of Canaan. Because there is no notion of an afterlife in Genesis and people were thought to live on through their children, the promise of numerous descendants is, in effect, a promise of immortality.

Ironically, Abraham and Sarah face a lifetime of infertility and transience. When Abraham finally produces sons—Ishmael (with Sarah's Egyptian slave Hagar), and Isaac (with Sarah)—God tells him to kill them, ordering him to abandon Ishmael and Hagar in the desert and to slaughter Isaac as a burnt offering. In both cases, God intervenes at the last minute to spare the children. In both cases, Abraham agrees to carry out the deity's gruesome order. Abraham's acquiescence to God's homicidal instructions, though troubling, appears in the biblical narratives to signal Abraham's proper respect for God. The only piece of the promised land Abraham actually acquires is a cave he buys in Hebron as a burial lot for Sarah. Virtually all the main characters of Genesis are buried there by book's end.

Abraham and Sarah's story begins in Genesis 12. YHWH orders Abram to go to "the land I will show you," promising to make him "a great nation" through whom all the families of earth will be blessed (vv. 2–3). Abram leaves Mesopotamia and goes to Canaan, continuing the immigrant journey his father already began from the heart of Babylonia (11:31–32). After YHWH promises to "give this land to your offspring" (v. 7), Abram begins to mark the territory by building YHWH altars, moving by stages from north to south.

In chapter 15, YHWH makes a covenant with Abram, reiterating the twofold promise and foretelling the distant future of Abram's family. "Your descendants will be resident aliens in a land not their own. They will slave away and be oppressed for four hundred years. But I will judge the nation they serve, and afterward they will come out with great wealth!" (vv. 13–14). In chapter 17, God, appearing as *El Shaddai* ("God Almighty" in NRSV's translation), renames the ancestral couple "Abraham" and "Sarah" and offers their family an "everlasting covenant" (v. 7), symbolized by male circumcision (vv. 10–14). Promising Abraham to "be God for you and your descendants after you" (v. 7), God blesses Ishmael (v. 20) but says that the covenant will be kept through Sarah's offspring: "I will bless her. She will be [mother] of nations! Kings of peoples will come from her!" (v. 16). Abraham falls on his face laughing because he is 100 years old and Sarah is 90. The promise to Sarah is reprised in chapter 18, the first of a two-part episode that concludes with the destruction of Sodom and Gomorrah in chapter 19.

Biblical tradition uniformly attributes the destruction of these cities to their irresponsible use of wealth and arrogant neglect of the vulnerable. Isaiah 1:8–17 condemns the rulers of Sodom who, though scrupulous about worship and sacrifice, fail to "seek justice, rescue the oppressed, defend the fatherless, and plead for the widow." Ezekiel 16:49 identifies the sin of Sodom as "pride, excess food, prosperous ease" and failure to "aid the poor and needy." Genesis 18—19 also explains the destruction of Sodom and Gomorrah as God's punishment for social injustice.

These chapters are mirror opposites. In chapter 18, YHWH and two angels appear to Abraham "in the heat of the day" (v. 1). Abraham offers the travelers extravagant hospitality, slaughtering a calf and having Sarah prepare cakes with a triple measure of choice flour. Abraham's behavior, though excessive, is rooted in the ancient Near Eastern custom of offering hospitality to travelers. Abraham's generosity leads to yet another prediction that his post-menopausal wife Sarah will get pregnant.

Abraham joins YHWH and the angels as they leave to investigate reports about "the outcry against Sodom and Gomorrah" (18:20). The word *outcry,* closely related to the terms used in connection with Abel's murder (4:10) and YHWH's liberation of Israel from Egyptian slavery (Ex. 3:7), refers to a victim's cry for help and justice: "If you close your ear to the *outcry* of the poor, you will cry out and not be heard" (Prov. 21:13). Abraham convinces YHWH to spare the cities if only ten righteous people are found there.

In chapter 19, YHWH's angels enter Sodom "in the evening." Only Abraham's nephew Lot, a resident alien, offers them lodging. This ominous failure of native citizens to provide hospitality turns to active hostility at bedtime. A mob gathers and threatens to gang rape the travelers, a violent act of humiliation associated with warfare: Defeated enemies often were raped. By treating the travelers as conquered enemies, Sodom confirms its reputation for injustice. By declaring war on the vulnerable, the men of Sodom inadvertently declare war on YHWH and bring destruction on themselves. Only Lot and his daughters escape the conflagration.

The Abraham and Sarah Narratives come to a troubling climax in the binding of Isaac story (22:1–19). A complex series of Hebrew wordplays brilliantly weaves the awful tale together. From the opening sentence, the reader is privy to knowledge hidden from the human characters: God (literally "the God," *ha'elohim*) "tested" Abraham (v. 1), ordering him to take his "only son" (*yehid*), Isaac, and burn him as a sacrifice on a mountain in Moriah (v. 2). Speechless, Abraham rises early in the morning, saddles his donkey, takes two servants and Isaac, splits wood for the offering, and goes to the place "the God" chose (v. 3). Sarah, who has figured prominently in other Abraham and Isaac stories, is silent and absent from this one. She never speaks again in Genesis. The next mention of her is her obituary.

Upon reaching the mountain (vv. 5–6), Abraham orders his servants to wait in camp while he and Isaac walk up the mountain "together, alone" (*yahdaw*, a slight variation on *yehid* in v. 2 above). Every step "together, alone" (*yahdaw*) is a reminder that Isaac is the "only son" (*yehid*). Partway up, Isaac asks where the offering is. "God [not "the God"] will provide the lamb for offering, my son," Abraham answers (v. 8). (An intricate play on similar Hebrew words translated "to provide," "to see," and "to fear" runs through the story. Even the name "Moriah" appears related to these words.) Abraham and Isaac keep walking "together, alone" (*yahdaw*, v. 8).

When they come to the place "the God" chooses, Abraham binds Isaac, puts him on the altar, and grabs the slaughtering knife (vv. 9–10). Just in time, "the angel of YHWH" (this is the first time "YHWH" has been used in the story) calls out from heaven, "Abraham! Abraham! Do not stretch out your hand against the boy or do anything to him. Now I know that you fear God [not "the God"]. You did not withhold your son, your only son [*yehid*], from me" (vv. 11–12). Abraham sees a ram trapped in a bush and offers it instead (v. 13). He names the place "YHWH will see," as "it is said to this day, 'In the mountain, YHWH will be seen'" (v. 14). (NRSV offers an equally plausible translation: "the LORD will provide…On the mount of the LORD it shall be provided.") The story comes full circle in the concluding verse 19: "Abraham returned to his boys, they got up and walked together [*yahdaw*] to Beer-sheba."

It is helpful to read this troubling story alongside Exodus 13's instructions for the Feast of Passover/Unleavened Bread. There God instructs Israel to sacrifice all firstborn males, except human firstborn, who are "redeemed" by sacrificing sheep in their place (v. 13). Substituting animal sacrifice for human sacrifice symbolizes that "YHWH brought us out of Egypt, away from the house of slavery" (v. 14).

Read in this light, Abraham's awful "test" finally reveals more about God than about Abraham: The God of Israel does not require human sacrifice, but redeems and rescues the victim. The story also makes another important point: In the end, God is trustworthy. God told Abraham that the promise would be fulfilled through Isaac. The horrifying "test" throws into question God's veracity: Can Abraham really believe what God has sworn? Throughout Genesis, God bends the rules to show mercy. The "test" asks whether God will alter course for bloodlust. The answer is no. God does not renege on promised blessing.

The Jacob Narratives (Genesis 25—36)

Rivalry, deception, and victory of the underdog are key themes surrounding the trickster Jacob. They appear already in the story of his birth. In 25:21, Isaac prays to YHWH for his wife "because she was barren," a chronic condition in Abraham's family since God first promised them countless descendants. YHWH grants his prayer, and Rebekah conceives twins. Suffering a difficult pregnancy, she seeks divine insight. God tells her that she is carrying "two nations," a plausible explanation for any woman in the late stages of pregnancy, but figuratively true in the case of Rebekah: Two peoples descended from her twins will be in conflict. One will be stronger than the other, and the elder will serve the younger (v. 23). This surprising prediction contradicts the ancient principle of "primogeniture," by which the firstborn son has the right and responsibility to rule the family and preserve its property after the father dies. This reversal of normal social order plays an important role in the Jacob stories and throughout Genesis.

The second child emerges from the womb gripping the heel of his brother. Rebekah names the first boy Esau and the second Jacob, a verbal form of *heel,* which means something like "to attack at the heel," that is, to overcome an opponent by sneaking up from behind and tripping him, to "hamstring" the competition. With a Jacob in the house, Esau would do well to watch his back. Esau grows up to be a rugged outdoorsman, his father's favored son. Jacob hangs around the women's tents.

Esau trades his rights as firstborn to Jacob for a bowl of soup, a shameful act, because preserving household property was a moral imperative. Later, Jacob successfully executes his mother's plan to steal his father's deathbed blessing from Esau (27:1–49). Although perhaps troubling to modern audiences, Rebekah's underhanded manipulation of her visionless husband serves God's intention, revealed to her during her pregnancy. With Jacob's help, she rescues the household property from the rash, selfish stupidity of Esau.

Furious, Esau consoles himself by plotting Jacob's murder. Rebekah intervenes, convincing Isaac to send Jacob to Mesopotamia to find a wife. The journey to and from Mesopotamia forms the heart of the Jacob stories and provides the setting in which YHWH's promise to Abraham begins to take noticeable shape.

On his way out of Canaan, Jacob has a vision of YHWH standing by the stairway angels use to move between heaven and earth (28:10–22). God reiterates the twofold promise and swears to "go with" Jacob into exile and to bring him back to Canaan. "I will not abandon you until I have accomplished what I have promised you!" (v. 15). When Jacob wakes, he builds an altar, anoints it, and names the place Bethel ("house of God") because it is the gateway to heaven. He vows that if God returns him safely to Canaan, "YHWH will be my God," the altar will become a temple, and Jacob will tithe there (vv. 20–22).

In Mesopotamia, Jacob finds his mother's brother Laban and arranges to work seven years to pay the bride-price for Laban's daughter Rachel. After seven years, at the end of the prenuptial party, Laban tricks him into consummating marriage with Rachel's older sister Leah. When Jacob discovers the switch (too late!) and objects, Laban gives him Rachel as well, for another seven years' work. Jacob prefers Rachel. YHWH, ever eager to side with the underdog, causes Leah to have numerous pregnancies and Rachel to have none. An intense sibling rivalry ensues. The sisters' competition and YHWH's capricious intervention in the reproductive process combine to net Jacob twelve sons, one daughter, and two concubines, Bilhah and Zilpah, the personal attendants of Rachel and Leah. YHWH's meddling unsettles household harmony and never satisfies Leah's desire to be loved by her husband. But it offers the first compelling evidence that God's covenant with Abraham is being kept. In Mesopotamian exile, the promise of numerous descendants finally comes true.

Jacob leaves Laban and returns to Canaan, where Esau meets him with a four-hundred-man army. Terrified, Jacob sends Esau extravagant gifts. The night before Jacob must face Esau, a "man" attacks him at the Jabbok River and wrestles with him until dawn (32:24–32), finally blessing Jacob and changing his name to Israel ("he strives with God" or "God will strive"), because he "has striven with God and with humans" and prevailed (v. 28). Jacob names the spot Peniel ("face of God") because, he says, "I saw God face to face and my life was spared!" (v. 30).

Jacob's gifts soften Esau. But when Esau invites Jacob to follow him home, Jacob tricks his brother and flees. He marks the end of his exile by returning to Bethel and building an altar where he first saw YHWH on his way out of Canaan (35:1–15). God appears to Jacob and, once again, changes his name to Israel. Urging him to "be fruitful and multiply" (v. 11), God repeats the twofold promise and "went up from him" (v. 13). The story of Jacob's exile comes full circle. At the beginning of the journey, YHWH had appeared to Jacob at Bethel and promised to be "with him" until he safely returned. The exile now ended, God ascends again to heaven at Bethel. With God's unfailing presence in exile, Jacob has become "Israel" and the promise to Abraham has begun to take shape.

The Joseph Novella (Genesis 37—50)

The Joseph story moves Jacob's family from famine in the promised land to prosperity in Egypt, continuing the theme of God's presence in exile. The narrative's smooth flow and rich character development lead scholars to call it a novella ("little novel"). The journey from Canaan to Egypt unfolds through a tightly connected series of events centered on Joseph, the visionary firstborn of Jacob's favored wife Rachel and the last child born to him in Mesopotamia. Born in exile, Joseph also dies in exile, his body preserved for eventual burial in the land of promise. The story's refrain reveals the key to Joseph's astonishing good fortune in Egypt: "YHWH was with him."

In the first episode (37:1–36), the reader learns that "Israel loved Joseph more than any of his sons" (v. 3). Joseph further complicates the dysfunction by snitching on his brothers (v. 2) and having dreams about ruling the family (vv. 5–10). Joseph's brothers loathe him and plot his murder. The eldest brother Reuben saves Joseph, but the others sell him to a caravan headed for Egypt, where he is sold as a slave to a high-ranking Egyptian official. The brothers convince Jacob that Joseph was killed by a wild animal.

Joseph rises from slavery to become governor of Egypt. Along the way, he lands in prison, falsely charged with attempted sexual assault. Joseph's astonishing ascent is the result of his unparalleled skill at interpreting dreams and the uncanny success that greets his every venture because "YHWH was with him" and "kept faith with him."

Joseph's supernatural insight and administrative skill provide the means for eventual reunion with his family. Interpreting dreams of Pharaoh, Joseph predicts a severe famine and recommends a strategy of preparation, earning his promotion to governor. When the famine strikes, Egypt has plenty of food. Jacob sends his sons to Egypt to buy grain. Joseph uses his political power and his brothers' failure to recognize him to trick them into bringing their youngest brother Benjamin to Egypt. Benjamin is the only other child of Joseph's mother, Rachel. When Benjamin arrives, Joseph announces that he is going to imprison the boy. Brother Judah, sure that God is punishing the brothers for an unnamed crime (presumably selling Joseph into slavery), begs for mercy and offers himself as a slave in Benjamin's place. Overcome with emotion, Joseph begins to cry and reveals his true identity. The brothers are terrified, but Joseph reassures them: "God sent me before you to preserve life...to preserve for you a remnant on earth, and to keep alive many survivors" (45:5–7).

Pharaoh invites Joseph's family to settle in the fertile region of Goshen in northeastern Egypt. At Beersheba, on his way to Egypt, Jacob builds an altar and has another vision (46:1–4). God promises that in Egyptian exile,

Israel will become "a great nation" (v. 3). Echoing the promise to Jacob at Bethel before Mesopotamian exile, God vows, "I myself will go down to Egypt with you, and I will also bring you up again" (v. 4).

When Jacob arrives in Egypt, he meets Pharaoh and blesses him (47:7, 10), recalling the promise that God will bless all the families of the earth through Abraham's lineage (12:3). Genesis comes full circle. Now settled in Goshen, the children of Israel "were fruitful and multiplied greatly" (47:27), words that echo the mandate to humans at creation (1:28) and to Noah after the flood (9:1, 7).

In chapter 48, Israel adopts and blesses Ephraim and Manasseh, Joseph's sons born in Egypt to an Egyptian mother. As grandchildren fathered by a late-born son with a foreign wife, Manasseh and Ephraim have no claim to privilege in the line of inheritance. Yet Israel says, "They will be mine like Reuben and Simeon [his first- and second-born sons]" (v. 5). This stunning subversion of primogeniture is compounded when Israel blesses the two boys. He puts his magically more powerful right hand on Ephraim, the secondborn, and his left hand on Manasseh, the firstborn (vv. 13–20). Jacob the "supplanter," the secondborn who began his narrative life by stealing his brother's birthright and his father's deathbed blessing, now closes his narrative life by elevating the second generation over the first and the secondborn over the firstborn.

In chapter 49, when he "blesses" his sons, Israel condemns the violence of Simeon and Levi (who in chapter 34 massacred an entire people to avenge the rape of their sister Dinah). As God undid creation in the Noah story because of the "violence" (*hamas*) that filled the earth (6:11), Israel now condemns Simeon and Levi because their swords are weapons of "violence" (*hamas*). As YHWH banished the murderer Cain, making him a permanent fugitive in "the land of wandering" (4:12–16), Israel now curses the violent anger of Simeon and Levi, promising never to "enter their council" or "be joined with their assembly." Like Cain, they will be scattered in Israel, with no settled home (49:5–7).

When Jacob dies, the brothers fear that Joseph will take revenge on them. They beg for their lives. In tears, Joseph offers surprising forgiveness: "Do not be afraid! Am I in the place of God?" (50:19). "You intended harm for me, but God intended it for good in order to preserve a numerous people!" (50:20).

Genesis ends with Joseph's deathbed wish to be buried in Canaan when God brings the children of Israel out of Egypt (50:24–25). The book closes with the stark notice that Joseph's corpse "was embalmed and placed in a coffin in Egypt" (50:26). The twofold promise that Abraham's descendants would become numerous and possess a homeland is only partly realized.

Israel's hope lies not in actual fulfillment but in the faith that God goes with them into exile and intends someday to bring them home.

Conclusion: Overarching Themes

Genesis is a complex narrative with many sometimes contradictory themes. Three stand out in the reading offered here. First, Genesis offers assurance of God's abiding presence in exile. Adam and Eve are exiled from Eden. Cain is exiled from farming. Noah is cut off from the land. Human civilization is expelled from Babel. Abraham leaves his homeland to sojourn in Canaan, Egypt, and Philistia as a resident alien until his death. Jacob is exiled to Mesopotamia and dies in Egypt. Joseph is born in exile and finally lies embalmed in a coffin in Egypt, waiting to be buried in the promised land. Yet through all these exiles, God is with the people.

Second, to fulfill the promise, God flouts social convention and subverts social order. God favors the secondborn and the underdog and in virtually every case works through the socially illegitimate power of women and younger children to save the chosen household and increase its prosperity. The pattern is set at the beginning of the book with the surprising note at the end of Genesis 2 that "a man will leave his father and mother and cling to his wife." Although this description reverses the social norm in ancient Israel, it introduces a pattern of reversal that becomes the narrative norm in Genesis.

Finally, God abhors human violence and injustice. A "Cain and Abel" theme punctuates the narrative throughout, but after the initial murder, the pattern is always interrupted. Cain is protected from murder by YHWH's special mark. God rescues Ishmael from the homicidal jealousy of Sarah. Esau fails to murder Jacob. Reuben derails his brothers' plan to murder Joseph. Finally, Joseph, with full knowledge of his brothers' crime and the full power of the state at his disposal, chooses compassion over retribution and spares the lives of the brothers who betrayed him.

Joseph's compassionate choice reflects the character of God in Genesis. Punishing violence, showing compassion for the oppressed and despised, and bringing blessing to all the families of the earth, God is finally a God of mercy, life, and hope, who does not require human sacrifice but desires human flourishing. Through days of exile, through the surprising turns of the never-ending journey home, the people of God can rest assured: "God is with you!"

Resources

Walter Brueggemann. *Genesis: Interpretation: A Bible Commentary for Teaching and Preaching.* Atlanta: John Knox Press, 1986.

Philip R. Davies. *In Search of "Ancient Israel."* Journal for the Study of the Old Testament, Supplement Series 148. Sheffield, U.K.: Sheffield Academic Press, 1992.

Baruch Halpern. *The First Historians: The Hebrew Bible and History.* San Francisco: Harper & Row, 1988.

Sharon Pace Jeansonne. *The Women of Genesis.* Minneapolis: Fortress Press, 1990.

John Van Seters. *Prologue to History: The Yahwist as Historian in Genesis.* Louisville, Ky.: Westminster/John Knox Press, 1992.

Claus Westermann. *Genesis: A Commentary.* 3 vols. Minneapolis: Augsburg Press, 1984.

4

Exodus, Leviticus, and Numbers

FRANK H. GORMAN, JR.

Exodus, Leviticus, and Numbers constitute the center of the Pentateuch, the Jewish *Torah* (a word often translated "Law" but also bearing the broader meaning "Instruction"). The books narrate Israel's deliverance from Egypt and journey to the plains of Moab, where the community anticipates entry into the land of Canaan. The story provides the context for the development of several important events and themes: YHWH's deliverance of the people from oppression and slavery, ratification of the Sinai covenant, construction of the tabernacle, founding of the sacrificial cult, provision of instructions concerning community life, and ongoing conflict between YHWH and Israel. The story narrates the negotiated, in-process nature of the YHWH-Israel relationship, with particular focus on YHWH's abiding presence in the midst of the Israelite community. The story speaks of a community that understands its origins and ongoing existence in terms of divine promise, divine acts of redemption, divine guidance, and divine presence.

The narratives and instructions in these books must be contextualized within the larger biblical story. The lives of the ancestors and the divine promises made to them (Genesis 12–50) provide the literary and theological contexts for the exodus, Sinai, and wilderness stories (see Ex. 2:23–25 and 3:6–10). The ancestral stories themselves are located within the context of creation (Genesis 1–11), so that the God who interacts with the Israelite community, who redeems them from oppression, who enters into covenant with them, and who seeks to dwell in their midst, is not only the God of promise but also the God of creation (compare Ex. 1:7 with Gen. 1:28). Numbers tells of Israel's arrival and encampment in the plains of Moab, the place where Moses bids farewell to the people and anticipates their life in the land (Deuteronomy). The book of Joshua narrates the realization of the ancestral promise of land.

Authorship and Social Setting

Although tradition has attributed the writing of the Pentateuch to Moses, the texts themselves suggest a more diverse and complex history of composition. They reflect a variety of theological viewpoints and perspectives on the ways of God, the ways of humans, and the nature of the world. The diversity of viewpoints and perspectives suggests that the texts reflect a lengthy history of composition (to be distinguished from the history of the events recounted and narrated in the text). Multiple writers and editors working in distinct social and historical contexts, reflecting distinct ideological and theological concerns, are responsible for the production of the present form of the Pentateuch. The multiple voices, however, come to the reader bound together in a larger structure, the Pentateuch, and that larger literary structure must be taken seriously. At the same time, critical reading of these texts must include recognition of, engagement with, and respect for the different theological perspectives found within the texts. Multiple voices speaking from diverse perspectives weave themselves together to tell the story of Israel's origins.

Just how the Pentateuch reached its present form remains uncertain. Traditional source criticism viewed the final text as a compilation of multiple sources—the Yahwistic, Elohistic, Deuteronomic, and Priestly writings— and located the origins of these sources somewhere between the 900s and 500s B.C.E. Although still providing a basic methodological framework, the traditional view is no longer able to account for the Pentateuch in its present form (see the discussion on Authorship and Social Setting in chap. 3, pp. 29–33). Recent analysis has concentrated on the composition and editorial history of individual blocks of material, such as the exodus story (Ex. 1— 15), the Sinai covenant (Ex. 19—24), the tabernacle material (Ex. 25—31, 35—40), the instructions for the sacrifices and offerings (Lev. 1—7), the purity instructions (Lev. 11—15), the Holiness Code (Lev. 17—26), and the Balaam story (Num. 22—24), and the ways in which these already edited blocks of material have been brought together into larger literary units. Recent work has also tended to locate more and more of the literary activity that produced the Pentateuch in the exilic and postexilic periods (500s and 400s B.C.E.).

The history of composition, however, involves more than a reconstruction of literary activity. The production of these texts took place in concrete social, cultural, and historical contexts. Israel's political and military interaction with other nations, particularly Assyria and Babylon, had a profound impact on Israel's thinking about God and the world. Social and political institutions within Israel had a stake in the telling of this story. Rulers and their families, priests, sages, and prophets all played a significant role in the life of the nation, and all would have wanted a voice in the production of their national story. This suggests that the texts point not only to diverse voices but also to voices of power that were able to "have their say." National stories speak of identity, power, and empowerment. By their very nature, they are therefore political. This does not necessarily mean that they are incorrect or wrong. Human perceptions of God, the self, and the world are always influenced and informed by values, hopes, ideals, and worldviews.

The Structure of Exodus through Leviticus

Exodus begins with Israel in Egypt, and Numbers concludes with Israel camped in the plains of Moab, anticipating entry into the land of Canaan. For purposes of discussion, the story may be viewed in terms of three primary units: (1) the exodus from Egypt (Ex. 1:1—15:21), (2) the journey to and the stay at Mount Sinai (Ex. 15:22—Num. 10:10), and (3) the journey from Sinai through the wilderness to the plains of Moab (Num. 10:11—36:13).

The exodus story consists of a description of the situation and the call of Moses to lead the Israelites out of Egypt (Ex. 1—7); the conflict between YHWH and Pharaoh played out in the Plague Narratives (Ex. 8—11); the death of Egypt's first born in the final plague, the observance of Passover, departure (Ex. 12—13); and the final victory of YHWH over Egypt at the Sea (Ex. 14—15). The redemption from Egypt is a continuation of God's interaction with the ancestors, and it anticipates Israel's ongoing life in relation to YHWH.

Israel's stay at Sinai begins in Exodus 19:1 and concludes in Numbers 10:10. The sojourn at Sinai is bracketed by journeys (to Sinai in Ex. 15:22—18:27 and from Sinai in Num. 10:11—22:1). Obviously, the Sinai material is central to the story. Mount Sinai provides the context for ratification of the covenant (Ex. 19—24); instructions for and construction of the tabernacle (Ex. 25—31, 35—40); Israel's rebellion against YHWH with the golden calf, followed by a new covenant (Ex. 32—34); divine instructions for sacrifices and offerings (Lev. 1—7); founding of and inauguration of the tabernacle cult (Lev. 8—9); the death of Nadab and Abihu (Lev. 10); purity instructions (Lev. 11—15); the ritual for the annual day of purification (Lev. 16); instructions for Israel's practice of holiness (the Holiness Code, Lev. 17—26); a census of the people (Num. 1; compare Num. 26); and instructions for Israel's departure from Sinai (Num. 2:1—10:10).

At Sinai, YHWH provides Israel with instructions for community life and identity. The fundamental requirements are simple: right relationship with YHWH and right relationship with others in the community (see Deut. 6:4, Lev. 19:18; compare Mk. 12:28–34, Mt. 22:37–40, and Lk. 10:25–28). Relationship is at the heart of Israel's religious and social life. *Torah* is an expression of life lived in the presence of YHWH, a life lived rightly and justly. It includes both ritual and social instructions; they are of one cloth. Rather than being "a burden," the instructions of YHWH are viewed in terms of redemption. Divine *torah* speaks of the good life, the life of holiness, the life of faith and hope.

Even so, Israel's journey through the wilderness is marked by complaint against and conflict with YHWH. Complaints concerning food, water, and leadership arise immediately following Israel's departure from Egypt (Ex. 15:22—18:27). Open rebellion—worship of the golden calf—follows immediately on the ratification of the covenant (Ex. 32). Israel's journey from Sinai to the plains of Moab is again marked by rebellion and complaint (Num. 11:1—25:18). Israel does indeed strive with YHWH in the wilderness (see Gen. 32:28).

Israel's encampment in the plains of Moab, anticipating entry into the land, closes the book of Numbers with a sense of hope. Through repeated conflict and rebellion, YHWH maintains relationship with Israel, remains present in the midst of this community, and continues to provide it with instruction. *Torah* is an ongoing reality in the covenant community (see, for example, Num. 15 and Ex. 25:22).

Themes in Exodus

The Story of Redemption

YHWH's deliverance of Israel from Egypt provides the primary narrative of redemption in the Pentateuch. The "act of redemption," however, must be understood as a two-part movement. YHWH will bring the Israelites "out of" Egypt *and* bring them "into" the land of promise. YHWH states this clearly at the burning bush (Ex. 3:8; compare 6:6–8). The development of the oppressive situation in Egypt raises questions concerning the ancestral promises of people and land (for instance, Gen. 12:1–9; 15:1–21; and 17:1–8). For the promises to be realized, YHWH must deliver the people from Egypt and bring them into the land. Israel experiences Egypt as a life-and-death struggle to survive (see Ex. 1:7 and 1:13–14). In the face of the oppressor, Israel looks to YHWH and cries out for help.

"Theology" and "narrative" intersect. In order for YHWH to "bring Israel out of Egypt" and to "bring them into the land of promise," in order for the Israelites to survive the harsh realities of oppression and enter into the landed experience of life, they will have to travel from Egypt to the land of promise. Thus redemption, as narrated in this story, is understood as a *process*. The departure from Egypt is followed by the journey to Sinai and the ratification of the covenant. From Sinai, the covenant people make their way through the wilderness toward the promised land. At the heart of Israel's story of redemption are narratives of a journey out of pain, a journey to a mountain, a journey through the wilderness, and ultimately a journey into the land of promise.

Israel's journey has several interesting features. First, the redemptive process requires human agency and activity. Moses' mother and sister preserve his life when he is a baby (Ex. 2:1–4). Pharaoh's daughter, an Egyptian woman, draws Moses from the water (Ex. 2:5–10). The midwives disobey the orders of Pharaoh and preserve the lives of male babies (Ex. 1:15–21). Moses leads Israel out of Egypt and through the wilderness (Ex. 14—Num. 36) and saves them from the wrath of YHWH (Ex. 32:1–14; Num. 14:1–25). The story of YHWH's redemption of Israel is, at the same time, a story about human acts of redemption.

Second, the journey provides the occasion for Israel to struggle with matters relating to power, authority, and leadership. On the way to Sinai, Moses appoints judges to help in the deciding of cases (Ex. 18:13–23). After their departure from Sinai, Moses appoints seventy elders to help him (Num. 11:16–30). Although YHWH provides numerous instructions concerning cultic leadership at Sinai (Ex. 29:1–37; Lev. 21; and Num. 3—4), the journey from Sinai narrates a series of conflicts and rebellions dealing with this issue: Miriam and Aaron ask who mediates YHWH's words (Num. 12); and Korah, Dathan, and Abiram ask who may enter into the presence of YHWH in the holy place (Num. 16—17, after which YHWH provides additional instructions concerning the priesthood [Num. 18]). The text makes clear that struggles revolving around community leadership are struggles about the leadership of YHWH. It suggests that civil, social, and cultic leadership are necessary for the life of the community.

Third, redemption includes Israel's reception of the instructions of YHWH. Divine instruction (*torah*) is an element of the initial covenant relationship (as shown, for instance, in the Covenant Code in Ex. 20—23). Commandments are given at Mount Sinai (Lev. 27:34), but God also speaks to Moses in the tent of meeting in the wilderness of Sinai (Num. 1:1), giving additional instructions concerning the sacrifices and offerings (Num. 15). Still more instructional rulings are recorded as Israel camps in the plains of Moab, on topics as diverse as the ritual "calendar" (Num. 28—29; compare Lev. 23), the vows of women (Num. 30:1–16), and the establishment of cities of refuge and other matters relating to murder and revenge (Num. 35:9–34). The ark, according to the final editors of Exodus, will provide a location for continuing meeting and commandment giving (Ex. 25:22). In sum, Israel views YHWH's delivery of *torah* not simply as a once-for-all-time event but as a central element in its ongoing experience of redemption. YHWH is the creator, redeemer, covenant maker, and *torah* speaker.

Fourth, Israel's journey provides the context for conflict between YHWH and Israel. Israel complains concerning the lack of food and water (Ex. 15:22–26; 16:1—17:7; Num. 11:1–15, 31–35; and Num. 20:1–13). YHWH provides. Following the report of the spies concerning the land of Canaan, the Israelites rebel and refuse to enter and occupy it (Num. 14:1–12). YHWH becomes angry and declares that the people who lived in and departed from Egypt, with the exception of Joshua and Caleb, will not enter the land. They will die in the wilderness (Num. 14:20–45). At Sinai the people worship a golden calf (Ex. 32); and while camping in the plains of Moab, the people participate in the cult of the Baal of Peor (Num. 25). YHWH and Israel struggle to understand the meaning and nature of their relationship, to negotiate and, when necessary, renegotiate it.

The Story of Divine Presence

Moses kills an Egyptian, flees to Midian, and marries. While going about the everyday business of shepherding his father-in-law's flock, he is confronted by a burning bush (Ex. 3:1—4:17). At the bush, Moses is commissioned by YHWH to bring the people out of Egypt. In the scene, God's name, YHWH, is declared. Although an earlier form of the scene may well have functioned to narrate the first revelation of the divine name, the story now functions primarily to declare the meaning of the name and, through that meaning, something about the God whose name is YHWH. Indeed, the sending of Moses and the meaning of the divine name are interwoven in this text.

The narrator reports that God has heard the cries of the Israelites, has remembered the covenant made with the ancestors (2:23–25), and has come down to bring the people out of Egypt and to lead them up into the promised land (3:6–10). Moses initially resists and asks to be told the divine name. Whether Moses' question is read as clever negotiation, subversive request for power, legitimate concern for knowledge, or fearful request made in light of the demands of the project, the scene shows YHWH and Moses negotiating a relationship within the larger framework of a YHWH/Israel relationship that is also negotiated.

God's initial response to Moses' request is, "I will be who I will be" (*ehyeh asher ehyeh*, v. 14). Repeating a word already used in promise to

Moses—"I will be [*ehyeh*] with you" (v. 12)—God states yet again, "Tell the Israelites, 'I will be [*ehyeh*] has sent me to you'" (v. 14b; translations in this chapter are by the author). Then, within the context of the promise of divine presence, God answers Moses' question directly: "Tell them, YHWH [note the similarity in sound to the word *ehyeh*], the God of your ancestors…has sent me to you" (v. 15). The text explains the meaning of the divine name in terms of the promise of divine presence and the ancestral story. God says, in effect, "I am the God who made promises to your ancestors and who will now be present in your story."

The parallel narrative in Exodus 6:2–8 takes place in Egypt following Pharaoh's refusal to let the people go. In a carefully constructed speech, God declares, "I am YHWH" (6:2, 8), and proceeds to promise both deliverance from Egypt *and* entry into the promised land. The declaration of the name functions to tell the reader something about the God who dwells in the midst of Israel's life and story. This is a God who is against the oppression of Israelites, a God who acts on their behalf, and a God who remembers and remains faithful to past promises. YHWH is a God who is experienced within the context of a real flesh-and-blood human history.

Two other texts are of interest in relationship to the meaning of the divine name. Following the exodus from Egypt (Ex. 12—15) and the ratification of the Sinai covenant (Ex. 19—24), the Israelites worship a golden calf, an unfaithful act that breaks the covenant relationship (Ex. 32). YHWH is prepared to destroy the Israelites and start a new people with Moses, but Moses, by reminding YHWH of the ancestral promises, brings about a change on the part of YHWH (32:11–14). YHWH makes a new covenant (Ex. 34) and declares to Moses, "YHWH, YHWH, a merciful and gracious God, slow to anger, and abounding in unfailing love and faithfulness…" (34:6). The declaration reflects YHWH's willingness to change and adapt in order to be able to remain in the midst of Israel's story. Confronted with Israel's unfaithfulness and rebellion, YHWH must construct new modes of relationship. In similar fashion, in Numbers 14, when the people refuse to enter the promised land because of the negative report of the spies, YHWH is ready to disinherit them and begin a new story with Moses. Moses responds by citing the words of YHWH found in Exodus 34:6–7 and calls on YHWH to remain faithful to the previously declared promise of forgiveness (Num. 14:13–19). Again, YHWH listens to Moses. Divine name and divine presence are woven together in Israel's ongoing, negotiated, and, when necessary, renegotiated relationship with YHWH.

YHWH's presence in Israel's story is nuanced by the concrete situations that arise in the story. YHWH adapts to Israel's story in such a way that the reader comes to know and experience YHWH in the unfolding of the story. The exodus story depicts YHWH as the redeemer who brings the Israelites out of oppression, pain, and slavery. YHWH is actively engaged in conflict with a political power, a context that demonstrates YHWH's real-world involvement. The unfolding story itself interweaves multiple images: The God who created the world, who made promises to Israel's ancestors, is the God who acts to redeem the Israelites. Both the plagues and the sea event suggest that YHWH accomplishes Israel's redemption in part through the use of "the world of nature." YHWH's creative powers will also be witnessed in the wilderness when water and food are provided for the Israelites (see, for instance, Ex. 15:22–26; 16:1—17:7; Num. 11:1–9, 31–35).

Israel associated images of YHWH as creator and ruler with the image of YHWH as warrior. Israel's song of victory at the sea (Ex. 15:1–18) identifies YHWH as warrior (v. 3), ruler (v. 18), redeemer (v. 13), and the God of the sanctuary (v. 17; compare Psalms 74, 77, 78, and 136). Following Israel's departure from the sea, YHWH leads the people to Mount Sinai and enters into a covenant relationship with them. The images all emphasize the importance of Israel's belief that YHWH was a God who participated in Israel's story. These images reflect a profound belief that YHWH desires to be present in the midst of this community and to share its story.

The Priestly traditions, composed in all probability during the Babylonian exile (500s B.C.E.), associate the presence of YHWH with the tabernacle, the sacred tent that served as divine dwelling place. Following the ratification of the covenant (Ex. 24:1–14), Moses ascends the mountain and enters the glory that rests on top of the mountain. The glory is described as a cloud and devouring fire and is seen by all of Israel (Ex. 24:15–18). The tabernacle is built so that YHWH might dwell in the midst of the people (Ex. 25:2–9). Interestingly, Exodus 29:44–46 states that YHWH brought the Israelites out of Egypt *in order to* dwell in their midst and be their God, the latter phrase reflecting the Priestly version of the ancestral promises (compare Gen. 17:4–8; Ex. 6:2–8). The God who dwells in the tabernacle is the God of promise and the God of the exodus.

YHWH provides Moses with instructions for the tabernacle (Ex. 25—31), and Moses constructs it "just as YHWH commanded" (Ex. 35—40). The larger tabernacle structure is located on an east-west axis with the entry facing east. The outer structure is 100 cubits by 50 cubits (approximately 150 feet by 75 feet) and contains an outer court, the altar of burnt offerings, the laver, and a smaller tent. The inner tent is 30 cubits by 10 cubits (approximately 45 feet by 15 feet), and is divided into two parts: (1) an outer area, 20 cubits (approximately 30 feet) in length, that contains a table, the menorah, and the altar of incense; and (2) the Holy of Holies.

The Holy of Holies, located at the back of the smaller tent, is a square of 10 cubits (approximately 15 feet) in which is located the ark of the covenant. The ark, a wooden box overlaid with gold, contains the tablets of the covenant and is covered by "the mercy seat" (the place where expiation takes place). When Moses finishes setting up the tabernacle, the glory of YHWH fills the structure in the sight of all Israel (Ex. 40:34–38; compare Ex. 24:15–18). The glory of YHWH takes up residence in the holy place. YHWH's journey is now materially and concretely bound up with Israel's journey.

The texts emphasize that YHWH is present in the tabernacle as the holy one. Leviticus will provide instructions concerned with safeguarding the holiness of the tabernacle and YHWH: sacrifice, purity practices and rituals, the practice of right social relations. YHWH's holy presence generates specific responsibilities for Israel, but the nature of these responsibilities makes clear that holiness is understood, to a large degree, in relational terms (for more about this, see the next section).

The Story of Covenant and Law, Ritual, Sacrifices and Offerings, and Purity

Covenant and Law. The Sinai covenant is a central moment in Israel's story. YHWH and Israel enter into a binding relationship in which both parties recognize rights and responsibilities. The Sinai covenant reflects the politics of kings and subjugated peoples in the ancient Near East. Although YHWH initiates the covenant and in large part controls the boundaries established by it, Israel is viewed not as a defeated and subjugated people but as a redeemed people called to mission and service in the world (see Ex. 19:3–6). YHWH seeks loving allegiance, obedience, just social relations, and cultic faithfulness. At the same time, YHWH offers protection, prosperity, fertility, and hope. The Sinai covenant is concerned with defining the YHWH-Israel relationship and, in and through this relationship, Israel's identity as a people.

The Sinai covenant is brought into being through ritual enactment. The blood of sacrificed animals is placed on an altar, and then, following the people's affirmation that they will obey YHWH, Moses throws the remainder of the blood on the people (24:3–8). In this ritual, the blood of the animals (or possibly the "life" of the animals found in the blood; see Gen. 9:4 and Lev. 17:11, 14) functions to bind YHWH and the people together. Following the blood ritual, a representative group gathers on the mountain to eat and drink, and in the context of that meal, they see God (Ex. 24:9–11). The blood of slaughtered animals, a ritual meal, and divine presence are interwoven to mark the ritual origins of Israel as the Priestly kingdom of YHWH (see Ex. 19:5–6).

The YHWH-Israel relationship is forged, however, not only in blood but also in word. The words of the covenant are concerned with Israel's identity, destiny, and mission. Divine instructions concerning Israel's covenant responsibilities (the Ten Commandments, sometimes referred to as the Decalogue, in Ex. 20:1–17, and the Covenant Code in Ex. 21–23) are enclosed textually within the preparations for and enactment of covenant. The Ten Commandments have traditionally been viewed as the heart of the divine instructions for the covenant (Ex. 20:1–22; see Deut. 5:6–21 and Ex. 34:11–28 for similar groupings of divine instructions). In relation to the sacred, the people are not to worship other gods, make idols, or misuse the name of YHWH. In addition, they are to observe the Sabbath. In the context of the family, the Israelites are to honor and respect mother and father. In community relations, the Israelites are not to murder, commit adultery, steal, bear false witness, or covet that which belongs to a neighbor. Relationship with YHWH requires not only proper actions in relation to the sacred but also proper attitudes and actions in relation to other members of the community. The Holiness Code in Leviticus 17—26 also emphasizes that holiness is constituted in large part through the practice of right social relationships. In this way, it speaks against any and all efforts to divide cultic from social practices. Justice is a relational issue that is concretized in life practices.

The Ten Commandments have played an important role in the construction of moral and legal discourse in Western culture. Christian faith has rather consistently maintained a commitment to these words, even while dismissing much of the rest of the Sinai instructional material. Matthew's gospel reports that in the Sermon on the Mount (Mt. 5—7), Jesus addressed several matters drawn from the Sinai material: murder (5:21–26; compare Ex. 20:13 and Deut. 5:17), adultery (5:27–30; compare Ex. 20:14 and Deut. 5:18), divorce (5:31–32; compare Deut. 24:1–4), the taking of oaths (5:33–37; compare Lev. 19:12; Num. 30:2; and Deut. 23:21), retaliation (5:38–42; compare Ex. 21:24; Lev. 24:20; and Deut. 19:21), and love and hate (5:43–48; compare Lev. 19:18 and Deut. 23:6). Jesus does not, in this context, set aside the covenant instructions, but seeks to make explicit the interior ground of human action. Those who make up the people of God must be guided by their hearts and their minds and must recognize the role that the will plays in human action. This stress on the interior side of human action was well-known and understood by Israel. Deuteronomy 6:5, a text the gospels suggest was well-known and embraced by Jesus (Mt. 22:34–40; compare Lk. 10:25–28), calls for the Israelites to love God with all their hearts, souls, and might. Jeremiah stated that YHWH would make a new covenant with Israel and would write it on the hearts of the people (Jer. 31:31–34). Jesus, in the context of God's coming reign (Mt. 12:28; Mk. 1:15; Lk. 8:1, and elsewhere), interprets *torah* so as to make radical demands on the new community he calls into being. His approach, which is not contrary to the call of the community being formed through covenant at Sinai, continues an interpretive tradition that seeks to think about divine instruction in terms of the human heart and will.

A careful reading of the range of biblical texts concerned with divine instruction or *torah* indicates that a variety of interpretive traditions and perspectives have developed around this material. Rather than seeking absolute statements of "truth" or searching for absolute "norms," the lengthy and diverse interpretive tradition suggests that *torah* functions more as a site of reflection and struggle than as a final repository of truth. Those communities that seek to locate and understand themselves in relation to and in terms of biblical texts and biblical images of community must struggle to make sense of *torah* in the context of the ever-changing realities of the world. Just as YHWH was caught up in and bound to the ever-changing story of Israel's journey as the people of God, so all those communities who look to that story of divine promise, redemption, covenant, and freedom must engage in ongoing reflection and discourse about the nature of human life and human practice.

Ritual. As presented in the final form of the pentateuchal text, sacrificial rituals and purity concerns are a significant part of YHWH's *torah* instructions to Israel at Mount Sinai. The texts make no distinction between instructions that are "moral and ethical," on the one hand, and "ritual and cultic," on the other. All of YHWH's instructions are of equal status and designed to guide the Israelite community in the shaping of life lived within the context of the divine presence.

Christian interpretations of this material, especially Protestant interpretations, have often constructed a dichotomy between ritual practice and matters of the heart, with a decidedly negative evaluation of "ritual" and "law." These arguments often appeal to biblical texts such as Jeremiah's promise of a new covenant written on the heart (Jer. 31:31–34). Jeremiah, however, does not do away with "the law" when he locates covenant obedience and faithfulness in the heart. Paul's discussions of "the law and faith" (especially Gal. 3—5 and Rom. 2—8), are also cited as sources for contrasting a "law-based Judaism" with "faith-based Christianity." But Paul is specifically working to construct a Christianity acceptable to a Gentile audience. He is *not* seeking to understand Israel's faith and cultic practices in their own terms. A certain rendering of Judaism becomes a foil by which Paul is able to offer an alternative understanding of religious faith and practice, one he believes to be more acceptable to a Gentile audience. The epistle of James takes a somewhat different approach to the same issue: Faith without works is dead (Jas. 2:17). The author of the book of Hebrews seeks to interpret the entire tabernacle and sacrificial system of Israel in light of Jesus as "the greater priest" who functioned as the mediator of a "better covenant" (see 4:15—8:13). The writer of Hebrews states that Christ's sacrifice was offered once for sins (10:12) and declares, in effect, that the Jewish sacrificial system is null and void in relation to Christianity.

The above reflect early Christian efforts to understand the nature of Christianity over and against Judaism. All too often, Christian efforts to invalidate "the Jewish law" reflect a desire to speak of Christianity as the "true" religion, which has displaced or overcome the "false" religion of Judaism. Contemporary readings of the Pentateuch must seek to understand Israel's texts on their own terms and in their own words, not from a perceived position of superiority and absolute certainty. An engaged and sensitive reading will struggle to understand how these texts and practices functioned for the Israelites, why these texts and practices were important for them, and how these texts and practices contributed to Israel's self-understanding and identity. It will also understand that today's Judaism is no more identical with ancient Israelite religion than is today's Christianity (which also claims roots in that ancient religion). Such engaged thinking, grounded in respect, approaches the texts as sites for theological discourse, reflection, and construction.

The observance of Passover provides an excellent opportunity to reflect on the ways in which Israel brought together ritual, history, and social practices. Passover demonstrates at least one way in which ritual provides a framework within which the heart is able to experience the presence and redemptive activity of God.

Described as both a family meal to be observed in the home (Ex. 12:1–13, 21–27) and a pilgrimage festival that required travel to the central shrine (Deut. 16:1–2), the observance of Passover is historically associated with Israel's departure from Egypt (see Ex. 12; Josh. 5:10–12 associates the observance with Israel's entry into the land). In Egypt, the Israelite families were to slaughter a lamb and place some of its blood around their doors to protect their firstborn from death. The lamb served as the center of a meal. At later observances, the children were expected to ask, "Why do we do this?" and the elders were to respond, "Because of YHWH's act of redemption for us" (Ex. 12:25–27). The Passover meal provides a context in which past events become present realities, when the redemption out of Egypt is experienced as a present reality by every generation. "Remembering" in the context of this meal becomes a means by, in, and through which past, present, and future generations experience a common identity through a common experience.

Sacrifices and Offerings. The book of Leviticus locates the presentation of sacrifices and offerings at the center of Israel's cultic life. Although these practices had a long history in Israel, the present shaping of the sacrificial material represents one of the latest layers of tradition in the Pentateuch. Two sets of instructions are included, Leviticus 1:1—6:7 and 6:8—7:36. Five basic types of sacrifices and offerings are identified: whole burnt offerings (1:3–17 and 6:8–13), grain offerings (2:1–16 and 6:14–23), well-being offerings (3:1–17 and 7:11–36), purification offerings (4:1—5:13 and 6:24–30), and reparation offerings (5:14—6:7 and 7:1–6). The instructions provide basic frameworks for cultic presentations, but they also allow for a certain amount of freedom in the actual enactment of the ritual. Prescriptive (what should be done) and descriptive (what was done) accounts of actual rituals, such as the ritual for the ordination of the priesthood (Lev. 8), the seven-day ritual for the return to camp of a person recovered from an unclean skin blemish (Lev. 13), and the annual day of purification (Lev. 16), provide additional information on the nature and purpose of these ritual presentations.

Sacrifices are associated with a range of emotional responses, including joy, thanksgiving, remorse, confession, and lament. They address a range of concerns associated with the YHWH-Israel relationship, including the turning of the anger of YHWH, expiation of sin, purification of impurity, and "setting right" when one human being has acted improperly against another. Sacrifice was one means by which the Israelites could enter into YHWH's presence, bring their flesh-and-blood existence and concerns into the context of the sacred, and take responsibility for setting things right after disruptions in the social and cultic realms.

Purity. Closely related to the sacrificial system is the purity system (Lev. 11—15). Purity instructions must not be confused with moral instructions, although the two were not unrelated in Israelite thought and practice. Childbirth (Lev. 12), the flow of menstrual blood (Lev. 15:19–24), and sexual intercourse in which the male ejaculates (Lev. 15:18) were all thought to generate impurity, although none of these common human experiences were considered sinful. The purity instructions are focused on the tabernacle. When impurity is generated, it is attracted to and defiles the tabernacle. If the defilement is left unattended, YHWH's ongoing presence is jeopardized. YHWH, the holy one, will not dwell in the midst of impurities. Thus, the purity instructions are concerned with safeguarding the purity and holiness of the tabernacle.

The specific purity/impurity issues addressed in these chapters include clean and unclean foods, identification of animals whose carcasses generate uncleanness (Lev. 11), childbirth (Lev. 12), "flesh-eating" skin conditions and contaminated walls within houses (a condition traditionally but incorrectly translated "leprosy"; Lev. 13—14), and bodily discharges (Lev. 15). The boundaries of the body associated with food and procreation are of particular concern.

The instructions concerning bodily emissions seek to maintain a distinction between the realms of life and death. Any encroachment of death into the realm of the living generates impurity. In giving birth, a woman loses blood, blood associated with life (see Gen. 9:4–7 and Lev. 17:10–16). She finds herself in an ambiguous situation: In the moment of generating life, she experiences a loss of life. Unclean skin conditions involve an eating away of the flesh associated with death (see Num. 12:10–12). Persons ruled "unclean" by the priest were to move outside the camp, an expression of social death, until the skin condition changed and was declared "clean" by a priest. Bodily "flows" from the reproductive parts of the body generated uncleanness (Lev. 15). These rulings are designed to "set watch" over the body. Although they may sound strange and at times bizarre to modern readers, the rulings take seriously the bodied nature of human existence and at the same time locate common human experiences within the context of the sacred.

Conclusion

The books of Exodus, Leviticus, and Numbers constitute an instructional narrative designed to provide Israel with at least part of its story of national identity, mission, and meaning. A journey is made from slavery toward freedom. YHWH, the God of creation, the promise, and redemption, travels with Israel. At the center of the story is a narrative imaging of the divine-human relationship.

The story in these books speaks of the nature and identity of both YHWH and Israel, and the relationship that exists between them—a relationship that is under constant negotiation and revision. In profound ways, the relationship is marked by redemption, covenant, presence, and instruction. A journey from Egypt to the plains of Moab provides the context for the unfolding of this relationship.

Redemption in this story is understood as a process. Israel comes out of Egypt and moves toward the land of promise. Redemption, however, consists of more than just movement out of slavery and a journey toward freedom. Redemption includes a call for Israel to be faithful to YHWH, to follow the instructions of *torah,* to practice holiness in relation to YHWH, and to enact relationships of justice and honesty with other Israelites.

Torah, associated with the words of YHWH at Sinai, is viewed as an ongoing process of divine instruction. The divine directives for community existence are engaged with ever-changing situations and are adaptable to the demands of Israel's community life. In the same way that YHWH and Israel change in the unfolding of the story, *torah* is open to new and changing possibilities. *Torah* calls for interpretation, adaptation, and engagement with the world of Israel's concrete existence.

In this story, Israel is "on the way." Likewise, the story tells the reader that YHWH, bound up in Israel's story, is "on the way" with Israel. The story of these books suggests that the YHWH-Israel relationship is, in profound fashion, "on the way" to actualization and realization. Numbers closes with hope, but with anticipation of what awaits Israel on the other side of the river.

Resources

Joseph Blenkinsopp. *The Pentateuch: An Introduction to the First Five Books of the Bible.* The Anchor Bible Reference Library. New York: Doubleday, 1992.

David J. A. Clines. *The Theme of the Pentateuch.* Sheffield, U.K.: JSOT Press, 1978.

Terence E. Fretheim. *The Pentateuch.* Interpreting Biblical Texts. Nashville: Abingdon Press, 1996.

Jon D. Levenson. *Sinai and Zion: An Entry into the Jewish Bible.* San Francisco: Harper & Row, 1987.

Thomas W. Mann. *The Book of the Torah: The Narrative Integrity of the Pentateuch.* Atlanta: John Knox Press, 1988.

Dennis T. Olson. *The Death of the Old and the Birth of the New: The Framework of the Book of Numbers and the Pentateuch.* Brown Judaic Studies 71. Chico, Calif.: Scholars Press, 1985.

5

Deuteronomy

DALE PATRICK

In Hebrew, the fifth book of the Torah is referred to by its opening phrase, "These [are the] Words." The name Deuteronomy comes from the Greek translation and means "second law." The book recapitulates the divine law given at Horeb (this book's name for Mount Sinai). Deuteronomy 1:5 terms Moses' address an "explanation" of God's Torah (teaching).

The first step in our quest to understand what Moses has to teach the reader is to read the book attentively, so this chapter begins with a look at Deuteronomy's style and contents. After that, we inquire into its history and background, returning once more at the end to the task of reading the book.

At the outset, let's take note of some "obvious" but easily overlooked aspects that may represent Deuteronomy's most important contribution to the message of the Pentateuch.

The book is chiefly given over to Moses' speaking.

"You" are addressed. Ostensibly, the addressees are the generation of Israelites who were born to the generation that came out of Egypt and entered into covenant with YHWH at Mount Horeb.

Now Moses speaks to the reader of scripture. Just as YHWH's covenant at Horeb was made "not with our fathers…but with us" (5:3), so the covenant made in the plain of Moab is "not only with you, but with those who are not here with us this day" (29:14–15). (Translations in this chapter are by the author.)

Moses instructs the common man and woman. "This commandment which I command you today is not too mysterious for you, neither is it far off…The word is very near you, in your mouth and in your heart, to do it" (30:11–14). Concepts are explained and repeated. The focus is on what is expected of the addressees; theological concepts are employed as backing. Moses not only explains, he motivates.

Moses constantly reviews the events of the past. When Moses rehearses these memories, he draws out the lessons the audience can learn. One now understands the plan of God running through the people's history. The individual can recognize who he or she is as a member of this people.

A sense of urgency hangs over this address. Every choice is a decision between life and death (11:26–28; 30:15–20). The addressees stand on the threshold of the next great action of YHWH's plan, the conquest and settlement of the land promised to Abraham. The Pentateuch ends on this note of incompleteness and expectation. Later Israelites are to imagine that moment of hopeful incompleteness and transfer that consciousness to their present.

The address is repetitious. Characteristic formulas exhorting the audience to listen up to what is being commanded and to follow it dutifully recur so often that one begins to read past them. These formulas, however, are sometimes clues to the structure of the discourse, somewhat like punctuation to signal the beginnings and ends of units. With them as our guide, let's survey the sections of the book.

Reading through Deuteronomy

The Introduction (Deuteronomy 1—11)

The first time we are told to attend to prescriptions and judgments is at the beginning of chapter 4. This command signals the end of Moses' narration of what has transpired since the people were commanded to leave Horeb (chaps. 1—3) and leads into a sermon on what sets Israel's religious tradition apart from all others.

The sermon (Deut. 4) appeals to Israel's pride. The prescriptions and judgments that Moses teaches them will show other peoples that Israel is "a wise and understanding people" (4:6). The people can learn the content of the divine will by attending to how the commandments were revealed. From this they should learn not to make any image of YHWH or to regard any heavenly being as anything but a creature (4:19–20). YHWH is without rival (4:32–35).

Deuteronomy 5:1 begins a new unit, calling the audience to hear prescriptions and judgments. What follows, surprisingly, is a story: the story of the revelation of the Ten Commandments. The Decalogue ("ten words" = Ten Commandments) is presented in a way that suggests that it is the primary content of the Horeb covenant, and indeed it is the only law text from Exodus actually reproduced in Deuteronomy. However, the wording in Deuteronomy 5 varies slightly from Exodus 20, indicating a certain nonchalance toward the literal. After hearing the Ten Commandments, we are told, Israel asked Moses to serve as mediator. Moses then received "all the commandments and the prescriptions and judgments" (5:31). This could well allude to the book of the covenant (Ex. 20:22—23:19), making Deuteronomy 12—26 an "interpretation" of that book for new conditions.

Deuteronomy 6:1–3 contains the most elaborate introductory exhortation in the book, prefacing its most famous passage: "Hear [*shema'*], O Israel, YHWH our God [is] one YHWH. And you shall love YHWH your God with all your heart, and with all your soul, and with all your might" (6:4–5). The exact meaning of these statements is to be filled out by the interpreter. It can well be considered the summary of Moses' teaching in this book.

Moses teaches his audience ways to teach their children. They are to tell the story of deliverance from Egypt and the gift of the land. The commandments are part of God's plan for Israel's good (6:20–25).

Deuteronomy 6—11 contains a series of "model sermons"; the first is 6:10–15. YHWH is about to give Israel a land that is already set up for living. Israel must remain loyal to him; YHWH will remove it if it does not. Chapter 8 expounds a similar theme, warning that pride in their own accomplishments must not lead the people to worship gods of their own making (8:17–19).

Chapter 7 admonishes Israel concerning the upcoming conquest. Conquered peoples must be wiped out lest they lead Israelites into apostasy (7:2–4). The effort to explain this policy calls forth the most profound theological teaching in the book. Israel is *holy,* set apart for intimate association with YHWH; Israel *as a whole* is holy, not just the priestly class. Israel's holiness is bestowed by election: "YHWH your God *has chosen* you to be a people for his own possession out of all the peoples that are on the face of the earth" (7:6). It was not some quality inherent in the people that moved YHWH to choose Israel; YHWH was simply moved by love (7:8).

Moses returns to the topic of election two more times in chapters 6 through 11. Deuteronomy 9:4–7 rules out any thought that Israel has earned YHWH's favor by its "righteousness." In 10:14–15, Moses sets forth election as a paradox: YHWH owns all creation, yet fell in love with one particular family and chooses to continue that relationship with the audience.

Chapter 11 draws together themes from the previous sermonic chapters and culminates in a call to decision: "See, I am setting before you today blessing and curse: the blessing when you obey the commandments of YHWH...the curse if you do not obey" (11:26–28). The purpose of this challenge is to make the audience realize that it forges its destiny as a people in the day-to-day decisions of its members.

Prescriptions and Judgments (Deuteronomy 12—26)

Although exhortation formulas appear in 8:1, 10:12, and 11:1, only in 12:1 does exhortation lead to the proclamation of law. Where will Israel worship YHWH? At the place YHWH chooses (12:5–7). Moses admits that he is requiring a change in religious practice (12:8). When only one legitimate altar is allowed, those who live at some distance from it will have to change their ways of slaughtering for food. Tithes of grains and oils and the sacrifice of firstborn male sheep, goats, and cattle must be done at the (distant) altar (12:17–18). Deuteronomy 14:22–29 and 15:19–23 explain how to do it.

There are also some changes to the celebration of major feasts (16:1–17). Feasts that were once celebrated at a local altar now entail a trip to the one legitimate altar. Even the home sacrifice of Passover (Ex. 12:21–28) is removed to the central sanctuary.

The institution of a triennial tithe (14:28–29 and 26:12–15) shows another emphasis of Deuteronomy 12—26: providing for the welfare of Israelites who lack sufficient income or are otherwise disadvantaged. Deuteronomy has extensive "humanitarian" provisions. Even animals are granted rights (22:6–7; 25:4).

Deuteronomy 13 commands the suppression of apostasy, whether advocated by individuals (13:1–5, 6–11) or a whole city (13:12–18). The primary concern of these laws is to strengthen the will to resist competing teachings. The penalty for the guilty is, of course, death. The motive clause, "so you shall purge the evil from your midst" (13:5; compare 13:11), assumes collective accountability and guilt: An offense by an individual or group can implicate the whole nation, but the execution of offenders has a quasi-atoning effect. Thus, capital punishment functions to avert collective guilt and national judgment (13:17b–18). Another apostasy case (17:2–7) seeks to protect the innocent from false accusations. Conviction and execution of an innocent person entails the same collective guilt as failing to convict the guilty, so one must guard against false witness (19:15–20), and cities of refuge are provided in case of accidental homicide (see 19:10 and 19:13).

Apostasy is not the only crime to entail collective guilt. Homicide (19:1–13), false testimony (19:15–19), kidnapping (24:7), adultery (22:22, 23–27), divination (18:9–11), and dishonoring parents (21:18–21) also implicate the community. For the case of an unsolved murder, Deuteronomy provides a rite that absolves the community's guilt (21:1–9).

To fulfill its legal responsibilities, the community must install conscientious and knowledgeable judges and clerks. Moses calls for this in 16:18–20 and then sets out the responsibilities of the courts in towns (17:2–7). A consulting body at the central shrine (17:8–13) advises the local courts on matters of legal principle and concept and hears cases involving suspect testimony (19:15–21).

The section governing the judiciary (16:18—17:13) is followed by provisions relating to kings, Levitical priests, and prophets. The law of the king (17:14–20) does not specify his function or authority, only the limits on his freedom of action. Deuteronomy 18:1–8 adjusts the rights and duties of priests to the provision for the centralization of worship. In 18:9–22, prophets are authorized as YHWH's living oracles, but the people must be able to judge who is abusing this authority (18:9–22).

These laws for officials constitute a rudimentary constitution. It was not customary for ancient Near Eastern law codes to spell out the powers and limits of the officials of the state; Deuteronomy is venturing into uncharted territory. The book assumes that YHWH is the sovereign in the full sense and that YHWH exercises sovereignty primarily through law.

Chapters 19 through 20 are organized by subject: homicide in 19:1–13, suspect testimony (which could amount to homicide) in 19:15–21, and the tribal militia in chapter 20. The laws in chapters 21 to 25 seem more haphazard, although 22:13–30 covers various aspects of marriage and adultery and 23:1–9 specifies categories of men who cannot "enter the assembly of YHWH" (presumably the sanctuary). Otherwise, the laws in these chapters alternate between humanitarian preachments, capital offenses, and customs. The very absence of conceptual order may be designed to keep the reader from dividing between weighty and inconsequential, moral and ritual, for officials and for laity.

After 12:1, we do not find formulaic exhortations signaling section breaks. There are a few introductory temporal clauses, such as "when you come into the land…" (12:1, 20; 17:14; 19:1; 21:1; 26:1), but they do not—except for the first and last—begin deliberately crafted units. Chapter 26 prescribes two rituals to celebrate once the people have settled in the land and begun to harvest grain crops (26:5–12 and 26:13–15). The chapter ends with a unit (26:16–19) that could belong to a covenant ceremony, but no rubrics are given to make that clear.

Concluding Scenes (Deuteronomy 27—34)

Deuteronomy 27 is a puzzle. Abruptly, Moses is joined by "elders." The text calls for construction of a sanctuary on Mount Ebal near Shechem.

After sacrifices and a feast, Moses is to declare that Israel has become the people of YHWH and therefore is obligated to keep these laws. He is to arrange for a ritual of blessing and cursing. Enter abruptly the Levites, who curse a series of twelve types of offenders, followed each time by an Amen.

Chapter 28 returns to Moses addressing Israel. He sets before them blessings for obedience and curses for disobedience. The vast majority of these apply to the people collectively. Dire threats lend urgency to the exhortations to obey YHWH's commandments. At the end of the blessings and curses, an impersonal narrator intervenes to characterize either the words just spoken or the words that follow as a "covenant" (29:1). This is the first time Moses' present address has been termed a "covenant." Moreover, this verse, unlike other covenant references in Deuteronomy (compare 5:2, 3; 17:2; even 29:12), speaks of a covenant between Moses and Israel rather than YHWH and Israel.

When Moses resumes speaking (29:2), it sounds as though he is making a new beginning. The speech (29:2—30:20) sounds as though Moses is addressing a future audience that has suffered the consequences he mentions.

In chapter 31, Moses prepares for his death by installing Joshua as his successor (31:7–8, 14–15, 23) and passing on his law to the Levites (31:9–13). Now, just before Moses' death, YHWH tells him of the coming judgment of his people and commands him to write it as the song in chapter 32. As if to counterbalance this dark vision, Moses blesses the tribes in another poem (chap. 33, something like an updating of Jacob's blessing in Gen. 49). Upon completing the blessing, Moses ascends Pisgah, views the promised land, and dies (chap. 34).

The Story Behind Moses' Address

A bit more than two hundred years ago, biblical scholars began to question the tradition, long held by Jews and Christians, that Moses wrote the Pentateuch. They sought evidence within the Pentateuch for when it was written and by whom. The first real breakthrough occurred when it was realized that the variation in the names or nouns for God in Genesis (long noted by Jewish scholars) could be coupled with style and vocabulary, repetitions and discrepancies, customs and laws, and depictions of God, to identify a multiplicity of authors from different times and places. The theory devised to account for the evidence was termed the *documentary hypothesis* because it understood the text to be made up of different documents or sources edited together. Deuteronomy provided criteria for sequencing the sources and a historical point of reference for locating the works on the calendar. Some church fathers had already recognized that Deuteronomy was the basis of Josiah's reform (2 Kings 22:3—23:25). In 1805, a German scholar named W.M.L. De Wette argued that Deuteronomy—or some portion of it—had been written just before this reform; it was a "pious fraud," composed to claim Mosaic authority for the reform of national religious life carried out by King Josiah.

Because the identification of Josiah's law book with Deuteronomy is so important for scholarship, let's look briefly at 2 Kings 22—23. During the renovation of the Jerusalem temple, about 621 B.C.E., a scroll of laws was found and read to Josiah. Josiah "rent his clothes," obviously distressed by what it said. He sent a delegation to the prophetess Huldah to determine its authenticity. She responded with a prophecy of judgment against the kingdom but said Josiah would die before it came about. Josiah convened a national assembly, at which he read the whole book and entered into a "covenant" (23:3). Then he began his reform.

We can reconstruct the contents of his book from the measures he took. Because all biblical law books forbid the worship of any god besides YHWH, Josiah's actions against other gods do not help us decide which book he was reading. His removal of the high places—local shrines—is another matter. Only Deuteronomy restricts sacrifice to one altar "at the place YHWH will cause his name to dwell." Centralization of sacrificial worship was an innovation, and celebration of Passover at the central shrine was a significant aspect. Other actions of Josiah also fit the provisions of Deuteronomy.

If De Wette's link between Deuteronomy and Josiah's reform is correct, then we have an absolute date (621 B.C.E.) for the publication of one part of the Pentateuch and a criterion for dating other parts. Those that do not know the centralization of worship—that is, the sources eventually named the Yahwist (J) and the Elohist (E)—must be earlier than Deuteronomy, whereas material that presumes such centralization—that is, what we now call the Priestly material (P)—must be later. (For more on J, E, and P, see pp. 29–33.)

Although other parts of the four-document hypothesis are under assault, De Wette's identification of Deuteronomy as the scroll of laws found by Josiah and made the basis of his reform has held up very well and is still in favor with a large majority of critical biblical scholars. This basic identification generates further questions. First, *What part of our present book of Deuteronomy was on the scroll read by Josiah?* The present book seems rather long to be read aloud in a single session. Moreover, some parts of Deuteronomy function mostly to weave it into its narrative setting; these parts would not have been needed in a stand-alone law book. Which parts of the book match up with Josiah's reforming activities? Deuteronomy 12—19 contains many provisions for the centralization of sacrifice. Chapters 20 through 25 do not deal with centralization, but the tithe ritual in chapter 26 does. The reaction of Josiah and Huldah to hearing the scroll suggests that the curses of chapter 28 were in the text they heard. This suggests that at least chapters 12–19, 26, and 28 were present in Josiah's book. How about chapters 4 to 11? Nothing in the report of the reform confirms them, but neither does anything exclude the possibility that they and 20 to 25 were present.

There is also the question, *How was the text that was read by Josiah supplemented and edited into the larger narrative complex to which it now belongs?* Martin Noth suggested that Deuteronomy begins a Deuteronomistic Historical Work that continues through Joshua, Judges, 1 and 2 Samuel, and 1 and 2 Kings. This work tells the story of how the people of God came into their inheritance and then lost it. Its authors incorporated and integrated older texts into the narrative. The legal document from Josiah's reform was incorporated to set the norms against which the people are judged and found wanting. Moses' narration in Deuteronomy 1—3 constitutes the introduction to the whole Deuteronomistic History, and chapters 29 to 34 link Deuteronomy to the next act of the drama.

Is there evidence that the text of Deuteronomy 5—28 was revised and supplemented between the time that Josiah promulgated it and the time when it was incorporated into the Deuteronomistic History? Some scholars scour the text for evidence of sequences of revisions, down to verse and part verse. Others feel that only a handful of passages (for instance, 14:3–20 and 27:1–26) interrupt the textual flow, style, and form abruptly enough to be considered additions. In this vein, Frank Crüsemann says that

> the regulations fit together in a compact, nearly contradiction-free whole. In spite of the many indications of editorial work, the whole appears to have been conceived as a whole and is juridically well conceived. (Crüsemann, 207)

The same can be said of the sermons in chapters 6 to 11.

When the Deuteronomic Law was incorporated into the Deuteronomistic History, it played an introductory role. When it came to be grouped with Genesis through Numbers as one of the five "books of Moses," its function shifted: Instead of an introduction to the books that followed, it became a wrap-up and recapitulation of the books that preceded it. Nevertheless, Deuteronomy plays this canonical role so well that the reader does not notice any discrepancy. The address of the Deuteronomic Moses becomes a homiletical re-presentation of earlier Pentateuchal narratives. Clearly, this "preacher" expects addressees to know some versions of Israel's story well and seeks to build on their memory. The preacher rewords (rather than simply referring to) many provisions of the book of the covenant (Ex. 20:22—23:19). In the process, Deuteronomy 12—26 adapts the older law code to the point of replacing it, not simply restating but revising divine law for settled life in the promised land.

The Roots of Josiah's Book

Was Josiah's law book itself composed entirely in the era of Josiah (De Wette's "pious fraud"), or was it assembled by editors from earlier documents? Scholarly thought on this question has undergone many twists and turns in the past century or so. Many scholars of an earlier generation thought they found evidence of earlier documents. For instance, one might suppose one source for laws written in "if...then..." style (such as 21:1–9, 15–17, 18–21; 22:13–29; 24:1–4; and 25:5–10), another source for commandments that identify acts as "abomination" (16:21—17:1; 18:9–12; 22:5; 23:18; 25:13–16), and another for humanitarian laws (such as 22:1–4; 23:15–16; and 19–20).

Another type of theory regarded the text as going back to some core series of laws that had then undergone amplifications and revisions. For instance, a scholar named Friedrich Horst proposed that Deuteronomy 12—18 grew from a list of YHWH's privileges similar to the one found in Exodus 34:11–26. Although no one proposal has carried the day, the idea that the legal section of Deuteronomy grew through layers of supplementation is still popular.

In the early 1900s, a number of scholars turned from the quest to reconstruct earlier written stages of Deuteronomy and began to ask instead about the traditions that might underlie it. *Tradition* here refers to anything that is passed on—practices as well as words, oral as well as written words, ideas as well as statements. Traditions are often local, bound to particular places, fostered by the groups associated with them. Some traditions are taken up by others; they may become the possession of a whole nation. Traditio-historical research seeks to discover the origin and dispersion of traditions.

Gerhard von Rad proposed that both the Deuteronomic and Sinaitic covenant traditions were rooted in a "covenant renewal" festival that would have drawn Israel's twelve tribes together as a confederation. He conjectured, on the basis of Deuteronomy 27 and Joshua 8:30–35 and 24:1–28, that such a festival would have involved recital of YHWH's saving deeds, proclamation of divine law, blessings and curses, and a ratification ritual. He suggested that it would have been performed regularly (perhaps every seven years, as commanded in Deuteronomy 31:9–13) at Shechem (a location mentioned in Deuteronomy 27). According to this explanation,

Deuteronomy 27—which doesn't fit too well in the book as it now stands—is a piece of older tradition that clung to the developing text even though Josiah's application assumed that the chosen place for sacrifice was Jerusalem.

An association between Deuteronomy and traditions of the northern regions of Israel (where Shechem is located) is also suggested by striking resemblances in wording and ideas between Deuteronomy and the northern prophet, Hosea. The sermon in Deuteronomy 8 virtually reproduces Hosea 13:4–8, and Deuteronomy 12:2 is strongly reminiscent of Hosea 4:13. Both books focus on loyalty to YHWH and characterize the proper relationship between YHWH and Israel as one of love. Tradition historians have speculated that Hosea might have been rooted in the covenant tradition associated with Shechem and his book preserved by the circles that produced Deuteronomy.

Observing that Deuteronomy has a very sermonic character and that the Levites are very prominent in its laws, von Rad also suggested that perhaps the book was rooted in the preaching of Levites who taught the law in country towns. Such Levites might have carried their traditions to the Southern Kingdom when they fled Assyrian subjugation of their own kingdom in 732 and 722 B.C.E.

Other scholars, in the middle decades of this century, inquired into the roots of the formal structure of Israel's covenant with YHWH. Klaus Baltzer and George Mendenhall were struck by the similarities between Sinaitic covenant texts and the forms and concepts used in ancient international treaties. But as decades passed and the details were examined more closely, the fit between those biblical texts and the purported treaty prototype came into question. D. J. McCarthy concluded that the covenant texts in Exodus did not really conform to the mentality of international power politics and did not have all the elements of the Hittite suzerain-vassal treaties to which Baltzer and Mendenhall had compared them. But treaty terminology and ideas do become prominent in the Deuteronomic covenant between YHWH and Israel, with a historical prologue in chapters 5 to 11, stipulations in chapters 12 to 26, provision for preservation and reading of the treaty in 31:9–13, and blessings and curses in chapter 28.

In recent decades, tradition history has fallen into disfavor, to be replaced by a revived, skeptical source criticism that tends to invert the order of influence and development assumed by earlier scholars. Lothar Perlitt, for example, traces all references to covenant and law in the Exodus account to the Deuteronomic school. According to Perlitt, the retelling of the revelation of the Ten Commandments (Deut. 5) produces the telling of it (Ex. 19—20).

Moshe Weinfeld looks for Deuteronomy's authors in the reign of Josiah, indeed, among the scribes of the Judean royal court. The sermonic tone of Moses' address is not, according to Weinfeld, evidence of otherwise unattested Levitical preaching, but of scribal training in wisdom and rhetoric. Life is most obvious in the Deuteronomic offers of reward for obedience (8:1; 11:9; 16:20; 22:7, etc.) and threats of punishment for disobedience (7:20; 8:19, etc.). For Weinfeld, the theme of parental teaching (6:7–8, 20–25) recalls the instructional pattern of Proverbs. He points out that some provisions of the code (Deut. 19:14; 23:16, 22–24; 25:13–16) have parallels in Proverbs rather than the book of the covenant.

Because royal scribes would have been trained in drafting treaties, we can easily imagine them adapting the international suzerain-vassal treaty (in its Assyrian-era form, not the older Hittite form) to the relationship between YHWH and Israel. Parts of the curses in Deuteronomy 28 follow the exact order of Assyrian curses, and in Assyrian treaties the relationship of vassal to suzerain is described as "love," "fear," "swear," "obey the voice," and "be perfect." The treaties describe treason as "going after others," "turning to others," and "serving others." This language was absorbed into theology with a minimum of alteration.

Although Weinfeld's views are currently popular, the traditio-historical studies should not be discarded out of hand. Some of the older hypotheses still illuminate aspects of the text. To reap the full benefit of this scholarship, we should suppress the urge toward a comprehensive, consistent explanation.

Research into Legal Innovation

Just what was new in the Deuteronomic law, and how did the supporters of innovation persuade people to accept it? To conclude our critical analysis of the book, let us survey the results of two recent studies.

Bernard Levinson has studied how the authors of Deuteronomy composed their proposal for cultic centralization. He accepts DeWette's identification of Deuteronomy (or, at least, a stratum of chaps. 12—18) as the document adopted by Josiah as the charter of his reform. He subscribes to Weinfeld's identification of the authors as royal scribes. He also assumes that the authors had the book of the covenant (now found in Ex. 20:22—23:19) in their possession and appropriated certain phrases from it. He then does an intertextual analysis, showing how one text cites and reapplies words from another. For example, Deuteronomy 12:13–15—which aims to ease problems created by the new centralized sacrificial policy—takes up the phrase "in every place" from Exodus 20:24 and uses it in three different ways. The citations make the innovation sound like it is an application of the old law to the present, whereas actually the innovation replaces the older law. Levinson finds the same "subversive" compositional technique in the Passover prescriptions (Deut. 16:1–8, citing phrases from Ex. 23:15, 18; 12:21–28; and 13:3–10). He also examines Deuteronomy 16:18—17:20 to show how the centralization of the cult affected the judicial system and monarchy.

Showing how the authors of Deuteronomy introduced their legal innovations is only half of Levinson's argument. He also wants to demonstrate how radical the innovation was.

> The Deuteronomic program of religious, legal, administrative, and ethical innovation was unprecedented...The Deuteronomic program...departed from and challenged conventions of thought, belief and action...Deuteronomy both promotes a radical innovation in ancient Israelite religion and represents a meditation upon what is necessary to accomplish a profound cultural transformation. (Levinson, 149–50)

Is the centralization of sacrificial worship, however, the great clue or a great trap for the interpreter of Deuteronomic law? Was it, as Levinson supposes, a radical innovation that drove everything else in Deuteronomy, or was it the culmination of an evolution, and perhaps a sideshow to Deuteronomy's most important innovations? Frank Crüsemann regards it as the latter. The clue for him is the little-noticed set of regulations of the tithe (a tenth of vegetable produce, discussed in 14:22–29 and 26:12–15). This tithe had probably once been paid to the monarchy or the sanctuary. Deuteronomy gives it to the producer to eat (with family and the needy) at the central shrine two of every three years; on the third year, it is distributed in the producer's town to the needy. (Thus, it becomes a welfare tax.) The tithe law stands at the center of Deuteronomic freedom theology (note how often Deuteronomy mentions Israel's liberation from Egyptian bondage). It ensures that Israelite farmers are obligated for payment to no one except the liberating God and those who do not share in the blessings of freedom and ownership of land (Crüsemann, 221). The addressees' gain in economic autonomy entails new responsibilities for the welfare of the vulnerable. Blessing is continually promised the addressees so that they can share it. According to Crüsemann, centralization boosted the temple's prestige and theological status while actually reducing royal and priestly revenues.

Crüsemann regards Deuteronomic law as a "democratization" of Israelite polity. The people initiate the institution of the monarchy, set up judges, scrutinize prophets, and make war. The law even limits the power of patriarchy within the family and the human exploitation of animals. Crüsemann calls this constitution a "theocracy as democracy." The

> deuteronomic law achieved its shape against the background of a situation in which the Judean *'am ha'ares* (lit., "people of the land," actually, "free property owners") themselves seized power. The law gave form and legitimation to this genuine popular rule. The collapse of Assyrian domination brought additional possibilities for the application of new political ideas (215).

Crüsemann's portrayal of the Deuteronomic reform as an incipient social gospel needs to be balanced by a recognition of its "conservative" side, emphasizing corporate accountability. Running through the laws are admonitions to the addressees to "purge the evil from your midst" (for instance, 13:5 and 17:7) and "not to show pity" (for instance, 13:8 and 19:13), so that "all Israel will hear, and fear, and never again do such an evil among you" (such as 19:20; 21:21b). These instructions are attached to serious offenses that entail capital punishment. These exhortations make the people and their courts of elders responsible for protecting their nation from guilt, and the laws are formulated from the community's perspective. Earlier laws are reworded to describe the case from the community's point of view for virtually all capital crimes recorded in Deuteronomy 12—26. The Deuteronomic law does not appear to change the judicial practice at this point, but it has framed it with a much more explicit corporate responsibility and accountability. Israel's failure to purge the evil from its midst will bring curse upon it (28:15–68).

Synthesis: Back to Scripture

Our task of understanding Deuteronomy is not complete until we return to the text printed in Bibles, the text read in the Jewish synagogue and Christian church, preserved after the book found by Josiah was taken up into the ongoing tradition. The Bible is not a library, but one work drawn from many sources. It was this one work that was received as God's work, God's word to the people of God. Hence, it is read as it comes in its composite form and is to be interpreted by the religious communities in this form. The final form is also the form that has had an impact on history. Good readers, whether religious or secular, open to learning what the text has to say, do not construct the text that they want, but interpret the received text as the best text it can be.

Can we go back to the final form? Have we not lost our innocence? We now know that it is not the historical Moses who addresses us. We are conscious of the composite character of the text and know something about the times various parts of it were composed. We know that Deuteronomy is not a simple recapitulation of the story told in the first four books of the Pentateuch, but a program for changing the community under the guise of restoring it. We now know that the clever strategies of Jewish and Christian interpreters for harmonizing Deuteronomic teaching with Exodus, Leviticus, and Numbers are rather futile: There is no way to construct, for example, a common doctrine of the tithe or the legitimacy of sanctuaries.

Perhaps we should settle for keeping the analytical and final form tracks of interpretation separate, forgetting what we have learned through critical scholarship when we read the final form as a kind of "poetic" work. When we do this, however, we know down deep that we are ignoring a dimension of the truth about the text. To set aside what we have learned from critical scholarship is to abandon all claim to historical revelation and to be satisfied with a fiction.

How, then, do we incorporate the knowledge we gain from critical analysis into our final form reading? I think we can discern an inner logic running through the evolution of a text from its original publication to its final form. Deuteronomy is a legal text that came into being at a particular moment of crisis and met that crisis with explosive power. It was a timely word; it prepared the people for exile and provided a way to maintain their religious vocation without king or temple or even land. It was taken up into the tragic Deuteronomistic History to provide the hermeneutical key for understanding what had happened. Then it was attached to the first four books of the Torah and became the recapitulation of the narrative of Israel's origins and the restatement of the law for the people who read the text as scripture.

The first thing that we noticed about Deuteronomy was that it addresses the reader from beginning to end. Direct address distinguishes Deuteronomy from the first four books of the Pentateuch and from the six books of history to follow. The address within the narrative world reaches out from that world to the reader. Such addresses to the book's audience do occur occasionally in Exodus—for instance, in the institution of the feasts of Passover and unleavened bread (Ex. 12—13) and in the proclamation of the commandments (Ex. 20). Deuteronomy raises this subtle rhetorical device to another level: History and law and admonition become the reader's story, "today" becomes our day. In the narratives of Exodus, Leviticus, and Numbers, Moses relays YHWH's words; in Deuteronomy he speaks, one human to another, as interpreter. The deeds that YHWH performed are also given a rhetorical function in Moses' preaching: They are filled with lessons for the reader. Moses thereby teaches us how to read the narratives of Genesis through Numbers, and Joshua too. The reader should take pride in being a Jew, set apart, holy; Israel should not, however, take pride in its own prowess or virtue. Whatever the people are is by divine grace, and they had better take care not to arouse YHWH's wrath.

The Pentateuch recounts YHWH's deeds to give authority and motive force to YHWH's commandments. When the Deuteronomic Moses reviews the story to instill the will to obey, he explicates this connection running through the first four books.

What are we to make of legal innovation that is couched as an interpretation of divine law that the people already know? Von Rad has helped us see that Deuteronomy had deep roots in northern tradition. If Crüsemann is right, ideas were abroad in Judah in Josiah's time, which prepared its people for this new law. King and people took ownership of the law and immediately took collective action to implement its programmatic provisions. Many scholars regard this whole transaction as a royal seizure of power. No doubt Josiah saw its advantages, but there is no reason to discount the enthusiasm of the people. Josiah revived the militia, enlisting the people in the defense of the kingdom and providing leadership opportunities. His reform was a national revival, which prepared the people for the coming years under weak kings and then without a king at all.

Josiah's book was designed to avert the exile, but it actually prepared the people to live without king or temple, even to live away from its land. When the sacrificial altars were removed from the cities and towns outside Jerusalem, people learned to live without altars. A new type of piety emerged, in which sacrifice was a distant symbol and everyday life was the practice of obedience. Out of it grew the sentiment expressed in Psalm 51:17:

> The sacrifice acceptable to God is a broken spirit;
> a broken and contrite heart, O God, thou wilt not despise.

These ruminations about the fate of Deuteronomy in the era of exile are not extraneous to the book we have now. The last chapters, especially chapters 30 and 32, speak to exiles. The bulk of Deuteronomy was probably designed to preserve Israel, settled on its land, ruled by its own king, sacrificing at the altar that bears YHWH's name, in YHWH's good graces. The closing chapters reshape this message into a call for repentance and rededication in the firm hope of return and restoration (30:1–10). This is, in fact, where the text leaves us: The reader is an exile who is still claimed by God, still a member of God's elect, still called to obedience, still on the threshold of the promised land.

Resources

Frank Crüsemann. *The Torah: Theology and Social History of Old Testament Law.* Translated by Allan Mahnke. Minneapolis: Fortress Press, 1996.

Bernard M. Levinson. *Deuteronomy and the Hermeneutics of Legal Innovation.* Oxford, U.K.: Oxford University Press, 1997.

E. W. Nicholson. *Deuteronomy and Tradition.* Oxford, U.K.: Clarendon Press, 1967.

Dennis T. Olson. *Deuteronomy and the Death of Moses: A Theological Reading.* Overtures to Biblical Theology. Minneapolis: Fortress Press, 1994.

Dale Patrick. *Old Testament Law: An Introduction.* Atlanta: John Knox Press, 1984.

Moshe Weinfeld. *Deuteronomy and the Deuteronomic School.* Oxford, U.K.: Clarendon Press, 1972.

6

Joshua and Judges

CAROLYN HIGGINBOTHAM

The book of Joshua picks up the story of the Israelite tribes at the very end of their wilderness wandering, after the death of Moses. It paints a memorable picture of their triumphant sweep into Canaan under Joshua's leadership. The book of Judges recounts additional stories of Israelites struggling with local enemies and one another in the period before their organization as a nation under a single king. Together, Joshua and Judges cover the history of the tribes from about 1200 to 1000 B.C.E.

This chapter begins by looking at historical-critical issues related to Joshua and Judges: When and why were these books written, and what do we know about the period they purport to describe? We then survey the contents, style, and theology of each book. The chapter closes with observations on the contemporary relevance of Joshua and Judges.

Historical-Critical Issues

Date and Audience

Joshua and Judges seem to have come into being in the context of a larger work, the Deuteronomistic History, which shows how the divine expectations and promises presented in Deuteronomy play out in the events of Joshua, Judges, 1 and 2 Samuel, and 1 and 2 Kings. When was this larger history composed? The final edition could not have been penned before the mid-500s B.C.E., because the last chapter of 2 Kings recounts the fall of Jerusalem in 587–586 B.C.E. and the release of King Jehoiachin from prison in 560 B.C.E., but the bulk of the work might have been compiled earlier. One way of dating it is to ask about the period into which it best fits. That is, what kinds of issues and problems does the Deuteronomistic History seem to be addressing, and when were those issues most pertinent? Two answers to these questions dominate the current debate. The most common theory is that the Deuteronomistic History was intended to support religious reforms carried out during the reign of Josiah (or perhaps even Hezekiah, decades earlier). Some scholars, however, contend that the Deuteronomistic History was written to provide a common history and ethnic identity for the postexilic community, which rebuilt the temple in the late 500s B.C.E., or for the diaspora community of the late Persian or Hellenistic Periods (400s or 300s B.C.E.).

Unfortunately, arguments based on "fit" are inherently speculative: How exactly does one measure the fit between a text and its proposed historical context? Because a literary work may serve powerful functions in multiple contexts, tying it to one particular context is virtually impossible. The language of the text provides an alternative basis for dating. Because vocabulary, syntax, and spelling change over time, they can serve as clues to the text's time of composition.

Overall, the language of the Deuteronomistic History seems reflective of the pre-exilic period (700s or 600s B.C.E.) for two reasons. First, it shows few Aramaic influences. Biblical books written in the late Persian and Hellenistic Periods, by contrast, contain both vocabulary and syntactic structures drawn from Aramaic, which was the lingua franca of the Persian Empire. Second, the Deuteronomistic History uses language like that found in archaeologically datable Israelite and Judean inscriptions of the 700s and 600s. On the other hand, 2 Kings ends with an account of events taking place in the reign of a Babylonian king, Evil-Merodach, who ruled from 562 to 560 B.C.E. That account could not have been written before the mid-500s.

Many scholars account for these various considerations by positing at least two editions of the Deuteronomistic History. The first, comprising the bulk of the history and probably incorporating some already-existent materials, would have been composed in the 600s B.C.E. in order to convince Judeans to support the centralization of religious and political authority in Jerusalem. This would account for linguistic features, as well as those aspects of "fit" related to centralization in a monarchic context. The final edition, which included the closing chapters of 2 Kings and probably some cautionary foreshadowing at earlier points in the text, was likely completed in the 500s B.C.E. This would be early enough that the language would still be similar, but late enough to account for the Evil-Merodach information and for the ways in which the history seems to address the concerns of life after the loss of land, temple, and kings.

Joshua and Judges as History

Joshua and Judges, like the rest of the Deuteronomistic History, appear at first to be very easy to interpret. These two books tell the story of premonarchic Israel. Their plot seems relatively straightforward. They recount how Israel came to possess the land and how the tribes survived in the land before the centralization of authority under the monarchy. The story is filled with much drama as repeated threats are overcome.

However, there is more to Joshua and Judges than an account of ancient history. In fact, these books are probably not intended as history at all. They certainly do not describe events exactly as they happened, and they offer two very different accounts of the conquest of the land.

Read Joshua 9—12 and Judges 1 for yourself. As you read, pay attention to the details. Ask yourself: How do their depictions of the conquest differ? For each account, make a list of the cities that were conquered and those that were not. How do these lists compare?

The book of Joshua presents an unambiguous account of the conquest of the entire land in the course of a single campaign, concluding: "So Joshua took the whole land, according to all that YHWH had spoken to Moses; and Joshua gave it for an inheritance to Israel according to their tribal allotments. And the land had rest from war" (Josh. 11:23). The book of Judges, however, clearly indicates that not all the cities and peoples were defeated: "Now these are the nations that YHWH left to test all those in Israel who had no experience of any war in Canaan…So the Israelites lived among the Canaanites, the Hittites, the Amorites, the Perizzites, the Hivites, and the Jebusites" (Judg. 3:1, 5). In fact, among the cities whose inhabitants Judges 1 claims were not driven out are six cities that Joshua 12 lists among those whose kings were conquered and whose territory was given to the tribes of Israel: Jerusalem, Taanach, Dor, Megiddo, Gezer, and Aphek.

These differences have given rise to a variety of theories about how Israel came to possess the land. Until recently, three theories—military conquest, peaceful infiltration, and peasant revolt—have dominated the discussion.

The military conquest theory follows the Joshua account most closely and is associated with such notable scholars as William Foxwell Albright, G. Ernest Wright, and John Bright. According to this model, the founders of Israel were a non-native population that entered Palestine from the east and conquered it relatively quickly, in the course of a single generation. The first archaeological excavations in Israel uncovered evidence of the destruction of many sites at the end of the Late Bronze Age, roughly 1200 B.C.E. This theory attributes those destructions to Joshua's campaigns.

The peaceful infiltration theory suggests that Judges more accurately reflects the process of Israel's emergence. Advocated especially by Albrecht Alt and Martin Noth, this theory draws on anthropological models of nomadism to explain Israel's origins. It asserts that the founders of Israel were nomads who migrated seasonally with their sheep and goats between the desert fringe and the mountain highlands. At the beginning of the Iron Age, these nomads began to establish permanent settlements in the highlands. As their population grew, their settlements expanded into the valleys and encroached on the established Canaanite cities. The Israelites conquered those cities one by one over a long period.

The peasant revolt theory draws its biblical support primarily from law codes rather than the narratives of Joshua or Judges. The egalitarianism of Israelite law codes led George Mendenhall and Norman Gottwald to propose that the founders of Israel belonged to the lowest strata of society. These peasants initiated a social and political revolution, overthrowing the ruling class of the cities and establishing an alternative egalitarian society in the highlands. In addition to the legal material, this theory finds evidence of social turmoil in Egyptian texts, which mention the presence in Palestine of a class of outcasts called Habiru who survived by robbing trade caravans and hiring themselves out as mercenaries.

These three theories agree that the history of Israel in the land of Palestine probably begins about 1200 B.C.E. A stone monument from Egypt claims that the Egyptian king Merneptah defeated a group of people called Israel during a military campaign in Palestine. Therefore, we can conclude that by the date of that monument's erection, 1208 B.C.E., a group going by the name Israel was present in Palestine. Because significant changes in the archaeology of the region begin at about the same time, the 1200 B.C.E. date seems relatively secure.

However, archaeological excavations and surveys of the past several decades have not supported the sudden-conquest picture painted by the book of Joshua and the military conquest theory. The transition from the Bronze Age to the Iron Age appears to have been gradual rather than cataclysmic. As earlier excavations showed, many cities and towns were destroyed during this transition, but (contrary to the conclusions of some earlier archaeologists) the destructions did not occur all at once. Some sites were destroyed as early as 1250 B.C.E., whereas others did not fall until at least a century later. The process did not take place within a single generation.

Archaeology also suggests problems with individual details given in Joshua. The most famous problem arises in connection with Jericho, where excavations suggest that the walls did *not* come tumbling down as described in Joshua 6, because Jericho *had* no walls during the Late Bronze Age. Joshua's conquest of Ai (Josh. 7—8) would hardly have been a glorious victory, because it had been uninhabited for almost two thousand years.

Aside from cities that were or were not destroyed, recent archaeology shows a broad shift in settlement patterns at around the time of Israel's emergence. During the Late Bronze Age (before Israel's arrival), most people in Palestine lived in cities and towns located in the fertile valleys and coastal plain. In the Early Iron Age (the time when the Israelite tribes are supposed to have established themselves in the land), the population was sparser and most people lived in small villages high in the mountains. These villages gave rise to the eventual nations of Israel and Judah.

The physical remains of the highland villages provide clues to the origins of their inhabitants. We do not find signs of a new and distinct culture, as the military conquest hypothesis or even the peaceful infiltration theory might lead us to expect. Instead, artifacts found in the villages are quite similar to those found in the lowland cities. The pottery is crudely made, but in the styles of Late Bronze Canaanite pottery. This evidence suggests that at least a significant portion of the population of the villages migrated from the cities—that is, they originated right there in Palestine.

Although a local origin for the "Israelites" would be consistent with the peasant revolt hypothesis, another reason for migration can be found in changes in the region's climate. In the late 1100s B.C.E., the entire Mediterranean region entered a period of drought. The valleys where the Canaanite cities were located no longer received enough rainfall to produce large surpluses of food. Some of the city dwellers moved to smaller villages in the surrounding hills, where they could raise enough food to feed their own families without putting too much pressure on the environment. At the same time, some of the sheep and goat herders whose grazing lands were drying up moved up into the hills and began to settle down as well (as per the Peaceful Infiltration theory, although that theory does not account for the whole picture). This mixed population of migrants from the cities and settling nomads eventually became the nation of Israel.

Social and Religious Context

In premonarchic times, Israel was a collection of tribes, with each tribe divided into clans. Each clan in turn would be composed of several extended families. Lists of the tribes always contain twelve names, but not all listings contain the same twelve (suggesting that symbolism of the number twelve is more important than the exact components of the list). Sometimes Levi, the priestly tribe, is counted among the twelve; at other times Levi is omitted and the Joseph tribe divided into Ephraim and Manasseh. We are not sure how unified the tribes were before the monarchy. Were the "judges" (who seem to have functioned as war leaders and governors, not just as judicial authorities) powerful central authorities, or was their authority temporary and restricted to at most a couple of neighboring tribes?

For answers to this question we turn to the book of Judges, our primary source for understanding the social and religious institutions of premonarchic Israel. The book gives extensive stories about some judges, and only the barest facts—name, lineage, length of service, and place of burial, in very formulaic language—for others (see, for instance, Judg. 10:1–5). Many historians believe the information about these "minor judges" comes from an authentic, early list of premonarchic rulers who ruled at least a substantial portion of Israel. The author of Judges would then have used this ancient source to structure the larger narrative, inserting longer tales of individual judges where appropriate. This line of reasoning suggests a strongly bound confederacy of tribes.

On the other hand, many literary critics see material such as 10:1–5 as a narrative device created by the author to link the larger heroic stories into a seamless whole. In this view, the list has no historical value; it is a literary fiction. It suggests that the tribes may have come together only in times of crisis and that they shared little sense of common identity.

The stories themselves hint at a degree of disunity. The tribes of Reuben, Gilead, Dan, and Asher fail to support Deborah and Barak (5:15–17); the Ephraimites fight against the Gileadites (12:4); and Benjamin is attacked by all the other tribes (20:35). Not one of the stories of the major judges mentions all twelve tribes by name.

Nevertheless, the present text of Judges is structured to create the impression of a strong tribal federation. Both the major and the minor judges are said to judge or deliver "Israel," not just a portion of Israel. The story of the Levite's concubine presupposes a twelve-tribe league when the Levite divides the woman's corpse into twelve pieces to be sent "throughout all the territory of Israel" (19:29).

The function served by the judges is no clearer than is the geographical range of their authority. Although these officials are often said to "judge" Israel, mostly they function as military rather than judicial leaders, delivering Israel from foreign oppressors. Many scholars question whether these "judges" played a significant role in the governance of Israel between military crises. Day-to-day administration of justice was probably in the hands of tribal, clan, and village leaders, especially the local elders. At most, the judges would have been called on to handle disputes that could not be resolved locally.

Both Joshua and Judges assert that the primary force binding the people together in this period was allegiance to YHWH, the God of Israel. Joshua closes with an elaborate ceremony in which the people of Israel commit themselves to the exclusive worship of YHWH. Although the people often fall away from the true faith, Yahwism is understood to be a marker of Israelite ethnicity. The Israelites are those people who have bound themselves to the service of YHWH.

Yet religion seems to have been chiefly a local affair in premonarchic Israel. The people and their leaders are portrayed as worshiping in a number of sacred sites scattered across the land. Some of these serve a single family, clan, or tribe—for example, the altar that Gideon built at Ophrah (Judg. 6) and the shrine that Micah set up in his own house (Judg. 17). Although Joshua seems to describe a succession of central shrines, first at Gilgal (Josh. 4:19–20; 5:2–12), then at Shiloh (Josh. 18:1, 8–10), religious assemblies continue to occur at other sites as well, most notably at Shechem (Josh. 24), Mizpah (Judg. 20:1, 3; 21:1, 5, 8), and Bethel (Judg. 21:2). Thus, we cannot be certain that there was a single, central shrine that was the focal point of a Yahwistic tribal league.

The plots of Joshua and Judges draw on religious practices, especially the casting of lots and the institution of naziriteship, to convey important theological points. The authors do not explain these practices because they assume that their intended audience, the people of Israel, is familiar with them.

Lots were cast to decide between two options. For the ancient Israelite, this practice did not mean leaving a decision to chance or luck, like flipping a coin. Lots were cast before God, usually by a priest, and the outcome was understood to be determined by God. Often the ephod, a priestly garment, was used to cast lots; the decision would depend on which of two sacred objects the priest drew out of the pocket of the ephod or how they fell when tossed. In Joshua, lots are cast to determine who has taken booty from Jericho (7:16–18) and which territory is given to which tribe (14:1–2).

The religious institution of naziriteship plays an important role in the story of Samson. The nazirite was an individual who took a voluntary oath to be set apart for God. According to Numbers 6, nazirites were forbidden to cut their hair, drink alcoholic beverages, eat grapes, or come into contact with a corpse while their oath was in effect. When they had fulfilled the vow and were ready to reenter secular society, they offered sacrifices to God, shaved their heads, and burned the shaved hair with their peace offering. Samson's case does not follow this pattern exactly, because his was not a temporary voluntary naziriteship, but a lifelong one declared before his birth (Judg. 13:7).

The act of "utterly destroying" the inhabitants of a conquered city, as described in Joshua and Judges, was not so much a military policy as a religious one. The practice is often termed the *ban,* in which case destroyed objects are said to have been "subjected to the ban." The Hebrew word for this practice literally means "devoted" and refers to anything that has been set aside for God's exclusive use and that therefore cannot be appropriated by human beings for other than sacred purposes. In Joshua and Judges, the spoils of battle were subject to the ban, which was carried out by slaughtering the people and animals, giving the precious metals to God's treasury, and burning the rest. However, in the case of Ai, only the conquered people were "devoted" (killed); livestock and valuables could be taken by soldiers for their own use (Josh. 8:2).

The concept of "devoting" a defeated populace was not unique to Israel. Other ancient Near Eastern nations also claimed to have utterly destroyed their enemies in an act of devotion to their god. Some scholars suggest that the practice may have originated as a means to prevent the spread of disease, whereas others suppose it simply provided a convenient excuse to exterminate enemies. In the Deuteronomistic History, the ban is practiced only during the period before David (the last account comes from the reign of Saul, a transitional figure between the judges and the hereditary kings).

Our assessment of the ban is complicated by other historical questions about Joshua and Judges: What are we to make of the details given about how the ban was applied at Ai, when archaeology suggests that the city was an unpopulated ruin in Joshua's time? There is no evidence, other than the narratives of the Deuteronomistic History, that the ban was actually carried out. Indeed, the continued presence of many ethnic groups within the boundaries of Israel, as indicated in Judges and elsewhere, suggests that it was not.

Scholars have offered many theories about why the conquest narratives include divine commands to exterminate those who resist Israel's invasion. The ban probably reflects theological and political concerns of the history's authors, late in the monarchy or even in exile. In their view, intercourse with Israel's neighbors led to religious contamination, which in turn brought divine disapproval. If only Israel had exterminated the Canaanite populace! The religious and political reforms of Hezekiah and Josiah sought to build a unified and centralized nation on the basis of religious purity. Nearly a century later the returning exiles laid claim to ownership of the land on the basis of ethnic, as well as religious, purity. The narratives of Joshua and Judges borrow the concept of the "ban" to give historical warrant to both these programs. As presented in these texts, separation and the avoidance of contamination are not new concerns: The God of Israel has commanded them from the earliest days of the nation.

Reading through Joshua

Narrative Overview

The book of Joshua is organized into four main sections: an introduction (1—5), the conquest of Canaan (6—12), the division of the land (13—21), and a conclusion (22—24).

Introduction (1—5)
> Instructions to Joshua and the people (1)
> The spies hidden by Rahab in Jericho (2)
> Crossing the Jordan (3:1—4:18)
> Encampment at Gilgal (4:19—5:12)
> Joshua's vision (5:13–15)

The conquest of Canaan (6—12)
> The southern and central campaigns (6—10)
> The northern campaign (11:1–15)
> The summary of the conquest (11:16—12:24)

The division of the land (13—19)
> Unconquered territory (13:1–7)
> Distribution of land east of the Jordan (13:8–33)
> Distribution of land to Judah and Joseph (14—17)
> Distribution of land to the remaining tribes (18—19)

Conclusion (20—24)
> Cities of refuge and provision for the Levites (20—21)
> Tensions between the eastern and western tribes (22)
> Joshua's farewell address (23)
> Covenant ceremony at Shechem (24)

Joshua tells the story of how God established the Israelites in their homeland, providing them with everything necessary so that they would have "rest" (security and prosperity) in the land. The dramatic stories of conquest and the dry (to most modern readers, anyway) accounts of the division of territory convey the same message: The people did not take the land; God gave it to them! Their role is to be strong and courageous and to act in accordance with God's law (1:7). God will do the rest.

Several passages make God's role in the conquest explicit. Jericho falls not because of the Israelites' military prowess, but because God gives them the city. At the sound of the trumpets' blast and the people's shout, the walls come tumbling down! When five kings of southern cities attack the Israelites and their Gibeonite allies, God throws the attacking kings into panic and bombards them with hailstones. At the end of the campaign in southern and central Canaan, we are informed that "Joshua took all these kings and their land at one time, because YHWH God of Israel fought for Israel" (10:42). These passages may be intended to reassure later audiences that God can protect them, even if their army is meager (late Judah) or nonexistent (exile and Persian Period).

Other passages highlight the importance of obedience to God's law. The first attempt to capture Ai is unsuccessful because Achan has broken God's law and taken some of the spoils from Jericho for himself. Once Achan is punished, victory over Ai comes easily. The account of the northern campaign stresses Joshua's obedience: "As YHWH had commanded his servant Moses, so Moses commanded Joshua, and so Joshua did; he left nothing undone of all YHWH had commanded Moses" (11:15).

Similarly, the distribution of the land is decided by God. Except for the two-and-a-half tribes to whom Moses had already assigned land east of the Jordan, the tribes now receive their inheritance by lot.

The book concludes with a covenant renewal ceremony at Shechem, which draws together the twin themes of divine provision and human obedience. Joshua recites the history of YHWH's actions on behalf of the people of Israel, from Abraham to the conquest. He then calls on the people to choose whom they will serve, YHWH or some other god. The Israelites respond: "YHWH our God we will serve, and him we will obey" (24:24).

Narrative Technique in Joshua

The entire book of Joshua is cast in a liturgical mode. Ritual pervades the story from beginning to end. The crossing of the Jordan and the fall of Jericho read like a ceremonial reenactment of the conquest. The people line up and parade around as though they are in a religious procession. The center of attention is always the priests bearing the ark, not the soldiers. After casting lots to assign the land, the community assembles at Shechem for one last ritual, an oath of allegiance to YHWH. Whether or not the Israelites regularly reenacted God's gift of the land or renewed their covenant with God, the ritualizing of the narrative serves as a unifying device and underscores the theological claim that this land belonged to the Israelites because God deeded it to them.

Theological Issues in Joshua

Joshua illustrates the reciprocity that lies at the heart of the divine-human relationship. Both God and humankind have expectations of each other. The God of Joshua is intimately involved in human affairs, guiding the Israelites and providing for their needs. YHWH is not an aloof, disinterested deity who lets the world unfold as it will or a whimsical, capricious god who toys with humankind. Israel's God is a partisan God who demonstrates loyalty, beneficence, and zealousness.

Although the gift of the land has clear political implications, theologically it has to do with God's provision for the people's basic needs. For Christians, this act finds an echo in the prayer, "Give us this day our daily bread." In an agrarian society such as ancient Israel, land is bread. To own a small plot of land is to be able to feed one's family. To be landless is to be at the mercy of others, especially the rich and powerful, for one's livelihood. The landless are always one step from poverty, enslavement, and starvation. Note that when the land is assigned in Joshua, it is given not just to large political units such as tribes and clans, but to each tribe "according to its families." Through this gracious act of God, then, each extended family is granted the means for its own subsistence. God provides for human need.

At the same time, YHWH is a demanding God, requiring absolute allegiance and adherence to an exacting set of moral and religious standards. Joshua warns the people: "If you transgress the covenant of YHWH your God...then the anger of YHWH will be kindled against you, and you shall perish quickly from the good land that he has given to you" (23:16). God expects the people to exhibit the same loyalty that God has shown toward them. The book of Joshua highlights the religious dimensions of the covenant, but the covenant incorporates a broader concern for moral human relationships as well. The people of God are enjoined to adopt a way of life that is centered around God and God's standards of justice. Such is the course that leads to a successful life.

Joshua speaks powerfully about God's relationship with Israel. Unlike some other books of the First Testament, however, it does not seem to conceive of God having responsibilities toward other peoples, especially the peoples whom Israel is displacing. This may reflect a context in which YHWH is still thought of more as a national patron God than as the sole deity of all the earth.

Reading through Judges

Narrative Overview

The book of Judges is organized into three main sections: a prologue (1:1—3:6), the stories of the judges (3:7—16:31), and a conclusion (17—21). The prologue introduces the seeds of the conflict that will drive the story: The Israelites have failed to drive out all the native inhabitants of the land. The consequences of this failure are developed through the successive stories of the individual judges. The book concludes with the stories of individuals who are not judges at all, but whose stories dramatize the full effects of Israel's dereliction.

Prologue (1:1—3:6)
> Conquest fails to drive out inhabitants of the land (1:1—2:5)
> Consequences of that failure outlined (2:6—3:6)

Stories of the judges (3:7—16:31)
> Othniel (3:7–11)
> Ehud (3:12–30)
> Shamgar (3:31)
> Deborah and Barak (4—5)
> Gideon (6—8)

[Interlude: Abimelech seeks kingship (9)]
> Tola and Jair (10:1–5)
> Jephthah (10:6—12:7)
> Ibzan, Elon, and Abdon (12:8–15)
> Samson (13—16)

Conclusion (17—21)
> Micah, his Levite, and the Danites (17—18)
> Another Levite, his concubine, and the Benjaminites (19—21)

It is easy to oversimplify the plot of Judges, reading it as a fixed cycle of apostasy, punishment, repentance, and deliverance. The pattern is laid out in Judges 2:11–19: The people sin by worshiping other gods; God punishes them through conquest and oppression; the people repent and call out to God; and God raises up a deliverer to defeat their enemies. As soon as that deliverer dies, the cycle seems to begin anew with the people returning to their worship of other gods.

In fact, the plot is somewhat more subtle and complex. Instead of a cycle, we have a downward spiral. With each turn of the spiral, the Israelites start at a lower level of spiritual and social health. There is a pattern, but not an endless repetition of the same fate. The story traces the spiritual and social degeneration of Israel. In the end, we have complete anarchy, civil war, moral depravity, and religious syncretism. The continued existence of Israel is in doubt, not because of foreign enemies but because of internal decay.

Of the six "major" judges, only the first, Othniel, is presented in an unambiguously positive light. Ehud uses diplomatic treachery and his own left-handedness (viewed as an unnatural trait) to accomplish his victory. Barak is shamed for his cowardly insistence that Deborah go into battle at his side: The opposing general is slain not by Barak but by a woman. Gideon makes a golden ephod (here, apparently, a kind of idol) from the spoils of war, thereby leading the people away from true faith. The tragic Jephthath is initially called to leadership by the elders of Gilead, not by God; he engages in human sacrifice (sacrificing his daughter to fulfill a rash vow) and becomes embroiled in an intertribal war between the Gileadites and the Ephraimites. With Samson, the level of leadership hits rock bottom. Although set apart for God as a nazirite from birth, Samson is inexorably drawn to foreign (Philistine) women, who are his undoing.

The conclusion reveals the depths to which Israel has sunk. The protagonists of the final two stories—Micah and his Levite, and the other Levite and the tribal elders whom he calls to assist him—are not good leaders. They are interested only in their own welfare, not in the broader welfare of the community. In this respect they are linked to the last of the judges, Samson, who was motivated by lust and revenge for personal injuries. Read Judges 19 to see the moral depravity that ensues. Notice the total lack of concern for others that most of the characters display. They violate not only the cultural norm of hospitality, but any sense of decency and humanity. The men of Gibeah are interested only in abusing the visitors. The old man and the Levite are quick to sacrifice women to save themselves. The Levite dismembers his brutalized concubine (was she already dead?) and sends the pieces throughout the land as a call to action. Each of these actors thinks only of himself. Society, in any meaningful sense, has ceased to exist.

Numerous female characters take the stage in Judges, but they do not tend to fare very well: They are sacrificed, raped, and abducted. What is the reader to make of the fact that the text never denounces their brutalization? Does the text condone the dehumanization of women, taking for granted that women are the property of men who can dispose of them as they wish? Perhaps. Or, as Tammi Schneider argues, perhaps the women in Judges serve as foils for the male characters, and their treatment is one of the criteria by which the men are to be evaluated. Then the increasing violence against women is one more sign of the disintegration of society.

Narrative Technique in Judges

The author of Judges uses irony to heighten the aura of tragedy and upheaval. The Levite travels late into the day to avoid spending the night in a foreign city, only to be victimized by fellow Israelites. Abimelech kills his brothers on a stone (9:5) and is himself killed when a woman throws a millstone on his head (9:53). Samson, who makes something of a sport of killing Philistines, kills more of them in his dying than he has during his life (16:30).

Links between Joshua and Judges

There are many echoes of Joshua in Judges, which suggests that the editor who compiled the Deuteronomistic History consciously linked the two books together. A careful examination of a couple of these echoes will help us see how our perceptions as readers are shaped by the recapitulation of previously narrated events.

The parallels between Judges 1 and Joshua 13—19 are especially significant because they address the central theme of Israel's failure to expel the Canaanites. K. Lawson Younger, Jr., observes that each passage devotes the longest accounts to the Judah and Joseph tribes and contrasts Judah's success with the failure of the other tribes, especially Dan. In both versions, Judah successfully displaces the Canaanites, whereas other tribes press the Canaanites into forced labor rather than driving them out. Dan actually loses its assigned territory.

Both books end with a (threatened) civil war. In Joshua, the tensions are between the tribes that live on the east bank of the Jordan River and those that live on the west bank. War is averted when the eastern tribes assure the western tribes that their construction of an altar is intended not to divide the community but to remind themselves that they, the easterners, belong to the larger Israelite community. In Judges, tensions run along a north-south divide and pit eleven tribes against Benjamin. In this case, negotiations break down and Benjamin is almost completely annihilated. The battle strategy used to defeat the Benjaminites in Judges 20 is strongly reminiscent of the tactics used to capture Ai. After losing the first one or two skirmishes, the Israelites lay an ambush. One army unit draws the enemy away from the city, pretending to give way in retreat. Then the unit that lays hidden seizes the city and burns it. The enemy is routed and slaughtered.

The recapitulation of elements of Joshua in Judges shapes our interpretation of the Judges narrative. The close paralleling of Joshua 13—19 in Judges 1 not only hints that the author of Judges had Joshua at hand but reinforces our perception that the source of the tribes' problems dates back to their very entry into the land. Similarly, the repetition of the civil war motif reminds us that impulses toward chaos and anarchy have haunted the community from the outset.

Theological Issues in Judges

Despite its political overtones, the book of Judges is preeminently about the divine-human relationship. The book returns again and again to the question of who will lead Israel. On the surface, this question seems to be about the character and actions of individual people who are called by God or their community to positions of leadership. On a deeper level, however, the text insists that Israel's true leader is YHWH. Israel and its leaders forget this truth at their peril.

Thus, the judges are not merely tragic individuals or examples of poor leadership. They represent Israel and Israel's own faltering relationship with God. Israel, like Samson, was set apart for God from birth. Yet despite its special status, Israel seeks its own path in the world, mixing freely with the surrounding peoples through foreign alliances and intermarriage with its neighbors. The downward spiral of the "judges" mirrors the downward spiral of the people of Israel as they turn further and further from God and descend into moral and spiritual chaos.

Judges revisits one of the great themes of Genesis: Human disobedience introduces chaos into the divinely ordered creation. When the people follow God's ways, the land has rest. Social harmony and prosperity are the norm. When the people turn from God, following human ideals, their world falls apart. Spiritual degeneracy leads to social and political anarchy. The people suffer, individually and collectively. At the heart of Judges' theology is the struggle to understand and realize a healthy relationship between God and human beings. In line with the larger program of the Deuteronomistic History, Judges contrasts the disasters that befall those who ignore God or who seek to manipulate God with the success that comes to those who acknowledge their dependence on YHWH.

Several of the stories in Judges raise questions about the extent to which human beings can induce God to do as they wish. Each time people call on God, they are trying to influence God to take their side and come to their rescue. In story after story, YHWH responds to such pleas with compassion and decisive action. Yet God will not be controlled even through religious means, as shown in the story of Micah. When Micah creates his own private house of worship, complete with silver idol and other religious paraphernalia, and hires a Levitical priest to serve it, he is sure that God will be bound to do whatever he asks. "Now I know that YHWH will prosper me, because the Levite has become my priest" (17:13). Shortly thereafter, the Levite leaves Micah's employ to accept a position with a bigger "congregation," the tribe of Dan, at a higher salary. To add insult to injury, he and the Danites take the shrine's furnishings with them. The story debunks "the false confidence men [*sic*] have that they know God in such a way that they can manipulate him by cultic and institutional means, and so secure their own futures" (Webb, 187).

Reading Joshua and Judges in the Twenty-First Century

One of the most troubling aspects of Joshua and Judges is the divine command to expel Canaanites from the land and to exterminate the populations of cities that resist the Israelites. Two theological motives can be adduced for this practice: fear of religious contamination and the belief that the spoils of this war belonged to YHWH. Neither, of course, justifies such treatment of other human beings.

In their own way, these texts address a problem that every religious community faces: the problem of acculturation. The Deuteronomistic writers fear that Israelites will learn foreign, non-Yahwistic practices from their neighbors. It is indeed difficult to live side by side with people who have different values, beliefs, and traditions without being influenced by them. The texts rightly recognize how hard it is to remain faithful to one's own traditions in a pluralistic world. Today's Christians might find it easier to sustain certain Christian values if they could wall themselves off in a Christian enclave, free of any other cultural influences. That, of course, is physically impossible. It would also violate other Christian commitments, such as being "a light to the nations" and going "into all the world." The church of the third millennium must relinquish illusory visions of a completely Christianized community without selling out its values. It must anchor itself to the gospel of Jesus Christ even as it lives out the gospel imperatives in an increasingly multiethnic, multifaith world.

The manner in which Joshua struggles with the distinction between us and them, insiders and outsiders, may offer us insights into the negotiation of similar boundaries in the world of the twenty-first century. We tend to think of the distinction in the First Testament as a purely ethnic one: The Israelites are the insiders; everyone else is an outsider. Yet in Joshua the dividing line is not quite so clear-cut. Insiders become outsiders, and outsiders become insiders. Thus, both Rahab of Jericho and the Gibeonites become part of "us" by their voluntary submission to the God of Israel. Achan, the Israelite, becomes one of "them" and subject to execution because he breaks faith with YHWH when he takes some of the spoils of Jericho for himself (Rowlett, 1992). Thus, the age-old categories of "us" and "them" are shown to be less about heritage, race, or ethnicity than about the commitments that people choose. In Joshua and Judges, anyone who sides with God is an insider, a member of God's community. This may have been an important point to exilic readers struggling to define their own community boundaries now that they had lost land and nationhood.

The theological picture is not all positive: These insider/outsider texts have been used to defend policies of colonialism, genocide, and "scorched earth" warfare. Colonial groups, such as the Boers in South Africa and the early European Americans, have modeled their claims to lands already occupied by an indigenous population after the book of Joshua. Sometimes the analogy has been extended to justify the eradication of indigenous populations when they resisted the incursions of the settlers. Other groups have found in Joshua and Judges a justification for military strategies that maximize civilian casualties and ecological destruction. These historical abuses of the biblical narrative should give us pause as we consider both our own tendency to read what we want to find into scripture and the culture of violence that persists in the world. "God's war against the Canaanites gives the interpreter more than the occasion for disavowing genocide. It prompts us to reflect on at least two major issues: the function of violence and the dynamics of genocide in our own world" (Coote, 617).

Resources

Robert B. Coote. *The Book of Joshua.* Vol. 12 of *The New Interpreter's Bible,* edited by Leander Keck. Nashville: Abingdon Press, 1998.

Lori Rowlett. "Inclusion, Exclusion and Marginality in the Book of Joshua." *Journal for the Study of the Old Testament* 55 (1992): 15–23.

Tammi Schneider. *Judges. Berit Olam.* Collegeville, Minn.: Liturgical Press, 2000.

Barry G. Webb. *The Book of Judges: An Integrated Reading.* Journal for the Study of the Old Testament Supplement Series 46. Sheffield, U.K.: JSOT Press, 1987.

K. Lawson Younger, Jr. "The Configuring of Judicial Preliminaries: Judges 1.1—2.5 and Its Dependence on the Book of Joshua." *Journal for the Study of the Old Testament* 68 (1995): 75–92.

7

Samuel and Kings

LISA W. DAVISON AND MARTI J. STEUSSY

The books of 1 and 2 Samuel recount how the Israelites unite under a king into a single nation. The books of 1 and 2 Kings tell how the single kingdom splits into two, Israel and Judah, and how each falls to foreign powers. (For more information on these historical events, see chap. 2, pp. 21–26.) The Jerusalem-oriented compilers of these books present the Northern Kingdom's fall as YHWH's punishment for that kingdom's secession from Judah and its worship of other deities. They portray the Southern Kingdom, Judah, as favored by YHWH, yet it also falls into foreign hands due to violation of its covenant with YHWH. The storyline ends with Jerusalem's exiles captive in Babylon. The Babylonians control the promised land, and Jerusalem's temple lies in ruins. Is it a sign of hope or hopelessness that at the end of the Deuteronomistic History (the books from Joshua through 2 Kings, not including Ruth), Jehoiachin, the exiled king of Judah, sits at the table of the king of Babylon (2 Kings 25:27–30; compare 2 Samuel 9:6–13)?

Date and Sources

Like Joshua and Judges, Samuel and Kings are not "history" in our sense of history as a recounting of objective facts. They are, like Joshua and Judges, theologically interpretive accounts. Some might call them religious propaganda. Certainly they promote a particular view of proper religious behavior. As we have seen (see pp. 79–80), many scholars believe that the first version of the Deuteronomistic History was composed in Judah during

King Josiah's reign (640–609 B.C.E.) to legitimate his reforms. This composition, however, probably drew on older materials. Samuel and Kings themselves claim to be drawing on older sources, such as the book of Jashar in 2 Samuel 1:18 and the annals of the kings of Judah in 1 Kings 14:29.

Beyond the sources named in the narrative, many scholars identify three component blocks that were probably composed before their incorporation in the books of Samuel. The Ark Narrative (1 Sam. 4:1—7:1 and perhaps 2 Sam. 6) tells how the ark of the covenant was lost to the Philistines and then recovered, perhaps continuing with the story of how David brought it to Jerusalem. The story of David's rise (1 Sam. 16—2 Sam. 1) is an enthusiastically pro-David account of David's activities and successes during the period when Saul was still king. Perhaps it was written to show that David was innocent of any plotting against Saul, in the face of suspicions to the contrary. The Court History (also referred to as the Succession Narrative, 2 Sam. 9—20 and 1 Kings 1—2) tells of events during David's reign in Jerusalem. In particular, it tells how David's adultery with Bathsheba and murder of her husband led to a series of rebellions, including one led by David's son Absalom, and how the throne eventually passed to Solomon (Bathsheba's son) rather than to one of David's older sons. The Court History portrays David in a realistic style as a very human person who makes a number of poor choices. When caught, however, he is willing to confess, and he never follows after foreign gods. Interpreters differ over whether this narrative legitimizes the kingship of David's son Solomon or underscores the differences between the two kings.

The books of Kings refer to the "Book of the Annals of the Kings of Judah" and the "Book of the Annals of the Kings of Israel" (see, for instance, 1 Kings 14:19, 29), and their information on regnal matters may indeed come from such court sources. The extended narratives about Elijah and Elisha, on the other hand, have the flavor of material that has circulated in oral folk form. The high words of praise for Josiah in 2 Kings and the parallels between Josiah's reforms and the program called for in Deuteronomy (compare especially Deut. 6:5 and 2 Kings 23:25) have suggested to many interpreters that these reforms might have been the occasion for drawing together the bulk of the history, as well as Deuteronomy itself (see also pp. 68–75 and 79–80). But because the end of Kings describes the Davidic king Jehoiachin's release from prison in Babylon (560 B.C.E.), the final compilation and editing must have taken place in exile or later. The use of phrases such as "to this day" (see, for instance, 2 Kings 16:6 and 17:34) in the writing supports the idea that there is a considerable distance between the narrators and the events they tell about.

Theology

The editors of the first (Josianic) edition of the Deuteronomistic History seem to have wanted to support Josiah's reforms by showing that the people's well-being depended on royal and popular adherence to YHWH's directive. The editors of the final edition (completed after Jerusalem's fall and Jehoiachin's release) needed to make sense of the disasters that had befallen a people and dynasties who understood themselves as recipients of special promises from God. It is not clear whether the writers reasoned forward from the picture of unmet covenant requirements to interpretation of Jerusalem's fall as punishment, or backward from Jerusalem's fall to the conclusion of covenant breaking. It may have been a bit of both. Both sets of editors, however, clearly assert that the fates of Israel and Judah were consequences of the religious behavior of those nations and especially their rulers. As they tell it, when a ruler did what was evil in God's sight (for instance, worshiped other deities or even worshiped YHWH but in the wrong way or in the wrong place), the whole country suffered. When a ruler did what was good in God's sight (for instance, maintained strict adherence to the covenant with YHWH, especially with regard to Deuteronomy's strictures about worshiping only YHWH and only at the chosen place), the people were blessed. According to the editors of the Deuteronomistic History, however, both curses and blessing were sometimes deferred. This allows them to explain why a bad ruler such as Manasseh (2 Kings 21:1–18) might have a long and prosperous reign, whereas a good ruler such as Josiah might die young:

> Before him [Josiah] there was no king like him, who turned to YHWH with all his heart, with all his soul, and with all his might, according to all the law of Moses; nor did any like him arise after him. Still YHWH did not turn from the fierceness of his great wrath, by which his anger was kindled against Judah, because of all the provocations with which Manasseh had provoked him. (2 Kings 23:25–26)

The Deuteronomists' explanation of Israel's and Judah's fates assumes that disastrous events such as famine, plague, and military defeat are directly controlled by God and that God uses them primarily to punish disobedience (albeit sometimes the disobedience of a previous generation). Not everyone has been persuaded by the Deuteronomists' explanations of historical events. The book of Jeremiah tells of Judean refugees who accepted the notion that Judah's fall was a divine punishment but drew the conclusion (quite different from that of the Deuteronomistic Historians or Jeremiah) that Josiah's reform had *invited* the punishment by interfering with the worship of the "queen of heaven":

> We used to have plenty of food, and prospered, and saw no misfortune. But from the time we stopped making offerings to the queen of heaven and pouring out libations to her, we have lacked everything and have perished by the sword and by famine. (Jer. 44:17–18)

The book of Job (see chap. 14, esp. pp. 234–35) accepts the premise of divine control but challenges the notion that suffering is always a punishment for sin. Poor Job's sufferings begin not with some terrible sin on his part, or that of an ancestor, but when God notices Job's exemplary righteousness. Questions continue to be raised today. Are not famine, plague, and war more the results of natural causes and human misdoing than of specific divine action? Others are willing to accept, for the sake of understanding the Bible at least, the interpretation of such events as divine action, but ask whether such harshness was merited even for rulers unfaithful to YHWH, especially in view of how such punishments affected persons other than the ones misbehaving.

Within the Bible, the Deuteronomistic History's explanation of the Israelite kingdoms' falls is the most widely accepted one. But the tension is strong between assertions of God's loving faithfulness (in the Deuteronomistic History and elsewhere) and the brutality of the punishment that God is said to inflict on the people of two tiny nations caught between rival empires. It is worth asking how much the "wrathful" character of God in the Deuteronomistic History is an inevitable result of the editors' assumption that natural and historical events directly reflect God's character and intentions.

Notable Characters

A look at some of the more important characters in Samuel and Kings helps illuminate the lengthy storyline. The first major player is *Samuel*, born in response to the prayers of his previously barren mother, Hannah (1 Sam. 1). She dedicates Samuel to service in the house of YHWH, leaving the child in the care of the priest Eli. Young Samuel ultimately displaces his mentor Eli as a spokesperson for YHWH (1 Sam. 3). In some respects, Samuel's role is similar to that of a judge (see pp. 83–84). He delivers prophetic oracles and provides guidance for the people. However, he does not participate in military combat, and he has the additional role of priest, one who presides over the religious rituals at Shiloh and Mizpah (old tribal sacred sites). To Samuel falls the task of anointing Saul and later David as kings-to-be, raising the potential for conflict between a divinely chosen king, who is instructed to "do whatever you see fit to do, for God is with you" (1 Sam. 10:7), and the prophet, who is no longer Israel's primary leader but still expects to be its intercessor and teacher (1 Sam. 12:23).

Saul is the first person identified by God and anointed by Samuel as a prospective "king." However, Saul does not seem to have the powers associated with full-fledged kingship. His status seems transitional between the charismatic judges and the later institutionalized royalty. His accomplishments are primarily in battle against Philistines, Moabites, Ammonites, Edomites, and Amalekites. Saul's downfall is blamed on two instances of disobedience: first, when he does not wait for Samuel to supervise a sacrifice before combat with the Philistines (1 Sam. 13), and second, when he captures the Amalekite king and some animals rather than slaughtering them on the spot (1 Sam. 15). After these incidents, the "spirit of YHWH" departs from Saul and an "evil spirit from YHWH" begins to torment him (1 Sam. 16:14), leading to depressed, paranoid behavior in subsequent chapters. Although the Deuteronomistic Historians apparently considered Saul's disobediences just cause for his disinheritance, many readers still come away from the tale feeling sympathy for Saul.

David is introduced in the biblical text three different times. The story of his anointing (1 Sam. 16:1–13) presents him, like the heroes of Genesis, as a youngest son chosen over his older brothers. David is characterized a little differently in the latter part of the same chapter, when Saul's servants recommend him as a courtier and valiant warrior (apparently full-grown) whose music will soothe Saul's troubled soul. The final introduction of David, and probably the most popular, has him showing up on the battlefield as an unknown, slingshot-armed lad who brings down the Philistine warrior Goliath (1 Sam. 17). Much of this chapter does not appear in the Greek version of Samuel. Because of this textual problem, and because a different story about Goliath's demise appears in 2 Samuel 21:19, many scholars view the story of David and Goliath as a later addition, a bit of hero folklore that has become detached from the lesser-known hero Elhanan and attached to the better-known figure of David.

According to 1 Samuel, David serves Saul loyally, although even Saul's own son, the heir apparent Jonathan, recognizes that David is destined to replace Saul as king. When Saul determines David to be a threat, the young commander flees to the wilderness and eventually becomes vassal to a Philistine king (1 Sam. 27). He returns home only after Saul's death. In 2 Samuel, David, acclaimed by both his native tribe of Judah and the tribes of Israel in the north, takes control as the first true king. We have already noted that the Court History section of 2 Samuel presents David's reign as a mixture of accomplishments and tragic mistakes. He unites Israel's tribes and expands its borders, but when he uses his royal power for adultery and murder, God declares that "the sword shall never depart from your house" (2 Sam. 12:10). The editors of 1 and 2 Kings seem to embrace David as a model king nonetheless, comparing all subsequent rulers to him and judging most of them as lesser.

David's son *Solomon* also receives a mixed report. Pronounced "beloved of YHWH" at his birth (2 Sam. 12:24–25), he asks only for wisdom when given the opportunity, near the beginning of his reign, to request anything from God (1 Kings 3:3–14). He builds a magnificent temple and presides over its dedication (1 Kings 3—8). Solomon proves to be gifted in foreign policy and establishes trade relationships with important empires of the ancient Near East. Whereas the biblical writers are proud of Solomon's international presence, they are less pleased by his numerous foreign wives and concubines and his provision of shrines to their gods (1 Kings 11:1–8). Although the Bible doesn't say this, international treaties were commonly accompanied by arranged marriages between members of the participating royal houses and also by erection of shrines to the gods of the participating nations (because each nation called on its god or gods to witness and guarantee the treaty). Thus, both the marriages and the shrines to foreign gods would have been natural accompaniments of Solomon's active foreign policy. In Solomon's own time, there was probably no sense whatsoever that this activity violated Solomon's commitments to his own patron God, YHWH. (Although the Torah laws that command exclusive worship of YHWH are said to be promulgated in Moses' time, they do not seem to have crystallized until several hundred years after the time of Solomon). But in the eyes of the Deuteronomistic Historians, it is Solomon's support of pagan worship that prompts God to divide the kingdom (1 Kings 11:9–13). A second explanation for the split, which occurs at the beginning of the reign of Solomon's son Rehoboam, appears in 1 Kings 12:1–19. Here, the breakaway tribes cite forced labor and high taxes as their causes for dissatisfaction.

The stories of the post-Solomonic kings of Israel and Judah appear in far less detail. In Judah, the kings Ahaz and Manasseh (2 Kings 16 and 21) are particularly condemned; Hezekiah and Josiah (2 Kings 18—20 and 22—23) receive special approval because of their worship reforms. More extensive, and more memorable to most readers, however, are the stories of the powerful northern prophets Elijah and Elisha. Like their predecessors

Samuel, Nathan (see especially 2 Sam. 12), and Gad (2 Sam. 24), these prophets have the courage and freedom to confront their kings with messages of God's disapproval.

Elijah (1 Kings 17—19 and 1 Kings 21—2 Kings 2) prophesies in the reign of the northern king Ahab (a different person than the Judean king Ahaz) and his Tyrean queen Jezebel (once again we see a diplomatic marriage leading to shrines for foreign gods). In the course of opposing the royal couple's policies on worship and their political machinations, Elijah is said to perform a number of flashy miracles, often involving fire from heaven. He is almost as famous, however, for a flight to the wilderness where he encounters YHWH *not* in wind, earthquake, or fire, but in "a sound of sheer silence" (in the *King James Version,* "a still small voice"; 1 Kings 19:12).

Elijah's successor, *Elisha,* assumes a slightly different prophetic role (1 Kings 19:15–21 and 2 Kings 1:1—9:10 and 13:14–21). Elisha is an even more prolific miracle worker than his mentor, so that even his corpse has power to resurrect the dead (2 Kings 13:20–21). He brings an end to Ahab's dynasty by instigating a coup (2 Kings 9:1–10).

Inserted in the narratives about Elijah and Elisha we find an interesting chapter about a lesser-known prophet, Micaiah ben Imlah (1 Kings 22). Large numbers of other prophets tell King Ahab what Ahab wants to hear, but Micaiah, after some prompting, prophesies tragedy for the king. Interestingly, Micaiah does not accuse the other prophets of fabricating their message. Instead, he reports that "YHWH has put a lying spirit" in them to goad Ahab into battle (1 Kings 22:23). In this depiction, YHWH uses the prophets not to communicate accurate information about the future but to accomplish certain changes of behavior on the part of the prophets' audience. We will see (pp. 135–36) that promoting behavioral change is also a primary function of the messages reported in the Hebrew Bible's prophetic books.

Reading through 1 and 2 Samuel

Overview

The book of Judges, which immediately precedes 1 Samuel in the Deuteronomistic History (remember that in the Hebrew Bible, Ruth appears in a different section; see p. 7), closes with a series of stories about idolatry, kidnapping, massacre, rape, and intertribal warfare (Judg. 17—21). The book ends with the words, "In those days there was no king in Israel; all the people did what was right in their own eyes" (Judg. 21:25). We are left thinking that perhaps a king would be a good idea. The books of 1 and 2 Samuel (originally a single book) pick up that theme, explaining how kingship finally came to Israel and detailing the career of the founder of Judah's Davidic dynasty. The following outline will help us follow the story of changes in Israel's leadership in the books of 1 and 2 Samuel:

> Samuel as prophet and judge of Israel (1 Sam. 1—7)
> Samuel's early life (1 Sam. 1—4)
> The ark of the covenant leaves and returns (1 Sam. 5—7)
> Samuel as prophet and Saul as king (1 Sam. 8—15)
> David rises while Saul declines (1 Sam. 16—2 Sam. 1)
> David becomes ruler over all Israel (2 Sam. 2—8)
> David's Court History (2 Sam. 9—20)
> Miscellaneous appendices (2 Sam. 21—24)

Samuel as Prophet and Judge of Israel (1 Samuel 1—7)

First Samuel opens with the common biblical motif of a barren woman (compare Sarah, Rebekah, and Rachel in Genesis) yearning for a child. Hannah reminds us especially of Samson's mother (Judg. 13), as she promises that if she has a child, no razor will touch his head (1 Sam. 1:11; compare Judg. 13:4–5). When she delivers him, as promised, to YHWH's temple, Hannah's prayer of exultation climaxes with statements that YHWH will give strength to "his king...his anointed" (1 Sam. 2:1–10, which seems to be the model for Mary's prayer in Lk. 1:46–55). Readers soon learn that this would indeed be a good time for new leadership, because the sons of the priest Eli, who will presumably succeed him, are corrupt (1 Sam. 2:12–25). Will Hannah's son Samuel become king? The audience can only hope that he will be a more responsible leader than Samson.

As we have already seen (see the Notable Characters section, 100–101), Hannah's son Samuel does not become king, but he does mature into a powerful leader who combines the roles of priest, prophet, and "judge" (as a decider of judicial cases and in the overall leadership sense of the book of Judges, although Samuel does little militarily). Meanwhile, Eli's family is cast off. The harsh language of the curses against Eli's line (1 Sam. 2:27–36 and 3:11–14) may well mean that the tellers of the story are members or supporters of a rival priestly family.

The story about how the ark of the covenant was lost to the Philistines and found its way back home (1 Sam. 4:1—7:2) is in some ways an interruption, providing comic relief (the Philistine god falling on his face in his own temple; the Philistines frantic to be rid of their "trophy"). In other ways it highlights important themes of Samuel. YHWH is more powerful than the gods of rival nations, but the Israelites must not assume that YHWH will always give them victory, and a wrong approach to

YHWH's sacred objects—even if well meant—will bring disaster. The narrative also explains how Eli and his sons die.

Samuel as Prophet and Saul as King (1 Samuel 8—15)

Ironically, Samuel turns out to have the same problem as Eli: His sons, designated to succeed him, are corrupt (1 Sam 8:1–3). The question of Israel's need for a king now emerges with full force. God's statement that "they have rejected me from being king over them" (8:7) and Samuel's warnings on the subject (8:11–18 and 12:1–25) suggest that the whole notion of having a king is unfaithful. But God's statement about Saul in 9:16–17 and the very positive summary of Saul's reign in 14:47–48 present kingship as part of God's positive plan to make Israel a "nation"—complete with land and king—living securely among the other nations. Interpreters often seize on just one side of this argument—that kings are sinful, or that Israel's kingship is a gift from God—as if it represented *the* biblical position. For a real understanding of 1 and 2 Samuel and the larger Deuteronomistic History, we must see that *both* positions are presented. We should also note that they are not presented abstractly but enmeshed with events and personalities. Samuel is not a neutral commentator, since the king will assume responsibilities previously held by Samuel and his sons. For his part, Saul seems to anticipate that the new job will spell his downfall (see especially 10:20–22). Despite his victories and his generosity—or perhaps even because of the latter—Saul ends up being condemned by both Samuel and YHWH, yet still on the throne and responsible for defending Israel against the Philistines.

David Rises While Saul Declines (1 Samuel 16—2 Samuel 1)

In 1 Samuel 16, God sends Samuel to anoint a new king-designate, David. "The spirit of YHWH came mightily upon David from that day forward," we hear, while "the spirit of YHWH departed from Saul, and an evil spirit from YHWH tormented him" (1 Sam. 16:13–14). The remainder of 1 Samuel traces the working out of this shift in divine support. Jealousy destabilizes Saul, who tries to kill even his own son Jonathan (20:33). David piously refrains from any move against Saul (see especially 1 Sam. 24 and 26), but those around him recognize that the popular young commander is destined for kingship. After one last condemnation by the ghost of the now-dead prophet Samuel, Saul dies, along with three of his sons, in a battle against the Philistines. David's lament for Saul and Jonathan in 2 Samuel 1 brings this part of the story to a close.

The narrative presents David as a clever, appealing, and oh-so-innocent hero, but most contemporary historians suspect it of being pro-David propaganda crafted to explain a somewhat more incriminating course of events. Notice, for instance, that it admits that David worked for a Philistine king and was even present in that king's army as it mustered for the battle in which Saul lost his life (1 Sam. 27 and 29). (We are indignant when we hear that "Saul planned to make David fall by the hand of the Philistines" but somehow fail to notice that David lets Saul fall by the hand of the Philistines; 18:17, 21, 25; 31:2.) First Samuel admits that not every city "liberated" by David during his wilderness days was grateful to him (23:1–12; see also 23:19–20) and shows him demanding supplies from a landholder in return for leaving the man's servants and livestock unmolested (25:5–8). Whereas Saul is condemned for taking Amalekite spoil, David not only takes it but uses it to buy favor among the elders of Judah, who will soon proclaim him king (1 Sam. 15 and 30). If we accept the principle that no one repeatedly denies an accusation unless the accusation is being made and is at least somewhat believable, then this section of the narrative bears witness that many people *did* believe that David plotted against Saul.

David Becomes Ruler Over All Israel (2 Samuel 2—8)

This section, even more than the previous one, reads like a defense of the legitimacy of David's kingship. He first becomes king of Judah (his own tribe, to whose elders he sent gifts in 1 Sam. 30:26). The way to his kingship over Israel (the northern tribes) is then cleared by two convenient assassinations, with David, of course, always outraged and never responsible. He relocates to a capital city, Jerusalem, that sits on the boundary between Judah and Israel and has hitherto belonged to neither. The king of Tyre sends gifts and laborers to build David a palace, and David accumulates a hefty set of wives, concubines, and children.

In 2 Samuel 6, David brings the traditional Israelite religious symbol, the ark of YHWH, into his new capital. During the initial attempt, one of the ark's caretakers is struck dead when the cart shakes and he reaches out to steady the ark. First Chronicles 15:12–13 suggests that this happened because proper protocol was not followed, but that explanation refers to legislation that was probably not in existence when 2 Samuel 6 was written. In Samuel, Uzzah's death is reminiscent of the deaths when the rejoicing Beth Shimshites look at the returned ark in the Hebrew text of 1 Samuel 6:19. (In the Hebrew text of that verse, 50,070 men are killed when they look at the ark. In the Greek text, the victims are descendants of Jeconiah, killed for not rejoicing at the ark's return. Your English translation should have a note indicating which text it follows.) The Uzzah incident perhaps echoes a point made in 1 Samuel's Ark Narrative: The ark does not constrain YHWH's choices. If David thinks that by bringing it to Jerusalem he can guarantee YHWH's support, then David had better rethink.

The subtle struggle to see who calls the shots continues in 2 Samuel 7, where David proposes to build a temple ("house") for YHWH. In the context of ancient Near Eastern thought, this might be construed as a favor done by David for God, for which David could expect return favors. God rebuffs the offer, declaring in strong terms that God has no want or need for a house and reminding David who it is that has chosen and supported Israel's leaders, including David himself. Then God turns the tables, declaring that God will make a "house" (meaning, this time, a dynasty) for David. This offer reaffirms God's affection for David while leaving no doubt as to who holds the power in this relationship. God promises to show familial loyalty ("I will be a father to him, and he shall be a son to me"; 2 Sam. 7:14) to David's offspring. While God reserves the right to discipline misbehavior "with blows inflicted by human beings" (7:14, following the Deuteronomistic assumption that political and military misfortunes result from God's action), the bottom line is that "I [YHWH] will establish the throne of his kingdom forever" (7:13). Although Christians have applied this promise to Jesus, the original authors and audience were surely thinking in more concrete terms of the Davidic dynasty's reign over Judah. God also promises that the deferred temple project will be taken up and completed by David's son.

The idea of a patron god standing in father/son relationship to a chosen king and his offspring is fairly common in the ancient Near East and may well represent the official theology of David's administration. The chapter as it stands, however, was almost certainly written later than David's own lifetime. In hindsight, it provides a theological rationale for the fact that Jerusalem's temple was built not by David, the dynasty founder, but by his successor, Solomon. Chronicles, written much later and reflecting a much more intensely pro-temple theology, provides a different explanation: There, David is disqualified because he has shed so much blood (1 Chron. 22:8). David is so important to the Chroniclers, however, that they nonetheless portray David himself as raising all the funds and finalizing all the planning for the temple, so that Solomon only follows the instructions given him by David. This is a different picture than that painted in the Deuteronomistic History, and the two should not be confused.

David's Court History (2 Samuel 9—20)

The Court History, or Succession Narrative (usually considered to extend into 1 Kings 1—2), is a brilliant piece of writing, so realistic that many have wondered whether it was written by an eyewitness. Others point out, however, that realism in a story is generally a mark of the teller's skill rather than a guarantee of knowledge or historicity. (A science fiction novel may seem vibrantly "realistic," while an unskilled storyteller's true account of events she has experienced may be totally unconvincing.) Although some scholars interpret this story as propaganda, perhaps intended to legitimize Solomon's kingship (because, as we learn in the narrative, most Israelites seem to have expected that David's older son, Adonijah, would inherit the throne), many wonder if it is not storytelling for its own sake, an exploration of character and events comparable to Shakespeare's plays or today's serious historical novels. At any event, the Court History brings us into a world where God acts subtly through "natural" causation and human impulse rather than by flashy miracles and in which the human actors show an all-too-familiar mix of good intentions and weakness or even downright corruption. In general, the characters of the Hebrew Bible are rounded, a realistic mix of good and bad rather than stereotyped examples of one or the other (even though preachers often try to present them in the latter style), but this humanness is particularly evident in the Court History.

The most famous incident in this section is probably David's adultery with Bathsheba, reported in 2 Samuel 11. Modern readers, accustomed to thinking of sex as a primary area of religious morality, may miss the fact that 2 Samuel seems to approach the incident more in terms of abuse of power. Trouble is foreshadowed as early as the opening verse, where the king (who would ordinarily be expected to be out leading his troops in person at this time of year) lounges in the capital city while his officers and soldiers are out doing the fighting. He sees the wife of a loyal officer, and desires her. Although it may seem that Bathsheba is asking for trouble by bathing on a rooftop, this may well have been ordinary custom in a crowded city with a mild climate. The Bible does not tell us whether she is a willing respondent to David's summons or was simply powerless to refuse the invitation of the king, although interpreters over the centuries have offered much speculation on the matter. What interests the storyteller are David's actions and motivations. Although he knows that Bathsheba is married to his soldier Uriah, the king sends for her. When she becomes pregnant, with her husband away at war, David attempts to cover his misdeed by summoning Uriah home. Uriah, however, refuses to return to the house to sleep with his wife, even after David has gotten him drunk. (Does he know why David is so eager for him to return home? We would love to know, but we don't.) David then sends Uriah back to the battlefield, bearing a note to the commander ordering that Uriah be left unsupported on the front lines of the fighting. The commander complies, and Uriah is killed. When Bathsheba completes her mourning, David marries her.

In the next chapter, the prophet Nathan confronts David about the incident, setting him up with a story about a rich man who takes a poor man's beloved and only ewe lamb. When David responds with outrage, Nathan tells him, "You are the man!" (2 Sam. 12:7). We might prefer that God's concern be for the citizens harmed by David's abuse of power, but Nathan, speaking for YHWH, seems to view the incident in more personal terms. "Why have you despised the word of YHWH?...You have utterly scorned YHWH" (12:9, 14). The taking of wives per se is not the problem—YHWH has already taken Saul's women and given them to David, "and if that had been too little, I would have added as much more" (12:8). YHWH is going to respond with further wife-taking: "I will take your wives before your eyes, and give them to your neighbor" (12:11). In response to the other part of David's crime, his arrangement for the sword to strike Uriah, YHWH declares that "the sword shall never depart from your [David's] house" (12:9–10). For the storyteller, the important point seems to be that these punishments parallel David's wrongdoings, but to modern sensibilities, it is problematic to see the punishment falling on David's wives and the many who will die because of the sword over David's house—again we note that in the Deuteronomistic History, wrongdoing is avenged within history but not necessarily on the actual wrongdoer. When David confesses, the *New Revised Standard Version* (NRSV) has Nathan telling him that his sin is "put away," but the term more literally means "made to cross over": David himself will not die, but the child conceived with Bathsheba will (12:13–14). Eventually, however, Bathsheba bears David a second son, the divinely favored Solomon.

The divine punishments announced in 2 Samuel 12 begin to take effect in chapters 13 to 20. David's daughter Tamar is raped by her half-brother, David's eldest son, Amnon. Tamar's full brother, Absalom, eventually kills Amnon. Later, Absalom leads a rebellion against David, who flees from Jerusalem. Absalom makes a point of having sex with the concubines left behind by David, in accordance with the statement that David's women would be given to his enemy (12:11–12; 16:21–22).

David apparently realizes that YHWH is the ultimate source of these troubles, and he has learned not to presume upon YHWH. He refuses to take the ark with him into exile (2 Sam. 15:25). When a member of Saul's tribe hurls stones and curses at the fleeing king, David responds, "Let him alone, and let him curse; for YHWH has bidden him" (16:11). On the other hand, David is not above leaving agents in Jerusalem to spy for him and provide bad advice to Absalom (15:27–28, 32–36). One of these agents—with God's covert support—persuades Absalom to adopt a ruinous strategy (17:1–14). Although David's troops eventually deal Absalom's a solid defeat, David continues in the vacillation that has dogged all his dealings with his grown children: Even as he sends the army out, he commands the soldiers not to harm Absalom, and word of Absalom's death (David's commander having ignored the no-harm order) affects David more than the news that his throne is secured (18:5; 18:33—19:4).

Miscellaneous Appendices

The last four chapters of 2 Samuel seem to contain miscellaneous materials displaced from their proper position in the story. The slaughter of Saul's male relatives (2 Sam. 21), for instance, is probably presumed by David's question, "Is there still anyone left of the house of Saul?" in 9:1. Verses 21:15–17 may explain why David remained in Jerusalem while his men went to battle in 11:1, but their more favorable account of his retirement from personal war leading has been deferred to here. An alternate account of Goliath's death, attributing the killing to someone other than David (some contend that "Elhanan" is another name for David, but this explanation has problems), appears in 21:19. Poems attributed to David appear in chapter 22 (closely paralleling Ps. 18) and 23:1–7.

The last chapter of 2 Samuel tells an interesting story about David's acquisition of what seems to be the eventual temple site. It begins when YHWH orders David to take a census and then punishes the nation for it with a plague. (Note that plague is interpreted as a direct act of God, as famine was in 2 Sam. 21.) Perhaps the problem with the census is that it represents too rapid a move toward the taxations and conscriptions about which Samuel warned in 1 Samuel 8:11–18, but our chapter does not say that. For YHWH to order something and then punish for it is fairly typical of the portrayal of God in Samuel, where God is an autocrat whose decisions are not to be challenged. One might compare the passage in 1 Samuel 2:22–25 where Eli rebukes his corrupt sons, "but they would not listen to the voice of their father; for it was the will of YHWH to kill them." In Chronicles, which is much more concerned about God's fairness, Satan or "an adversary" incites the census (1 Chron. 21:1).

Seventy thousand people die (another instance of punishment falling on persons other than the evildoer), but when the plague hits Jerusalem, God issues a "hold" order. David, stricken by the suffering, confesses the sinfulness of his census a second time, then prays that God's hand might be against him rather than against the people (2 Sam. 24:17; contrast vv. 10–14). The prophet Gad then tells David to erect an altar on a certain threshing floor (an open rocky hilltop area). After he makes offerings on the new altar, "YHWH answered his supplication for the land, and the plague was averted" (2 Sam. 24:25). This story probably tells us something important about ancient understandings of the role of the king (who may be responsible both for bringing trouble on the people and/or for averting it) and the temple (a place for supplication on behalf of the land and people).

Reading through 1 and 2 Kings

Overview

First and Second Kings (originally a single book) tell the story of kingship in Israel and Judah after David (who is still alive, but impotent, at the beginning of 1 Kings). Early in 1 Kings, the tribes that had comprised David's and Solomon's "united kingdom" split into the two kingdoms of Israel and Judah. In 2 Kings, we see first Israel and then Judah captured by Mesopotamian armies. Interwoven with stories about and evaluations of the reigns of individual kings are stories of prophetic figures.

Solomon's reign over a united kingdom (1 Kings 1—11)
  Solomon gains the throne (1 Kings 1—2)
  Solomon's reign (1 Kings 3—11)
Two Kingdoms: Israel and Judah (1 Kings 12—2 Kings 17)
  Early kings of Israel and Judah (1 Kings 12—16)
  Prophets in the north (1 Kings 17:1—2 Kings 7:15)
      Elijah (1 Kings 17–21; 2 Kings 1:1—2:12)
      Micaiah ben Imlah (1 Kings 22)
      Elisha (2 Kings 2:13—10:31)
    Instability and the fall of Israel (2 Kings 10:32—17:41)
Reform and collapse in Judah (2 Kings 18—25)
  Good King Hezekiah (2 Kings 18—20)
  Evil King Manasseh and his son (2 Kings 21)
  Good King Josiah (2 Kings 22:1—23:30)
  Judah falls (2 Kings 23:31—25:30)

Solomon's Reign Over a United Kingdom (1 Kings 1—11)

Although many regard the first two chapters of Kings as a continuation of the Succession Narrative begun in 2 Samuel 9—20 (see p. 98), they portray a situation in which David's rule has effectively ended. The question has become, Who will succeed David? Most, including the powerful general Joab (commander of David's citizen army) and the priest Abiathar (who joined David in the wilderness days before David became king), expect that David's oldest living son, Adonijah, will become king. But Bathsheba and the prophet Nathan ask the failing David to make good on a promise (not elsewhere recorded—did he really promise, or are they manipulating a senile old man?) to appoint Solomon to the throne. David agrees. Nathan, the priest Zadok (who seems to have joined David after the move to Jerusalem), and Benaiah (commander of the Cherethites and Pelethites, foreign mercenary troops) move immediately to anoint Solomon. By the end of 1 Kings 2, Benaiah has executed Adonijah and Joab (among others), and Abiathar has been banished to his family estate. One wonders, reading this strikingly bloody account, whether it does not protest Solomon's innocence too much. Did he seize power in a coup?

As we have already observed (see the Notable Characters section, p. 102), Solomon's reign receives a mixed review. He is praised for his wisdom, wealth, and international influence, and above all for building a temple for YHWH in Jerusalem, the building and dedication of which are described in loving detail in 1 Kings 5—8 (the clear reference to exile in 8:46–53 suggests that some of this material was composed much later than Solomon's own time). But the northern tribes fret under Solomon's taxation and labor policies, and the Deuteronomistic editors frown on his foreign wives and the shrines that he establishes for their gods. Because YHWH loved David so much, we hear, full accounting will be delayed until after Solomon's lifetime, but already in 1 Kings 11 we see international unrest and domestic rebellion.

Two Kingdoms: Israel and Judah (1 Kings 12—2 Kings 17)

Early Kings of Israel and Judah (1 Kings 12—16). According to the somewhat stylized account in 1 Kings 12:1–19 (one gets the impression that the narrators might be disgruntled elder advisors), Solomon's heir Rehoboam foolishly and rudely refuses to lighten the tax and forced labor burdens imposed by his father (1 Kings 12:1–19), angering the northern tribes and triggering the revolt announced by the prophet Ahijah in 1 Kings 11:26–40. Rehoboam remains in control of Judah and Jerusalem in the south, while one of Solomon's former officials, Jeroboam, becomes king of the larger, more prosperous, northern kingdom, Israel.

Jeroboam, fearing that worship in the Davidic family's temple in Jerusalem will compromise his people's political loyalties, quickly provides the new nation with its own temples (1 Kings 12:26–29). In the thought-world of the ancient Near East, where national temples were also treasuries and symbols of national power, and in which a king curried the favor of his patron god by constructing a temple or temples for the god, Jeroboam's action makes perfect sense. For him, worship only in Jerusalem would have been tantamount to declaring himself a vassal of Rehoboam. The Deuteronomistic History's editors, however, are loyal to Jerusalem and David's line, and they harshly condemn the temples at Bethel and Dan (12:30).

We see, in these stories of the early kings, two features that will characterize the remainder of the Deuteronomistic History. First, the editors organize their work king by king, describing and assessing each one's reign before moving to either his successor or any kings who may have come to power in the other kingdom during his reign. They judge each monarch by his adherence to YHWH's commands as understood at the time of Josiah's reform. Because that reform emphasized worship at Jerusalem alone, the northern kings fare poorly. Although we get hints of nonreligious aspects of various reigns, we do not receive all the information that a modern historian might consider relevant. With only Kings to go by, for instance, one would not know that Omri (1 Kings 16:21–28) had a widespread and long-lasting international reputation for wealth and power.

Second, Kings shows a special interest in the activities of prophets. Sometimes they make theological speeches that reflect the agendas of the editors. The "prediction" that Josiah will destroy Bethel's altar (1 Kings 13:2–3) is probably an example of the editors' work, inserted with benefit of hindsight (the technical term for this is *ex eventu,* or "after the event" that the prophecy purports to describe). If we think that the point of prophecy is predicting the future, it may be troubling to think that such prophecies have likely been composed after the fact, but if we understand that prophets are, above all, theological interpreters who point out the religious meaning of events (see pp. 135–36), then it does not matter so much whether the statement of this anonymous prophet was actually made at the time or written later for the benefit of a later audience.

Prophets in the North (1 Kings 17:1—2 Kings 10:31). Prophets play an especially prominent role in the portion of the narrative that bridges 1 and 2 Kings. The powerful northern king Ahab and his spirited Phoenician queen Jezebel appear as little more than foils for the mighty Elijah and audacious Micaiah (see the Notable Characters section, pp. 102–3). Most often, Elijah quarrels with the royal couple for their honoring of the deities Baal and Asherah, but in 1 Kings 21, we encounter a different kind of story. Here, Jezebel arranges for false witnesses to testify against a man in order that Ahab may gain possession of the man's vineyard. Two important themes of the Deuteronomistic History come into play here: first, the king's responsibility (violated, in this case) as an administrator of justice, and second, the sacredness of each family's hold on the land granted to it by God.

In 2 Kings 2, Elijah departs for heaven in a fiery chariot (a story that gave rise to traditions, mentioned in the Second Testament, that he had never died and would eventually return to earth). His mantle is taken up—literally—by the prophet Elisha. Like his predecessor, Elisha provides food for a woman who shelters him, and he raises a dead child (2 Kings 4; compare 1 Kings 17). He multiplies loaves and cures leprosy (2 Kings 4:42—5:14). He also consorts with kings, including the kings of other countries. In particular, Elisha is credited with instigating a coup in the neighboring country of Syria (Aram) and commissioning other prophets to instigate a coup by Israel's army commander, Jehu (2 Kings 8:7–15; 9:1—10:31). Although 2 Kings presents Jehu's revolt as a divinely commissioned judgment against Omri's dynasty, Hosea 1:4 portrays God as more critical of Jehu's action: "In a little while I will punish the house of Jehu for the blood of Jezreel, and I will put an end to the kingdom of the house of Israel." This reminds us again that the biblical books present us with theological interpretations of events—interpretations that may even vary—and not simply with the facts.

Instability and the Fall of Israel (2 Kings 10:32—17:41). In the course of seizing Israel's throne, Jehu also slaughters the reigning king of Judah. Judah's queen mother—a member, ironically enough, of the Israelite ruling family that Jehu has just deposed (2 Kings 8:26)—assumes control of the country. She attempts to eliminate rival claimants to the throne, but according to 2 Kings, another royal woman conspires with the priests and royal guard to protect a legitimate heir. Seven years later, the young Davidic prince is brought out of hiding to assume Judah's throne.

Although a few kings (notably Jeroboam II of Israel and Azariah, also known as Uzziah, of Judah) still enjoy long and prosperous reigns, trouble is on its way from Mesopotamia. When Tiglath-pileser of Assyria threatens Syria and Israel, the rulers of those small countries form an alliance (2 Kings 16). They pressure Judah's King Ahaz to join, but he faces a rebellion by Edom on his southeastern border. Perhaps he also fears that Syria and Israel are fighting a losing battle. In any case, he pays tribute to the Assyrian king in return for that king's support against Ahaz and his confederates. Although Isaiah 7 condemns Ahaz for making this alliance (see pp. 141–42) rather than trusting solely in YHWH, Judah does survive when its northern neighbor Israel falls to the Assyrians in 722 B.C.E.

In 2 Kings 17, Deuteronomistic editors comment on the history of Israel and the fall of the north, noting that both Judah and Israel persisted in sin (a comment inserted in light of Jerusalem's later fall?) but blaming the north's demise especially on the "sins that Jereboam committed" (17:22, referring especially to the erection of temples outside of Jerusalem). Although it is historically quite credible that, as this chapter asserts, Israelites were taken to Assyria and persons from other places were settled in the formerly Israelite territory, it is unlikely that this exchange involved the entire population (other parts of the Bible clearly assert that some of the population continued to live in the region). Some of the "impure worship" customs with which occupants of the region are charged in 17:32–41 may actually be indigenous Israelite customs of which the Deuteronomistic reformers in Jerusalem (or Babylonian exile) disapprove, rather than truly foreign imports. To put it another way, we may be hearing one side of an intra-Israelite quarrel over the proper methods of worship, and it might be that the population of the north would have judged Jerusalem's worship as unacceptable to YHWH as the writers here judge the northern worship.

Reform and Collapse in Judah (2 Kings 18—25). Judah survives for almost a century and a half after the fall of Israel. The history's editors single out two of this period's kings, Hezekiah and Josiah, for special praise, while heaping particularly bitter condemnation on another king, Manasseh.

The dates given in Kings for events of King Hezekiah's reign are difficult to correlate with information given in Assyrian and Babylonian records and elsewhere in the Bible; it seems likely that the editors of Kings have arranged their story to serve theological purposes rather than to provide an accurate chronological sequence. They report that Hezekiah destroys all places of worship other than the Jerusalem temple, and purifies the temple itself by removing such objects as a bronze serpent to which offerings had hitherto been made (2 Kings 18:4). Even David and Solomon had not been so zealous. Although the editors present Hezekiah's program as a return to the "commandments that YHWH commanded Moses" (18:6), we must wonder whether those commandments had really been so clearly set forth before Hezekiah's time. The history clearly states that prior Davidic kings had engaged in a whole variety of forbidden practices, and surely they would not have done so had they possessed a clear tradition that those practices were abhorrent to the patron deity, YHWH, whose favor they sought.

The editors do not mention, perhaps because it would have been obvious to their ancient audience, that Hezekiah's efforts on behalf of Judah's national God were tied up with a rejection of the Assyrian superpower that his father Ahaz had courted. Hezekiah also made other preparations for rebellion: He made Jerusalem more siege-worthy by providing it with an internal water supply (2 Kings 20:20, probably referring to the Siloam tunnel, which can still be seen today), and he negotiated with a Babylonian king who also desired Assyria's downfall (20:12–15, likely occurring before some events in previous chapters). In 2 Kings 18:13–16, Assyria responds to his defiance and forces Hezekiah to cough up withheld tribute (recall that ancient temples were not just houses of worship but also treasuries). Assyrian records make no mention of the slaughter reported in 19:35. They do claim that Hezekiah was "shut up like a bird in a cage," consistent with the biblical account of siege, and they do *not* claim that Sennacharib captured Hezekiah, although they do report Assyrian victories over other important Judean cities such as Lachish (18:14).

Although the report on Hezekiah is mostly favorable, 2 Kings shows no such fondness for his son Manasseh. A secular historian might speculate that Manasseh's rebuilding of local shrines and respect for a variety of gods contributed to the peacefulness of his fifty-five year reign by honoring the sensibilities of both the Judean populace and Judah's Assyrian overlords. In the eyes of the Deuteronomistic Historians, however, Manasseh's policies seal the fate of Judah; the punishment for such idolatry might be delayed but could no longer be averted. Chronicles, by the way, finds it incomprehensible that a king so evil could have had so long a reign; it attempts to explain the riddle by inserting a story of repentance on Manasseh's part (2 Chron. 33:12–16).

The second great reformer of Judah was Josiah (2 Kings 22:1—23:30), who receives greater praise from the editors than does any other king, even David (see especially 23:25). Like Hezekiah, he seems to have hoped to throw off the Assyrian yoke, and in connection with this he initiates great religious reforms. Second Kings reports that during repairs to the temple, Josiah's high priest finds a scroll, "the book of the law" (22:8). High officials take this book to the woman prophet Huldah, who declares it authentic. Josiah then reads it in the presence of all the people and, according to 2 Kings 23:1–3, they repent. However, other biblical texts (such as the books of Jeremiah and Ezekiel) lament ongoing polytheism in Judah, suggesting that the account in Kings may be exaggerated. The book's contents seem new and startling to its readers (note, for instance, the admission in 23:21–23 that through the entire history of the monarchy Passover had never been observed in the manner prescribed by this book). It may have been composed precisely to support Josiah's reform, and many suppose it looked much like the core of our present book of Deuteronomy (see pp. 68–71). We have noted previously that the first edition of the Deuteronomistic History may also have been composed to support this reform.

Josiah, however, dies at the age of forty-one. Judah's fall is now close at hand. Josiah's first successor, his son Jehoahaz, lasts only three months before Egypt's pharaoh replaces him with another of Josiah's sons, Jehoiakim. Jehoiakim soon becomes subject instead to the Babylonians (who have meanwhile conquered Assyria). He dies in an attempted rebellion against them. In 597 B.C.E., his successor, Jehoiachin, is taken to Babylon as a captive.

(He and fellow upper-class deportees of 597 are described as "good figs" in Jer. 24:1–7.) The Babylonians install another Davidic prince, Zedekiah, on Judah's throne, but he too tries to rebel. This time, the Babylonian king Nebuchadnezzer decides to make an example of rebellion-prone Judah. Nebuchadnezzar and his troops flatten Jerusalem and take still more of its upper class into exile (2 Kings 25:1–21). The last vestige of Judean home rule crumbles when the native-born governor appointed by the Babylonians, Gedaliah, falls to assassins.

At the end of 2 Kings, the Judean king Jehoiachin (captured in 597) is released from prison and given a place of honor at the table of Babylon's ruler, King Evil-merodach (25:27–30). Is this a glimmer of hope for the Davidic dynasty, or a final confirmation of its subjugation to Babylon? The reader is left to decide.

Summary

The books of Samuel and Kings provide modern readers with an odd (to us) mix of exciting storytelling, tedious detail, and didactic sermonizing. The whole is suffused by the convictions that Israel and Judah are locked, for better or worse, in covenant relationship with a passionate and demanding God, that God's judgments upon them are played out in natural events and political history. For ancient readers of a first, Josianic edition, the lesson would have been that their nation's only hope lay in rallying to Josiah's reform. The subsequent exilic edition would have supplied its readers with an explanation for their nation's fall and, perhaps, with hope that faithfulness on their own part might yet lead to restoration. Surely the God who had brought down might also be able to rebuild! Some readers today still find in these books motivation for adherence to God's law. Others are left questioning a theology that reads history's vicissitudes as the judgment of God.

Resources

Walter Brueggemann. *David's Truth in Israel's History and Imagination*. Rev. ed. Minneapolis: Fortress Press, 2002.

Terence E. Fretheim. *First and Second Kings*. Westminster Bible Companion. Louisville, Ky.: Westminster John Knox Press, 1999.

David M. Gunn. *The Fate of King Saul*. Journal for the Study of the Old Testament. Supplement Series 6. Sheffield, U.K.: Sheffield Academic Press, 1980.

Gary N. Knoppers and J. Gordon McConville, eds. *Reconsidering Israel and Judah: Recent Studies on the Deuteronomistic History*. Sources for Biblical and Theological Study. Winona Lake, Ind.: Eisenbrauns, 2000.

P. Kyle McCarter. *I Samuel* and *II Samuel.* Vols. 8 and 9 of *The Anchor Bible.* Garden City, N.Y.: Doubleday, 1980 and 1984.

Marti J. Steussy. *David: Biblical Portraits of Power.* Studies on Personalities of the Old Testament. Columbia, S.C.: University of South Carolina Press, 1999.

8

Ezra, Nehemiah, and Chronicles

SAMUEL PAGÁN

First and Second Chronicles (which were originally a single work) tell the story of Judah from its genealogical beginnings in Adam through Cyrus' edict authorizing the return of the exiles from Babylon (2 Chron. 36:22–23). Ezra and Nehemiah (also originally a single work) begin with the edict (Ezra 1:1–4) and tell how leaders of the returnee community rebuilt the temple and Jerusalem's walls. Chronicles and Ezra–Nehemiah are united not only by the almost-verbatim words in which they report Cyrus' edict, but by their Second Temple Period outlook and intense interest in the formal worship life of the community, including the roles of particular groups of priests and Levites. Because of these similarities, rabbinic Judaism and medieval Christianity attributed both works to one author, Ezra the scribe.

Today, however, most scholars think that the books in their present forms come from considerably later than the time of Ezra. Differences in vocabulary, style, theology, and methodology also suggest that Chronicles may come from a different source than Ezra–Nehemiah, despite some important common interests shared by the sources. The books represent two different types of historiography. Ezra–Nehemiah speaks directly of the bitter experience of exile in Babylon and later efforts to rebuild the Jerusalem temple. It analyzes the life of a people that has undergone military defeat and deportation but is now engaged in dramatic national reconstruction. Chronicles also addresses issues of national reconstruction, but in a different way. Like the Deuteronomistic History, it tells stories of the past to emphasize general principles important for its own day. From the Chronicler's perspective, "history" is the concrete expression of divine authority in the world.

Because the books covered by this chapter are closely related to their historical context and each other, we begin with a discussion of their common historical background. Next, we discuss matters of date and authorship. After that, we discuss the distinctive features of the individual books, first Ezra–Nehemiah and then 1 and 2 Chronicles.

Historical Background

Exile in Babylon

King Nebuchadnezzar's military campaigns in Palestine brought pain, death, destruction, captivity, deportation, and exile. Defeated peoples saw some of their leaders die and others taken captive into exile. Royal institutions gave way to new structures imposed by the Babylonian Empire. Nationally associated temples, worship services and sacrifices, and priestly groups were also hit hard. Judah's sense of history and identity was permanently affected by these defeats. We mark this change in identity by referring to Judah's people in the time of exile and thereafter as "Jewish" rather than "Judean." (In the biblical languages of Hebrew and Greek, however, "Jewish" and "Judean" are the same word.)

Two or possibly three agonizing experiences of deportation took place during the years 598–597 B.C.E., 587–586 B.C.E., and 582 B.C.E. The economic, political, social, and religious scaffolding of Judah collapsed. Jerusalem's poor people were left behind, as were most Judeans who dwelt outside the capital city. These nonexiles faced social disorder; a ruined temple; political and administrative disorganization; economic difficulties; and the physical, emotional, and spiritual consequences of all these calamities.

Meanwhile, Jerusalem's elite had been taken to Babylon. These former national leaders felt oppressed and humiliated by their captive situation. Nonetheless, they were allowed to live in community, to devote themselves to agriculture and business, to build homes, and to earn their livings in diverse ways (Jer. 29). King Jehoiakim, who was taken into exile in the year 598–597 B.C.E., was treated with some respect and consideration. Even as they settled into life in Babylon, the deportees nurtured memories of their homeland and hoped for a restoration of Judah and Israel.

Cyrus the Great: The Politics of Conquest and Tolerance

For all its power, Babylon soon fell into social, spiritual, and political decay. Internal conflicts and discontent interrupted its external conquests. Eventually it found itself under an emperor, Nabonidus, who lacked the people's trust and respect. In 539 B.C.E., the armies of a neighboring emperor,

Cyrus of Persia (also known as Cyrus II and Cyrus the Great), entered Babylon without difficulty.

Rather than trying to intimidate conquered peoples by razing their cities and removing their leaders, Cyrus left the cities intact (insofar as military requirements allowed) and respected the life, religious feelings, and culture of vanquished peoples. He worked to better the empire's social and economic conditions and declared himself an envoy of Marduk, the god of Babylon. In 538 B.C.E., in accordance with his policy of respect and affirmation for national cults—as long as those cults did not interfere with subject peoples' loyalty to the empire—he issued an edict regarding the exiled Jews.

Ezra 6:3–5 gives an Aramaic text of the edict. It stipulates that the temple be rebuilt with the financial help of the Persian Empire, states some regulations concerning reconstruction, and adds that the royal treasures taken from the temple by Nebuchadnezzar must be returned to their proper place in Jerusalem. Ezra 1:2–4 quotes the edict in Hebrew. This version says that Jews who want to return to their homeland may do so, and it invites those who remain in Babylon to cooperate financially toward the restoration.

The First Return of Jews from Babylon to Jerusalem

To guide the return to Palestine and to direct the tasks of reconstruction, Cyrus appointed Sheshbazzar (perhaps an alternate name for King Jehoiachin's son Shenazzar; 1 Chron. 3:18) as governor (Ezra 5:14). Apparently, only a small number of people accompanied Sheshbazzar on the initial return to Jerusalem. Neither the Bible nor archaeological sources tell us what happened to Sheshbazzar, but at some point the Davidic prince Zerubbabel took his place.

As soon as the returnees arrived in Jerusalem, they began the work of reconstruction and possibly resumed worship at the site of the ruined temple. They had come full of hopes and dreams, expecting fulfillment of the promises of Deutero-Isaiah and Ezekiel. Instead, they experienced difficulties, deprivation, insecurity, crises, and violence. Although the books of Ezra–Nehemiah talk about these difficulties from the point of view of the returnees, we may imagine that the local people, the ones whose families had never gone into exile and who had been surviving and reestablishing themselves in this ruined land for fifty years already, had their own feelings about the strangers who arrived from Babylon to take over the show.

Reconstruction of the Temple

Cyrus died in 530 B.C.E. His eldest son, Cambyses, succeeded him. Cambyses' death in 522 B.C.E. brought instability and crisis to the empire.

It took his successor, Darius I, several years to reorganize the empire and consolidate power.

These internal conflicts in the Persian Empire doubtless contributed to Jewish hopes that the nation would soon break free from Persian rule. Messianic hopes (that is, hopes for renewed national independence under a Davidic king) grew up around Zerubbabel. The prophets Haggai and Zechariah rallied support for Zerubbabel and the restoration effort. The Second Temple, central symbol of the returnees' hopes and identity, was finished and inaugurated in 515 B.C.E. (It stood—with some additions and improvements—until the Romans burned Jerusalem in 70 C.E.)

Life After the Temple's Reconstruction

As the Persian Empire reorganized, the returnees' dreams of independence and their messianic hopes for Zerubbabel did not come true. Although the first phase of reconstruction had been accomplished, both the returnee Jewish leaders and the local people displaced by them felt frustrated and insecure.

After the reconstruction of the temple, additional Jews returned to Jerusalem from their diaspora communities. (*Diaspora* means "scattering" and refers to the communities and culture of Jews choosing to live outside Palestine in this period and thereafter.) The lists set forth in Ezra 2 and Nehemiah 7 are probably related to a census of the population of Judah held during the days of Nehemiah. A large number of these approximately 50,000 inhabitants must have arrived after the temple had been rebuilt and inaugurated.

During the Persian administration, Judah was a part of the Fifth Satrapy (a Persian administrative district) known as "Beyond the River" (referring to the Euphrates). Jerusalem may have been governed from Samaria, with local affairs in the hands of the Jewish priests. According to Ezra 4:6, the officials in Samaria promoted confrontation between the Jewish community and the Persian Empire. At the same time, the Egyptians were organizing to recover lost territories. Their military incursions prompted the Edomites to move from their ancestral lands and resettle in southern Palestine, as far as the north side of Hebron.

With all this going on, the Jewish community decided to rebuild the walls of Jerusalem and fortify the city. At this point, Nehemiah probably arrived in Jerusalem, in King Artaxerxes' twentieth year, in 445 B.C.E. (Neh. 2:1–10).

The Condition of the Jewish Community

Ezra–Nehemiah and Malachi (which seems to be of similar age and theological outlook) paint a bleak picture of the people's moral and spiritual condition in the mid-400s B.C.E. We read that priests neglected the Torah and offered stolen, sick, blind, and lame animals for sacrifice (Mal. 1:6–14); that the Torah was interpreted with partiality and injustice (Mal. 2:1–9); that Sabbath, which had become a central covenant symbol during the exilic period, was not kept properly (Neh. 13:15–22); that the community forgot its economic responsibilities, such as tithes and offerings (Mal. 3:7–10); that loyalty to the Torah was questioned (Mal. 2:17; 3:13–15); that the divorce rate was scandalous (Mal. 2:13–16); that employees were cheated and the weak were oppressed (Mal. 3:5); that the belongings of the poor were embargoed in times of scarcity and crisis and the poor were made slaves in order to pay their taxes and debts (Neh. 5:1–5); and that marriages between Jews and pagans threatened the integrity of the community (Neh. 13:23–27). It is probably worth asking whose point of view we get as we read such texts. For instance, Haggai and Zechariah, who call so zealously for generosity toward the temple, may well have been staffers who were paid with cuts from the sacrificial offerings. Ezra and Nehemiah call for divorce of foreign wives, but Nehemiah 13:28 tells us that the high priest's family did not agree with Nehemiah's views about marriage to "foreign" women, and Malachi speaks against divorce and thrusting aside of the alien (Mal. 2:16; 3:5). The very fact that the Bible records more than one side to the story underscores that this was an economically stressed and socially fractured community.

The Question of Ezra's Date

Ezra 7:6–7 tells us that Ezra went to Jerusalem "in the seventh year of King Artaxerxes." But *which* Artaxerxes? Did Ezra's time in Jerusalem come before, after, or during Nehemiah's administration, and if during, why is there so little mention of interaction between the two leaders? Scholars have proposed several answers to the question of Ezra's date.

One possibility is that the king is Artaxerxes I (465–424 B.C.E.). In this scenario, *Ezra arrived before Nehemiah, in 458 B.C.E.,* and began his reforms about thirteen years before Nehemiah came to Jerusalem. This dating agrees with the book's suggestion that Ezra's religious reforms preceded Nehemiah's administrative and political ones. Also, Ezra's surprise at finding mixed marriages in Jerusalem makes more sense if it comes before Nehemiah's actions against such marriages (Ezra 9—10; Neh. 10:30). On the other hand, Nehemiah's "memoirs" make no mention of religious reforms under Ezra, and for Jerusalem's situation to have been as bad as it was by the time Nehemiah arrived, we would have to suppose that Ezra's mission had failed almost completely.

Another possibility is that the king is Artaxerxes II (405–358 B.C.E.), in which case *Ezra arrived in Jerusalem after Nehemiah's work, in 398 B.C.E.*

This reckoning would explain Ezra's allusion to Nehemiah's labors (Neh. 3:1; 13:4), the social and political situation of Jerusalem at Ezra's arrival (Ezra 8:29; 10:5), and the fact that when Ezra and Nehemiah appear together, Ezra seems to play the junior role (Neh. 8:2, 4, 9; 12:36).

However, descriptions of Jerusalem's situation at this time, in contemporary documents from a Jewish community in Egypt, do not agree with the Ezra–Nehemiah literature's description of conditions at the time of Ezra's arrival. Also, if Ezra came so late, it is surprising that we even find verses that place him alongside Nehemiah.

These difficulties have led a few scholars to propose that *Ezra arrived during Nehemiah's second mission, in the year 428 B.C.E.* This affirms the biblical tradition that places Ezra and Nehemiah as contemporaries (Neh. 8:9; 12:26, 36), working together for the physical and spiritual reconstruction of the community. However, this dating requires an important textual correction, changing Ezra 7:6–8 to refer to the thirty-seventh year of King Artaxerxes I (428 B.C.E.) instead of the seventh year (458 B.C.E.). This adjustment eases the difficulties related to an early (458 B.C.E.) or late (398 B.C.E.) arrival of Ezra in Jerusalem. However, there is no manuscript evidence in any language to support this amendment of the biblical text.

All things considered, the traditional early dating of Ezra seems the most satisfactory, and that dating will be followed in this chapter.

Authorship and Dates of Composition

Rabbinical teachers in the early centuries of the Common Era greatly respected Ezra and regarded him as the author of Ezra–Nehemiah and also Chronicles. Some modern scholars accept this theory, especially with regard to Ezra–Nehemiah, but it does not adequately explain some features within that body of writing, especially the mixed signals about who (Ezra or Nehemiah) arrived in Jerusalem first.

Given the problems with the hypothesis of Ezra as author, a second theory attributes the whole set of books (Chronicles and Ezra–Nehemiah) to an otherwise anonymous source referred to as "the Chronicler." Supporters of this theory point to the literary, thematic, and historical continuities between Chronicles and Ezra–Nehemiah, which together present the history of Israel in a generally continuous form. They also point out that these books use sources in a similar way.

A third theory attributes both Chronicles and Ezra–Nehemiah to Second Temple priestly circles (thus accounting for similarities between the books) but not to the same author. Supporters of this theory argue that the writer of Chronicles views some important priestly controversies differently than does the writer of Ezra–Nehemiah. The controversies involve the responsibilities of particular priestly and Levitical families and—of more interest to most readers today—the status of "foreigners" in the community. Chronicles may even have been written as a deliberate response to Ezra–Nehemiah, attempting to show that some of the policies promoted in Ezra–Nehemiah are a departure from the true spirit of Israel as understood by the Chronicler.

Ezra–Nehemiah and Chronicles seem to have been written in the late 400s or early 300s B.C.E. They cannot have been written much before this, because the list of David's descendants in 1 Chronicles 3:24 includes the sons of Elioenai, whose youngest son was born around 405 B.C.E. The last Persian king mentioned in the books is Darius II (mentioned in Neh. 12:22), who reigned 424–405 B.C.E. The last high priest mentioned in Ezra 10:6 is Jehohanan, and Jewish documents from Egypt tell us that he was priest in 411 B.C.E. These documents also tell us that Bigvai was governor of Judah in 408 B.C.E., but his governorship is not mentioned in Ezra–Nehemiah. All this suggests that the material in Ezra–Nehemiah was gathered around 400 B.C.E., although some portions may have been added during the first part of the 300s B.C.E. The fact that Chronicles uses Ezra–Nehemiah as a source (see below) suggests that it was likely written later than Ezra–Nehemiah.

Ezra–Nehemiah

Overview

The following outline of the books of Ezra and Nehemiah may contribute to the process of studying and understanding these books.

Return of the captives under Sheshbazzar (Ezra 1—2)
  Cyrus' edict (1:1–4)
  Return to Jerusalem (1:5–11)
  List of those returning with Zerubbabel (2:1–70)

Reconstruction of the Jerusalem temple (Ezra 3—6)
  Restoration of the altar and worship (3:1–7)
  Laying the foundation (3:8–13)
  Enemies stop the work (4:1–24)
  Rebuilding the temple (5:1—6:22)

Ezra's reforms (Ezra 7—10)
  Ezra and his companions arrive in Jerusalem (7:1—8:36)
  Ezra's prayer of confession (9:1–15)
  Foreign women expelled (10:1–44)

Rebuilding the walls of Jerusalem (Neh. 1:1—7:73a)
    Nehemiah's prayer concerning Jerusalem (1:1–11)
    Artaxerxes sends Nehemiah to Jerusalem (2:1–10)
    Nehemiah encourages the people to rebuild the walls (2:11–20)
    Distribution of the rebuilding tasks (3:1–32)
    Protection against enemies (4:1–23)
    Abolition of usury (5:1–19)
    Enemies' machinations (6:1–19)
    Nehemiah appoints leaders (7:1–4)
    List of those returning with Zerubbabel (7:5–73a)
Other reforms by Ezra (Neh. 7:73b—10:39)
    Ezra reads the Torah to the people (7:73b—8:18)
    Ezra confesses Israel's sins (9:1–37)
    The people vow to follow the Torah (9:38—10:39)
Miscellaneous information on Nehemiah's term (Neh. 11—13)
    Inhabitants of Jerusalem (11:1–24)
    Inhabited places outside Jerusalem (11:25–36)
    Priests and Levites (12:1–26)
    Dedication of the walls (12:27–43)
    Portions for priests and Levites (12:44–47)
    Nehemiah's reforms (13:1–31)

The Theology of Ezra–Nehemiah

In the theological traditions of monarchic Judah, religious and national identity had been closely identified with each other, and national protection had been one significant means by which people expected YHWH to show love and care for them. The fall of Jerusalem had posed a terrible theological crisis. Was YHWH trustworthy? What did YHWH want from the people? How could the people show faithfulness to YHWH? and how would YHWH care for the people in the context of exile, or even in the context of return under continuing foreign imperial control? These are some of the theological questions that Ezra–Nehemiah must address.

The answer begins with an emphasis on God's authority as creator. The books of Ezra and Nehemiah identify Israel's God with the titles "God of heaven and earth" (Ezra 5:11) and "God of heaven" (Ezra 1:2; 5:11; 6:9–10; 7:12, 21, 23; Neh. 1:4–5; 2:4, 20). As "God of heaven and earth," YHWH has the capacity to create and establish order in the world (not just one small corner of it) and to ensure the triumph of good over the forces of evil.

Ezra–Nehemiah, like chapters 40 to 55 of Isaiah, pays special attention to God's exercise of international dominion through the Persian authorities (who, we should note, also use the language of the "God of heaven" in Ezra—for instance, 1:2 and 6:9–10—and in documents outside the Bible). God stirs up the spirit of Cyrus (Ezra 1:1) and inspires Artaxerxes to grant permission to Nehemiah to return to Jerusalem (Neh. 13:6). This theology allows the returnees to portray the mighty Persian empire as God's tool at work for their own benefit, while also politely dovetailing with the emperors' own claims of divine support.

However, the "God of heaven" portrayed in Ezra–Nehemiah also maintains a special covenant relationship with Israel (Neh. 9). Even as Judah was falling, promises of restoration had been announced by Jeremiah and Ezekiel. Ezra 1:1 declares Cyrus' edict a fulfillment of those promises. The lists of returnees in Ezra 2 and Nehemiah 7 are intended to demonstrate that those who accompany Zerubbabel are legitimate heirs of the promises, the faithful remnant (Ezra 9:8, 15) of Israel. The restored community is portrayed as continuous with the ancient people of God.

In First Temple Judah, religion and national identity had been tightly interwoven. In the Second Temple community, which lacked political independence, religious identity became all the more important. A new Temple was rebuilt over the ruins of the ancient one; old walls were reconstructed; and religious leaders emphasized that the community's worship patterns, offerings, and festivals were based on pre-exilic patterns. God's great acts in history were hailed in worship and festivals, educational experiences where color, music, singers, priests, and Levites contributed to the community's process of education. The exodus in particular was viewed (again in agreement with Isa. 40—55) not simply as a piece of history but as a "type" (foreshadowing or pattern-setting precedent) of the returnees' own deliverance from exile and return to the promised land.

One particularly striking aspect of the faith taught by Ezra and Nehemiah is allegiance to the Torah (the law of Moses). As we have seen in chapters 3 to 5, there is good reason to believe that the Torah was not simply written by Moses. Indeed, the five books do not seem to have assumed their present forms until the exile or later. But for the writer of Ezra–Nehemiah, the Torah books represent the true essence of the tradition. They are regarded as both law to be obeyed and revelation to be understood. In the attitude of Ezra–Nehemiah toward the Torah, we see the beginnings of the concept of an authoritative written scripture.

Another feature of Ezra–Nehemiah's focus on ethnic identity, a feature that many modern readers find problematic, is the demand that Israelite men divorce their foreign wives. This demand becomes more disturbing when we realize that in Ezra–Nehemiah, "Israelite" refers only to members of the returnee community, so the so-called foreigners probably included

Judeans whose families had not gone into exile. On the positive side, the policy against mixed marriages may be defended as a move to maintain ethnic, cultural, and religious identity in a multicultural situation full of pressures for assimilation. On the negative side, we should note that by prohibiting intermarriage with locals, members of the elite "remnant" returnee group—to whom the Persians had entrusted governance of the area—could keep power concentrated within their own ranks.

This tension notwithstanding, Ezra–Nehemiah displays a spirituality not completely alien to Jews and Christians today. This spirituality is particularly evident in the prayers recorded in the books. The prayers reveal a profound sense of solidarity with ancient Israel, a serious attitude of humility, and a precise knowledge of what is being asked of God—in short, a serious and mature faith.

1 and 2 Chronicles

Overview

Rather than directly telling the story of their own Second Temple time, the books of Chronicles recount Israel's political and religious life from the beginning of humanity's history to the people's new beginning after the exile. The story ends with Cyrus' famous edict of liberation. The Chronicler's work sets forth the fundamental events that endow the people Israel with a reason for being, covering the same period as Genesis to Kings. The Chronicler revises this history from a point of view of hope, restoration, redemption, and renewal. The work has three main parts:

- Genealogy from Adam to Israel (1 Chronicles 1—9), including Noah, Abraham, and Jacob (Israel), along with their children
- History of Israel (1 Chronicles 10—2 Chronicles 9) under David and Solomon
- History of Judah (2 Chronicles 10—36) from the crisis with the northern tribes to the reconstruction period

The first major section (1 Chron. 1—9) provides a sort of introduction. Ethnic, geographical, and chronological references introduce the people, define their territory, and allude to fundamental religious institutions. This section ends with a list of the inhabitants of Jerusalem (9:3–34) and adds a genealogy of King Saul (9:35–44).

Already this section shows the Chronicler's view of God's plan for humanity: All human history converges in King David and the temple priesthood, placing the tribe of Judah at the center of Israel. This first section also implicitly articulates the Chronicler's theological conviction that Israel's future may be discovered through a careful analysis of its past.

The second major section (1 Chron. 10—2 Chron. 9) portrays the reigns of David and Solomon as a single period in which, according to the Chronicler, Israel attains its highest prosperity and greatest military achievements. Both kings are portrayed as virtuous, making wise administrative decisions supported by the entire populace. David founds the dynasty and begins administrative processes that bring success, growth, and prosperity to the people. Solomon continues and enacts the political and administrative plans of his predecessor.

David's history contains four parts: the beginning of his reign in Israel (1 Chron. 10—12), the establishment of worship in Jerusalem (1 Chron. 13—17), wars (1 Chron. 18—20), and the organization and stabilization of the kingdom (1 Chron. 21—29). Unpleasant incidents related in the Deuteronomistic History, such as the Bathsheba affair and Absalom's rebellion, are omitted here. Rather than emphasizing David's human individuality, the Chronicler portrays him as a model of the kind of political and religious leadership that the postexilic Jewish community needs in order to project itself with vigor and authority toward the future.

References to Solomon are set forth in three great blocks: Solomon's confirmation in kingship (2 Chron. 1), construction and dedication of the Temple (2 Chron. 2—7), and Solomon's enterprises and achievements (2 Chron. 8—9). These sections show how the new monarch continued in David's path, just as the Chronicler's community does.

The final section of the Chronicler's work (2 Chron. 10—36) sets forth the history of the kings of Judah, highlighting the life and work of Asa, Jehoshaphat, Hezekiah, and Josiah. The Chronicler is not interested in the history of the Northern Kingdom, because he interprets Judah as the legitimate heir of God's promises to Israel.

The Chronicler's Use of Sources

Chronicles gives us a fascinating insight into the methods of biblical writers/editors, because some of the sources that the Chronicler draws on are actually available to us. Specifically, the Chronicler quotes sections of the Torah, the Former Prophets (Joshua through 2 Kings), and Ezra–Nehemiah. Chronicles quotes these directly, alludes to them, or even rewrites them to support the Chronicler's theological and historical aims. The most famous modification he or she makes—aside from omission of the entire Bathsheba/Uriah sequence—is probably his or her adaptation of the introduction to the story of David's plague and census. The source (2 Sam.

24:1) reads, "Again the anger of YHWH was kindled against Israel, and he incited David against them, saying, 'Go, count the people of Israel and Judah.'" This suits the Deuteronomistic History's portrayal of God as inscrutable and sometimes violent. But the Chronicler refuses to entertain the idea that YHWH might punish someone (as happens later in the chapter) for an act that YHWH had ordered. In 1 Chronicles 21:1, the verse becomes, "Satan [or 'an adversary'; see pp. 224–25] stood up against Israel, and incited David to count the people of Israel."

The Chronicler's omissions are as interesting as the inclusions and changes. The Chronicler omits stories of David's sins and personal problems, almost all the history of the Northern Kingdom, and, strikingly, the fundamental narratives of the exodus. Although Chronicles clearly respects the Torah of Moses, it remembers David as the nation's real founder and authoritative model leader.

From Ezra–Nehemiah, the Chronicler cites Cyrus' edict of liberation (2 Chron. 36:22–23, paralleling Ezra 1:1–3a) and a list of the inhabitants of Jerusalem (1 Chron. 9:2–17a, paralleling Neh. 11:3–19). The inclusion of these items is a clue that although the Chronicler speaks mostly *about* Judah's First Temple past, the message is *directed* at its Second Temple future. The Chronicler adds other materials, not present in the biblical source narratives. These include large blocks about the Jerusalem temple, David's administration, and Solomon's accession to the throne (1 Chron. 22:1—29:25). Legitimization of Second Temple practices is surely at stake in the Chronicler's discussion of the organization of temple servants into four basic liturgical divisions (priests, Levites, cantors, and gatekeepers).

The Theology of Chronicles

The Chronicler's theological purpose in writing this history of Israel is manifold. The author recognizes that, after the exile in Babylon and the prophetic and priestly efforts to rebuild the city, the people's social, political, and religious dynamics have to be changed to serve the new reality. The Chronicler emphasizes Jerusalem's claim as the sole legitimate center of worship and works hard to show that the policies of the new priestly worship leaders and governors are continuous with those of the house of David, implying that they inherit the authority of David's house.

For the Chronicler, history is the concrete expression of the relationship between God and Israel, and that particular concept of history is set forth in a systematic and continuous manner. The Chronicler's historical work touches only lightly on some theological themes important for Israel (for instance, monotheism and divine authority over the world), perhaps because the writer takes these for granted. Some others, however, receive great emphasis.

In keeping with the general Second Temple Period emphasis on God's authority as creator, the Chronicler relates Israel's election directly to the creation of the world. It is not seen as a specific historical act that may be associated with any particular character within the nation's history (such as Abraham or Moses). Israel's election as God's people is the result of divine initiative from the very beginning of human history. Israel, from the Chronicler's point of view, was chosen and elected by God since the creation of the world.

The Chronicler takes pains to show how God's capacity to intervene has been manifested concretely in human history, in ways that reveal and emphasize God's justice and righteousness (2 Chron. 12:6). Justice in Chronicles is not an abstract and philosophical concept, which only serves to be pondered, admired, and debated. It is a serious manifestation of human obedience to the divine will.

Chronicles also emphasizes the ways in which humans respond to their relationship with God in worship. The Chronicler highlights the people's religious life and affirms the importance of the people's commitment to the divine revelation, shown through their following the statutes and by their religious practices in the temple. Worship is the space provided for the encounter between divinity and humanity.

Although some biblical texts (for instance, Am. 5:21–24 and Mic. 6:6–8) hint at possible conflict between the claims of temple worship and social justice, the Chronicler views these as mutually necessary aspects of a unified loyalty to God. The cultic experience should have concrete and specific repercussions in the daily life of the people; the theology of worship has to be translated into concrete manifestations of justice. For the Chronicler, righteousness and justice require a person's entire effort and dedication. Knowledge, trust, humility, and fear of God are important values for the Chronicler, and according to Chronicles, they are cultivated in temple worship.

The Chronicler also affirms and celebrates the contribution of prophets to the life of the community, both as agents who transmit God's will to the community and as intercessors with God on behalf of the community. The prophets are appreciated and respected persons who embody, in their lives and ministries, YHWH's will and YHWH's firm commitment to communicating divine principles and values to humanity in general and Israel in particular.

Divine inspiration is not only related to religious figures, but it is also manifested in David and Solomon and in the temple's musicians (1 Chron. 25:1–5). God's relationship with the people acquires new degrees of revelation when it includes not only the traditional leaders in revelatory processes (such as priests, kings, and prophets) but also musicians. This component brings to the Chronicler's theology an important element of democratization.

Our awareness of that "democratization" should not blind us to the enormously important role that the institution of the monarchy plays in the Chronicler's history. Through the kings' actions and decisions, God intervenes in the public and political life of the community. Even though the true king is YHWH (2 Chron. 13:8), the authority to exercise power has been conferred upon David and his dynasty. The importance of the Davidic kings and the potency of God's support for them are shown, in Chronicles, by the physical frontiers of Israel. As portrayed in 1 Chronicles 13:5, the boundaries stretch from Shihor in Egypt to Lebo-hamath in upper Syria—an area far beyond the territorial limits that seem actually to have been conquered by David and Solomon. The Chronicler's depiction of these boundaries shows us again that he or she was less interested in geographical exactitude than in the theological perspective of grandeur, affirming the people's prosperity and expansion, which were in turn eloquent signs of divine goodness.

Finally, although the Chronicler precisely identifies the ethnic and geographical limits of Israel, the work's perspective of the "great Israel" surpasses the limits of the twelve tribes and includes the non-Jewish population, the "sojourners." "Israel" is understood to include not only members of the twelve traditional tribes but also the foreigners living in their midst. In contrast to the insistence on genealogical purity in Ezra–Nehemiah, Chronicles reminds us that some of Israel's most foundational figures, such as the patriarch Judah (1 Chron. 2:3–4), had children by women of the land. The great David himself proclaims, "We are aliens and transients before you, as were all our ancestors" (1 Chron. 29:15).

Canonical Placement

In the Hebrew Bible, the books of Ezra–Nehemiah and 1 and 2 Chronicles are included after Daniel, and they occupy the final position in the Jewish canon. In the Greek and Latin versions of the Old Testament used by Christians, and in the translations descended from them, these works appear at the end of the so-called historical books. (They precede Esther and the Deutero-canonical books of Tobit, Judith, and 1 and 2 Maccabees and are placed before the wisdom literature and the Prophets.) The Greek/Latin placement (followed by most standard English translations) has encouraged Christians to view Ezra–Nehemiah and Chronicles as historical sources, in contrast to the Jewish order, which emphasizes literary and theological qualities by placing these books among the Writings.

Additionally, in contrast to the Christian ordering, which closes the Old Testament with a vision of the "great and terrible day of YHWH" (Mal. 4:5), the present Jewish arrangement gives the closing word to Cyrus' proclamation: "Whoever is among you of all his people, may YHWH his God be with him! Let him go up" (2 Chr. 36:23).

Resources

Peter Ackroyd. *I & II Chronicles, Ezra, Nehemiah*. London: SCM Press, 1973.

Joseph Blenkinsopp. *Ezra–Nehemiah*. Old Testament Library. Philadelphia: Westminster Press, 1988.

Enzo Cortese. "Introduction to 1 and 2 Chronicles, Ezra–Nehemiah." In *The International Bible Commentary*. Collegeville, Minn.: Liturgical Press, 1998.

Sara Japhet. *I & II Chronicles: A Commentary*. Old Testament Library. Louisville, Ky.: Westminster/John Knox Press, 1993.

Samuel Pagán. *Esdras, Nehemías y Ester*. Miami: Caribe, 1993.

9

Isaiah

MARY DONOVAN TURNER

Isaiah is the first of the Latter Prophets, a division of the Hebrew Bible (see p. 7) that also contains Jeremiah, Ezekiel, and the twelve shorter books from Hosea through Malachi. (Daniel appears, in the Hebrew Bible, with the Writings rather than the Prophets.) Isaiah's sixty-six chapters make up a full quarter of this prophetic collection. The book is quoted twenty times in the New Testament, more than all the other so-called writing prophets (another term for the Latter Prophets) together. Its oracles and narratives grow out of the experiences of the Judean people over a period of nearly two hundred and fifty years. Through its words, the reader glimpses the political, religious, and social life of a small nation trying to live in relation to a holy God.

Prophets such as Isaiah were called forth to speak against religious and political establishments. Their words are often introduced by a messenger formula, "Thus says YHWH," which both claims God's authority and explains their compulsion to speak. The covenantal relationship between God and people—*I am yours and you are mine*—often undergirds their words of judgment and redemption. They borrow oral and literary forms of expression and use metaphors that grow from their everyday experiences to stir the moral imagination and invite a lived response from their hearers.

Prophets were called forth in a particular context to name the realities of life and interpret them from a theological perspective; they were interpreters of the national story. Prophets were mediators between God and humanity, consultants to kings, and preachers to the religious and political establishments. Their words were at times heavy and ponderous, calling the community back to right relationship with a holy and just God. At other times, they spoke comfort and hope to a wayward, persecuted, and forgetful people being called back by their loving God. The prophet was neither priest nor pastor, but instead a spokesperson, speaking paradoxical, perplexing words of both judgment and redemption. The prophets sharply assessed communal behavior and passionately appealed for change. Their oracles were designed to teach and to give praise to God. The heyday of this kind of prophecy was 750–500 B.C.E. This period roughly corresponds to the dates within which the texts in Isaiah seem to have been collected, edited, and recorded.

Information about the nation, the monarchy, the wars, and the intrigue during this time is found in the books of Kings, Chronicles, Ezra, and Nehemiah. Reading these together with the prophetic books, discovering consistencies and dissonance alike, we as readers can piece together at least one perspective of the life and times of a nation and the prophetic word that befell it.

Changing Understandings of the Book

Isaiah was a favorite of the Dead Sea community of Qumran. New Testament writers found in it time-honored words that spoke to their understandings of the myriad ways God was working through Jesus Christ in their own contemporary world. The words of Isaiah inspired the early church fathers, rabbinical scholars, reformers, and more. When historical and textual criticisms were brought to bear on biblical texts in the 1700s C.E., the understandings of the prophet Isaiah and his word took interesting new turns.

As early as the Middle Ages, the Jewish scholar Ibn Ezra asked whether Isaiah, the prophet of eighth-century Jerusalem, had really written the latter chapters of the Isaiah scroll. For the most part, however, interpreters believed that God had verbally inspired the biblical text (that is, that God had dictated its words to the prophet). They saw no problem in attributing the entire Isaiah scroll to Isaiah of Jerusalem. After the Renaissance, scholars began to analyze and ask questions more freely. The material in Isaiah 40—66, many noticed, bore evidence of different historical contexts, different geographies, different moods, language, and themes. (For instance, the name Isaiah occurs sixteen times in chaps. 1—39, but never in the last twenty-seven chapters of the book. This in itself creates a possibility that the latter chapters are anonymous and added to the eighth-century collection.) By the late 1700s, other scholars were joining Ibn Ezra in questioning whether the Isaiah scroll really came from a single author (for details, see Seitz, 473).

From these beginnings, it was ultimately suggested in 1872 by Bernhard Duhm that chapters 1—39 (First Isaiah) were pre-exilic in nature, 40—55 (Second Isaiah) were written during the exile, and 56—66 (Third Isaiah) were written in the years after the exile when the Israelites were allowed to return and begin the rebuilding of Jerusalem. This three-part division of the book has enjoyed widespread, though not unanimous, support in scholarly circles. A few scholars still attribute the sixty-six chapters to one prophet having foreknowledge of historical events centuries before their occurrence, but this approach fails to recognize the importance of the prophetic word's historical context and communal foundations.

Although Duhm's tripartite outline will be used in this discussion, we will not draw tight or rigid boundaries between the divisions. Surely the words of First Isaiah were read and edited by later prophets or groups of prophets who found in the earlier prophetic word seeds for their own understandings. And surely the words of First Isaiah were backdrop for new words of judgment and redemption to a different generation. These recognitions give witness to a complex and variegated history. Traces of both earlier and later words meld into a curious mixture of looking forward and back on the same events. Thus, although some distinctions between the units are clear, it is wise to consider not only the differences between them but also the strands of tradition that bind them together in a loosely fashioned but organized whole. Themes and motifs such as exodus, Zion, and the Davidic line form both tenuous and tenacious bonds within and between units.

First Isaiah (Isaiah 1—39)

Isaiah of Jerusalem

Isaiah of Jerusalem (the primary source of "First Isaiah") was one of the earliest writing prophets, his ministry taking place in the Southern Kingdom of Judah over about four decades in the 700s B.C.E. (During this time, Micah also prophesied in the Southern Kingdom, while Amos and Hosea were active in the Northern Kingdom.) The name Isaiah means "YHWH saves" or "YHWH is salvation" or "YHWH gives salvation." Isaiah 1:1 calls him "son of Amoz." The book mentions that he experienced a conversion or call, was married, and had children who were given symbolic names that spoke a prophetic word to the community around them. We know little more, perhaps because what was important for those who collected and remembered these words was not the person of the prophet. To provide biography was neither the motivation nor intent. What was important was that the word of God was altered and rendered new in successive generations as it came to speak differently in changing contexts.

The Historical Context

Isaiah 1:1 tells us that the prophet brought a word to Judah under the rulership of four kings—Uzziah, Jotham, Ahaz, and Hezekiah. At the beginning of Isaiah's time of prophecy, the nation was wealthy and prosperous. The "good days" faded, however, into fear and war as the Assyrian empire gained power under Tiglath-pileser from about 745 to 727 B.C.E. From the Syro-Ephraimatic War of 734 to the invasion by Sennacherib in 701, the small Southern Kingdom of Judah was caught in a crucible of conflict and crisis with the nations that surrounded her. We see this in two Isaiah narratives. One concerns Ahaz and the rulers Pekah of Israel and Rezin of Aram (Syria), who try to convince the Judean king to ally with them against the Assyrians (Isa. 7—9). The second (Isa. 36—39) shows King Hezekiah miraculously warding off the powerful ruler of Assyria. In these stories, we become aware that the desires of YHWH dictate a ruler's success or lack of it. The great messianic hope is that a Davidic ruler will come to the throne who will embody the spirit and the wisdom of YHWH, bringing a time when there is no more war. In the book of Isaiah, political relationships and the tenuous life of a small nation are the arenas in which God's care and challenge are played out. YHWH's vision, it is thought, can transform moral and political life; the prophet's task is to bring that vision to the people.

Literary Structure and Genre

Untangling the varied layers and strands of tradition within Isaiah 1—39 is at least as difficult as unraveling the relationships between the three major parts of the book of Isaiah. Some consider 1—39 to come entirely from the 700s B.C.E. Others suspect that an eighth-century core has been greatly expanded on by later editors. This raises further questions: What did the core look like? When and why were changes made? How did later editors alter or enhance the core to speak to their new and different contexts?

Scholars do not even agree about the organizational logic of our present Isaiah 1—39. Some look for a chronological sequence (for instance, chaps. 1—6 spoken during the reigns of Uzziah and Jotham, 7—14 during the time of Ahaz, and 15—39 during the reign of Hezekiah). Others see thematic organization, and still others stress the role of "catchwords" in binding units. These theories are complex, and none fully account for the internal movement in First Isaiah. Nevertheless, various groupings of texts lend themselves to categorization and analysis:

Isaiah 1—12

Isaiah 1—12 defines the essence of Isaiah of Jerusalem's thought and describes for us a vision from a holy God. These chapters move abruptly from words of judgment to visions and hopes of grandeur. Many scholars view the strong contrasts as evidence of a second, later hand trying to modify the harshness of Isaiah's original words.

There are some other puzzles in Isaiah 1—12. Isaiah 1 introduces the prophet Isaiah, his lineage, and his historical context. Why then do we find another introductory statement in Isaiah 2:1? And why does the call narrative not come until chapter 6? Not all call narratives come at the beginning of prophetic collections, but here Isaiah's vision comes after he has already voiced a harsh indictment of the nation. We may also wonder why there is such a marked interruption between two series of refrains, the woes (5:8–23 and 10:1–4) and the acknowledgment that God's hands are outstretched still (5:25 and 10:4) respectively. These questions about the complex relationship between pieces of Isaiah 1—12 cannot be easily answered.

Call Narrative. In the year King Uzziah died (742 B.C.E.), Isaiah had a vision. He is standing in the temple and sees YHWH on a throne, high and lifted up. The seraphim are singing "Holy, holy, holy is the LORD" (Isa. 6:3). *Holy* (a word often used to describe God in 1 Isaiah) means "separate from that which is common"—wholly good and pure. The building shakes and is filled with smoke, and in response to this magnificent vision of YHWH, Isaiah is called to confession: "Woe is me" (v. 5). In contrast with the holiness and glory that he witnesses, Isaiah understands that he and the community in which he lives have "unclean lips." The seraphim swoops down with a live coal, pressing it against his lips. Now he is purified and readied to respond to the callings of God. His sin is seared away. God asks, "Whom shall I send"? Isaiah replies, "Here am I; send me" (v. 8).

This is a "fiery" call narrative. The seraphim are fiery serpentlike creatures. The vision is filled with God's "glory," a bright, illuminating, light-filled, burning presence (see Isaiah 10:16). There is smoke, and Isaiah is cleansed with a live coal. This picture of the fiery cleansing of Isaiah foreshadows or works symbolically to depict the condition, fate, and mission of the community. This vision is about Isaiah *and* the people of God. Through burning, he is made ready, and the community is made ready (see 4:4, 6:13), to serve. Herein lies a difficult theological concept. Hope lies on the far side of disaster! Isaiah's repentance is immediate, but something disastrous is needed to change the course and fate of the nation. For Isaiah, the good news is that after disaster, a remnant will remain. Isaiah uses the image of the holy seed and a stump (6:13) to describe former times and the possibility of new life to come. A remnant will remain to begin life anew. A seed can sprout. A new tree can be born from the remains of the felled trunk. The relationship between God and new people filled with justice and righteousness will be restored. Again.

Oracles of Judgment: Naming the Realities of the Sinful Life. One of the primary tasks or callings of the prophet was to *name* the realities of life as the community was living it. We therefore begin our analysis with several texts in which the prophet brings words from YHWH—oracles of judgment—that name in daring and perhaps offensive ways the sins and transgressions of God's people. The prophet uses a variety of metaphors, images, and literary devices in an effort to communicate his sense of urgency.

The oracles of judgment collected in chapter 1 provide the starting place for First Isaiah in its entirety. The predominant metaphor for the broken relationship between YHWH and the people is that of a parent's relationship to a rebellious child. "Ah, sinful nation, people laden with iniquity, offspring who do evil, children who deal corruptly, who have forsaken YHWH, who have despised the Holy One of Israel, who are utterly estranged!" (1:4). YHWH witnesses people living in self-destructive, unproductive ways.

This parent metaphor plays a crucial role in communicating the argument of the prophet. As Lakoff and Johnson point out:

> Our concepts structure what we perceive, how we get around in the world. Our conceptual system thus plays a central role in defining our everyday realities…the way we think, what we experience…is very much a matter of metaphor. (Lakoff and Johnson, 3)

Isaiah's imagery moves subtly between the fractured relationship between parent and child and images of the land—the desolate, devoured, overthrown land. Daughter Zion is left like a booth in a vineyard. She is like a besieged city. She has lost her faithfulness; she is like a whore. The metaphors of wounded child and city form the backdrop for a series of complaints that

God has against the people that God has reared. God complains of dishonesty and shallow allegiance. The people have performed unsatisfying rituals. The hands of the one who prays are "full of blood"—the blood of the forgotten and oppressed. Bloody hands betray shallow devotion, a hypocritical posture.

In Isaiah 5:1–7, commonly titled the Song of the Vineyard, the prophet again brings moral indictment but in radically different form and imagery, using a narrative about a farmer and a vineyard, a story of love gone awry. Caretaker YHWH does everything possible to tend the soil and plant a bountiful crop, but the field yields unsuitable grapes. "And now, inhabitants of Jerusalem and people of Judah, judge between me and my vineyard. What more was there to do for my vineyard that I have not done in it?" (5:3–4). Judgment on the field that does not produce becomes judgment on YHWH's people, once so rich with promise. YHWH expected justice from them but got bloodshed. Instead of righteousness, YHWH heard cries. Six cries of mourning follow (5:8, 11, 18, 20–22; 10:1) for those who are living unjust and unrighteous lives—those who have no room around their homes for others, who do not know the deeds of YHWH, who call evil good and good evil and who are wise in their own eyes, who deprive the innocent of their rights. As in chapter l, Isaiah portrays a God who is deeply invested in the lives of the people God has created. God experiences great anger and anguish when disappointed by the people.

Visions of Hope/Oracles of Salvation/Messianic Promises of Peace. First Isaiah intersperses words of future promise between its words of judgment and indictment. Chapter 1 spoke of the present and the past. Chapter 2 sees the future. It dreams of a new age, pregnant with possibility and rich with promise. It describes a mountain toward which *all nations* are moving, a place where all can learn YHWH's ways, Torah, the word. Here, there will be peace: "They shall beat their swords into plowshares, and their spears into pruning hooks; nation shall not lift up sword against nation, neither shall they learn war any more" (2:4). Chapter 1's besieged city of Zion becomes the glorious place to which nations stream.

Another word of hope comes in Isaiah 9, which describes the current plight of the Judean people and the transformation that God will bring for them. After a preface (8:11–22) that tells of YHWH's strong-handed instructions to Isaiah himself, darkness becomes a metaphor for the experience of wayward ones who know warriors and garments rolled in blood. Amid the darkness comes a great light: "For a child has been born for us, a son given to us; authority rests upon his shoulders; and he is named Wonderful Counselor, Mighty God, Everlasting Father, Prince of Peace" (9:6). Are these words of a familiar liturgy used when a king takes the throne, a description of a leader who is to come in the end time, or even a description of Hezekiah, the successor to Ahaz? Each possibility has scholarly endorsement, but in all, hope lies in the ruler's faithfulness to the nation's god. Here and in chapter 11, the ruler comes from the line of David.

As chapter 11 begins, the people of Judah are only a tree stump, left behind and forgotten. Suddenly and without warning, a shoot grows from the stump; there is a new world. "The wolf shall live with the lamb, the leopard shall lie down with the kid, the calf and the lion and the fatling together, and a little child shall lead them" (11:6). Isaiah brings the word of hope in many forms: a light penetrating the darkness, a high mountain to which nations stream, a small shoot growing from an apparently dying and useless stump. All these metaphors arise from the experiences of a small nation that longs for peace and for a leader to bring them to it.

A Narrative. The crux of Isaiah 1—12 is a story about King Ahaz and Judah's political situation. The threat of the mighty Assyrians raised perplexing theological questions and dilemmas. How could an ungodly nation advance and be successful? Hadn't God promised that Zion/Jerusalem would be protected? Did God have a plan, and was God in control?

Ahaz was only twenty years old when he began to reign, although perhaps that was not a young age in Jerusalem in the 700s. Second Kings tells us that Ahaz made offerings on high places to other gods. Around 734 B.C.E., King Rezin of Aram and King Pekah of Israel mounted an attack on Jerusalem, trying to force Ahaz to join their coalition. The hearts of Ahaz and his people shook as the trees of the forest shake before the wind (Isa. 7:2). Isaiah spoke God's word to Ahaz: "Take heed, be quiet, do not fear, and do not let your heart be faint" (7:4). But Ahaz found it difficult to trust in God's word; he needed a sign. Isaiah spoke of the birth of a child (future king? child of the prophet? any child?) whose name would be Immanuel (meaning "God with us"). This child, said Isaiah, would be God's sign to Ahaz. But Ahaz was not willing to rely on spiritual insight to fight the threat of a foreign army. Instead, he put his trust in military might.

The Doxology. The hymns in Isaiah 12:1–2 and 3–6 look deceptively simple, but they announce with certainty and for the first time in Isaiah that the *salvation* promised in Isaiah's own name will come to pass. Against declarations of judgment and destruction such as those in Isaiah 1 and 5, the hymns affirm ultimate deliverance. The first section of First Isaiah thus closes with a picture of a gracious, abundant, generous God who provides the water of salvation.

Isaiah 13—35

In Isaiah 13—35, the reader encounters several collections of oracles of judgment and salvation delivered to other nations, to Judah, and to the world.

Oracles against the Nations. Identical superscriptions in Isaiah 13:1, 15:1, 17:1, 19:1, 21:1, 22:1, and 23:1 indicate that the vision accounts in chapters 13 to 23 may have been gathered together before their placement in the book of Isaiah. Each vision indicts a different nation—large faraway nations capable of overthrowing the small country of Judah and smaller nearby nations threatening Judah's peace and security. It is as if the onslaught of the Assyrians in chapters 1 to 12 foreshadows a global assault in chapters 13 to 23. Oracles from the 700s B.C.E. speak against Assyria, Philistia, Syro-Ephraim, Egypt, and Judah. Later additions condemn enemies of the 400s: Babylon, Persia, Moab, and Tyre.

This cataloging of nations and their grim destinies is not particular to Isaiah. Similar lists are found in Ezekiel 25—32 and Jeremiah 46—51. Each prophet singles out nations and describes the harsh treatment they will receive from YHWH for their pride, arrogance, violence, and idolatry. These oracles are similar to prophetic oracles against Judah and Israel, except that the oracles against other nations are seldom balanced by promises of salvation.

The Little Apocalypse. The oracles against the nations culminate in Isaiah 24 with a potent description of the end of Earth. Thus begins the four-chapter Isaiah Apocalypse (Isa. 24—27). These chapters are described as apocalyptic because they foretell the end of the existing world order and its replacement by a new order, one grounded in God. (For more on apocalyptic themes, see pp. 246–47 and 261–62.) God brings victory on behalf of a city that is besieged by threatening powers. In poetic repetition, the end result is proclaimed: "The earth is utterly broken, the earth is torn asunder, the earth is violently shaken. The earth staggers like a drunkard, it sways like a hut; its transgression lies heavy upon it, and it falls, and will not rise again" (24:19–20). These chapters are more extreme than other parts of First Isaiah in that they seem to proclaim God's judgment *on* history, rather than merely God's judgment *within* history. Their historical context, authorship, date, and relationship with the larger literary context remain uncertain.

Oracles against Judah. Isaiah 28—33 contains six poetic compositions introduced with the interjection *hôy* (28:1; 29:1; 29:15; 30:1; 31:1; 33:1), perhaps a cry of mourning. The oracles speak of the arrogance and misplaced trust of the people from every walk of life; they remind us of descriptions of the people's rebelliousness in chapters 1 to 12. Yet again, redemption is proclaimed for the people who live in Zion. "And when you turn to the right or when you turn to the left, your ears shall hear a word behind you, saying, 'This is the way; walk in it'" (30:21).

Apocalypse Revisited. In Isaiah 34—35, as in 24—27, we encounter a raging, furious God who brings the world to virtual collapse. In 35, with imagery akin to that of Second Isaiah, the Israelites are brought home. In these two chapters, First Isaiah's contrast between judgment and salvation reaches a crescendo.

Isaiah 36—39

In the final four chapters of First Isaiah, we hear of an encounter between a prophet and a king and of the sparing of sinful Jerusalem. Chapters 36 to 37 are set by the conduit of the upper pool on the highway to Fuller's Field (36:2), the same spot where Ahaz rejected prophetic counsel. Hezekiah, in clear contrast to his predecessor Ahaz, responds to God's word in prayer and penitence. The story as it is told here vindicates Isaiah's message of salvation, offering a powerful example of what the royal house can accomplish when a king like Hezekiah occupies the throne. (Second Kings 18:17—19:37, however, gives a different version of events.)

In First Isaiah, the Assyrian king has been YHWH's instrument to punish Jerusalem for unfaithfulness. In chapter 39, we begin to hear about Babylon, the next mighty power with which Judah will have to contend, the one that will bring demise and devastation. These words form a transition to Second Isaiah that speaks to those who, decades later, find themselves living in Babylon in exile.

The Theology of First Isaiah

In First Isaiah, the repeated exclamation *hôy*, an outcry of lament and agony, leaves the reader with the sense of pain and horror expressed by the eighth-century prophet as he looks upon and evaluates the world around him. He is plagued by perplexing observations and questions: (1) A pervasive external threat from the Assyrian empire could easily overwhelm and perhaps even destroy the small country of Judah. Assyria was chosen to be the "rod of God's anger." Would the king trust and be faithful to God, or would the king, out of an overwhelming fear of this powerful nation, put trust in military might, strategy, and alliance? (2) Would God protect Zion/Jerusalem from external threat, war, and destruction? Was Jerusalem a "chosen" city and "invincible"? (3) What would the future of the nation be? The nation was prone to injustice, unrighteous behavior, and idolatry. Would God punish them? This constellation of questions poses thorny theological issues and challenges. For Isaiah, these issues were resolved in the understanding of the remnant that would be purified and become the seed for a new community.

Compelling messages of judgment and salvation are thus interwoven in Isaiah, images both local and cosmic, in poetry and narrative, collected and edited from various places and times. Isaiah's God recognizes oppression and works to overthrow it. Isaiah's God is offended by injustice. This God stirs the imagination of those whom God has called, pulling the community toward an envisioned day without tears.

Isaiah speaks in compelling metaphor in an effort to get the people to hear the stark condition and urgency of his appeal. His metaphors (God as parent, farmer, or overseer of the vineyard) often involve caring relationships that require continued nurture. Isaiah, however, most often names this God "the Holy One of Israel," who is one wholly other and separate from the human condition.

Isaiah relentlessly unveils oppression and calls the people to justice and righteousness. Always believing that tomorrow could be too late, the prophet foresees the demise of a ruler and a people who misplace trust and break covenant promises. Still, he sees a better day, when a faithful ruler from the line of David comes to the throne. He sees a glorious day in the "end times," when the world, all nations, will know a fully restored relationship to God. A prophet must know and live in the tension between the reality of the present condition and the hope of a better time to come.

Second Isaiah (Isaiah 40—55)

To even the earliest of readers, the differences between Isaiah 1—39 and 40—66 were apparent. Chapters 1 to 39 focus on impending punishment for the people of Judah. God's tool for punishment in these chapters is Assyria. In Isaiah 40, however, the mood, language, and perspectives change. Assyria has fallen; Babylon has taken its place as God's tool and has destroyed Judah, but that judgment is past. For Second Isaiah, the temple's destruction and the deportations to Babylon lie in the past. This new prophetic voice speaks not of impending judgment but, exuberantly and confidently, of return for the exiles. Beyond chapter 55, we will see, the tone changes yet again. Distinct in tone and context, the words of Isaiah 40—55 invite separate consideration and analysis.

The Prophet and Historical Setting

Isaiah 40—55 has no introduction identifying the speaker, his lineage, or the kings reigning in his lifetime. Yet the speeches of this anonymous prophet contain historical allusions that help us identify the historical context. As foreshadowed in Isaiah 39, the Babylonians had conquered the small country of Judah and carried Jerusalem's leaders into exile. Second Isaiah's speeches assume that the hearers know of Cyrus, king of Persia, who will conquer the Babylonian Empire (see 44:28 and 45:1). Second

Isaiah sees Cyrus' amazing rise to power as God's intervention. Is this not the one through whom God will liberate the exiled Israelites and bring them home? The prophet invites the exilic community to participate in a new exodus by making the journey from Babylon back to Zion/Jerusalem. In chapter 40, a herald—either Zion herself or a female prophet (the word for herald has a feminine form here)—is commissioned to get up on a mountain and announce the good news that punishment is over. Through Second Isaiah, God announces salvation, a new exodus, a procession through the wilderness, and a grand homecoming. About the prophet as a person we know little more.

Literary Structure and Genre

Although we know little about Jewish life in the exile, Jerusalem's deportees appear to have been smoothly integrated into Babylon's business and governmental life. Second Isaiah's task, then, was to persuade those who were now comfortably entrenched (who may indeed have been born and raised in Babylon) that the time had come to return "home." Home was Zion. Second Isaiah seeks to demonstrate through ancestral traditions that Cyrus' defeat of Babylon is a sign that the appointed time of favor has come. To bring this compelling message, Second Isaiah uses genres (literary forms) borrowed from the liturgical poetry of Israel: laments, oracles of salvation, thanksgivings, hymns, and victory songs. Second Isaiah also makes use of "trial scenes" (41:1—42:9; 43:9—44:5; 44:6–23; 45:21). Israel's reemergence as a people, through its return to Zion, witnesses to YHWH's sole sovereignty. The silent gods of other nations have no comparable power.

Second Isaiah's prophesies take the form of Hebrew poetry. Although such poetry has no rhyme, its lines often have regular numbers of accented syllables and almost always exhibit *parallelism,* where a thought is restated in the following line in different words.

> Seek YHWH while he may be found,
> call upon him while he is near;
> let the wicked forsake their way,
> and the unrighteous their thoughts;
> let them return to YHWH, that he may have mercy on them,
> and to our God, for he will abundantly pardon. (Isa. 55:6–7)

Poetic repetition underscores the beauty and urgency of Second Isaiah's appeal to the community.

The first collection of poems to be identified in Second Isaiah were the "servant songs." The word *servant* occurs twenty times in chapters 40 to 55 (once in the plural). In thirteen instances, the word clearly refers to Israel. The remaining seven occur in what have been labeled the servant songs (42:1–4; 49:1–6; 50:4–9; 52:13—53:12). Several theories regarding the identity of the "servant" have been offered: the prophet, a messiah to come, or Israel. These theories are complex and are rooted in the scholars' understandings of the historical and literary contexts in which the songs are found. Recently, J. Severino Croatto has written about the songs from the perspective of one who lives among an oppressed people. He emphasizes Israel's status as "servant" within a political and social context of domination (Croatto, 221–36).

Form critics have since defined and collated other "genre sets" in Second Isaiah. Other scholars traced threads of tradition—particularly creation and exodus. James Muilenburg analyzed the work's rhetorical structure and concluded that chapters 40 to 55 consisted of twenty-one poems, each with a different theme and each divided into a number of carefully formed strophes. Additionally, he analyzed assonance, imagery, contrast, repetition, and wordplay. Finding fourteen units in chapters 40 to 48 and seven in 49 to 55, he analyzed the work's internal unity. In later studies, scholars have analyzed the message of Second Isaiah by examining theological categories found in the text. Richard Clifford, for instance, examines the "polarities" found in Second Isaiah:

- First and Last Things.
- Babylon and Zion. (Zion rises in 40:9; 47:1 orders Babylon to sit in the dust.)
- YHWH and the Gods.
- Israel and the Nations.
- The Servant and Israel. Here, Second Isaiah exploits a familiar theme. The servant in Second Isaiah is a chosen individual and what all Israel is called to be and do. When Israel becomes the servant, Israel embraces the divine will and plan. When the people do not obey God's word, then the servant stands over against the people as a rebuke and as an invitation to conversion. (Clifford, 498–99)

More recently, those texts that speak of Zion as a woman have been isolated and explored. The Zion songs, foreshadowed by 40:1–11, cluster mostly in the second half of Second Isaiah (49:14–26; 50:1–3; 51:1–8; 51:9—52:12; 54:1–17). Although they are not consistent in genre, each of them follows the long prophetic tradition of symbolizing Jerusalem and the community in female terms. More specifically, they speak of Zion as "daughter." Perhaps Second Isaiah means for hearers to recall the sections of Lamentations in which female Zion mourns her devastated condition. In Lamentations 1, she has "no one to comfort" her. But in Second Isaiah the situation changes. "Comfort, O comfort my people, says your God. Speak tenderly to Jerusalem, and cry to her that she has served her term, that her penalty is paid, that she has received from YHWH's hand double for all her sins" (Isa. 40:1–2).

The prophet's gendered portrayal involves violence, female Zion having received YHWH's wrath for her unfaithfulness. Chapters 49:14–26 and 54 portray an apologetic YHWH, now bent on restoring his relationship with the spouse and returning the children to her. "For a brief moment I abandoned you, but with great compassion I will gather you. In overflowing wrath for a moment I hid my face from you, but with everlasting love I will have compassion on you, says YHWH, your Redeemer" (54:7–8). The question for feminist, womanist, and *mujerista* scholars has been whether these texts, which portray YHWH apologizing for his anger, are powerful enough to redeem the lasting effects of the graphic images of the violence the female Zion experienced. What does it mean to have these images of violence in our canon?

The Theology of Second Isaiah

A sense of the remembered past suffuses Second Isaiah's rhetoric. For him, the remembered past is not simply a recording of facts, but a consciousness of God's mighty acts of deliverance, as in the exodus and in a continuous call to be a faithful people. The people of Judah have lost their symbols, their land, and their temple. Second Isaiah must convince the community that YHWH intends to save them, a difficult task because the people believe they have been forgotten (40:27). He must also convince the community that YHWH has the ability to save, which is why he emphasizes YHWH's ability to create, make, and fashion. It is YHWH, not Marduk (god of the Babylonians), who is the true creator and who can do "new things." The prophet has to convince the community that there will be a different end to the story because YHWH is their God. This is the purpose of Isaiah 40:1—49:13, which addresses the communities of Israel and Judah and names Cyrus as the one who will bring deliverance on behalf of YHWH, the living God. In Isaiah 49:14—55:13, the purpose of the orations is to console Zion with the hope that she will be restored. Of interest in both sections is Second Isaiah's use of maternal imagery to describe the nurture and care of YHWH (see 42:14; 46:3–4; and 49:15).

Like First Isaiah, Second Isaiah names God as "the Holy One of Israel." The Holy One is a transcendent other, who upholds high and lofty standards for God's people. But Second Isaiah also refers often to God as Redeemer

(41:14; 43:14; 44:6, 24; 47:4; 48:17; 49:7, 26; 54:5, 8). In Hebrew, this term describes a kinsman who rescues his relatives from danger or difficulty. God is Israel's redeemer, who will stand up for the people and vindicate them. In Second Isaiah, "redemption" describes deliverance from Babylonian captivity, a new exodus. It is connected with forgiveness, and it is the cause of great rejoicing. The redeemer reclaims, recovers, regains, repossesses, gets back, buys back, absolves, and sets free.

Third Isaiah (Isaiah 56—66)

Bernhard Duhm, we have seen, was the first to suggest that Isaiah 56—66 should be separated for analysis from Isaiah 40—55. He argued, on the basis of historical references, literary allusions, and theological considerations, that chapters 56 to 66 were the work of a prophet living in Jerusalem after exile.

Clearly, the historical setting reflected in Isaiah 56—66 is later than that of Second Isaiah. The setting for the work is Jerusalem. The exiles have returned, and the community is dealing with the frustrations of living in and rebuilding Jerusalem. Conditions were more severe than the returnees had anticipated (see Haggai). Second Isaiah had spoken about a great light coming to the people. In Third Isaiah we read, "We wait for light, and lo! there is darkness; and for brightness, but we walk in gloom" (59:9b). Numerous other differences can be found between Second and Third Isaiah, such as the latter's focus on worship and temple. Some believe that the differences in tone and style suggest separate authors, whereas others believe that a change of context for the same author could account for the differences. Third Isaiah lacks historical indicators that would resolve this question. At any rate, the division between chapters 55 and 56 of Isaiah is not as clear and forceful as the division between chapters 39 and 40. Streams of tradition interwoven in the texts of Second Isaiah are adopted and revised in Third Isaiah to bring the prophetic word to the community in Jerusalem.

The Prophet

If one posits a separate prophet for the last eleven chapters of Isaiah, he or she, like Second Isaiah, remains anonymous. First-person reflection in chapters 61 and 62 tells us something of the prophet's understanding of his call.

> The spirit of the Lord YHWH is upon me, because YHWH has anointed me; he has sent me to bring good news to the oppressed, to bind up the brokenhearted, to proclaim liberty to the captives, and release to the prisoners; to proclaim the year of YHWH's favor, and the day of vengeance of our God; to comfort all who mourn;

to provide for those who mourn in Zion—to give them a garland instead of ashes, the oil of gladness instead of mourning, the mantle of praise instead of a faint spirit. (61:1–3)

Like other prophets, he tells of his compulsion to bring the news. He cannot keep silent (62:1). Little else is known about him except for his interest in proper worship, purity, restoration of the Sabbath, and proper sacrifice.

Literary Features and Structure

Isaiah 56—59 calls the community to exercise justice and let the oppressed go free. Community members must take care of one another. Through this care, light breaks and healing springs forth (58:8). The image of Daughter Zion again accompanies words of restoration to the struggling community, in a three-chapter unit (Isa. 60—62) that concerns the reestablishment of Jerusalem. This powerful message of reconciliation contrasts sharply with the threats of judgment and imperative calls to repent in 56—59. Zion's sons and daughters return home. The words "come," "gather," and "bring" are repeated often. The daughter will be glorified; she is called to arise from the dust. Her days of mourning are ended. Third Isaiah, like Second Isaiah, exploits the female metaphor by describing the female Zion as a mother waiting for the return of children. He also uses bridal imagery, bringing to listeners' minds the early idyllic covenantal relationship between YHWH and spouse. At the conclusion of Third Isaiah, Zion gives birth to a son. She is described as a mother with many children, whom she feeds at her breast and dandles on her knee.

The Theology of Third Isaiah

Third Isaiah is replete with themes from Second Isaiah: the ingathering of the dispersed, the return of God's glory, and the participation of the nations in rebuilding Zion and praising God. In other passages, however, Third Isaiah gives evidence of painful conflict within the community. In Third Isaiah, God enters again into the harsh realities of human struggle and suffering. There has been no magical transformation; Judah has not instantly become the land of peace and prosperity. Yet God continues to be present with the people in the form of the prophet's word.

Though the form varies considerably from that of the oracles of First Isaiah, Third Isaiah's message is remarkably similar. Though the people have now suffered the loss of their temple, deportation to a foreign land, and then return to Zion, they must still be reminded, as the eighth-century community needed to be reminded, of the constant demands of living in covenant with God. Coming full circle, the word is brought again to the city of Jerusalem.

Reading Isaiah as a Whole

For more than a century, the scholarly world has analyzed, defined, and scrutinized the differences between First, Second, and Third Isaiah. The historical, literary, and theological differences between them are immense and significant. However, approaches that emphasize only those differences sometimes miss the literary skill with which the parts have been assembled. Recently, scholarship has taken a fruitful turn toward analyzing Isaiah's sixty-six chapters as a whole (for a compilation of such studies, see Broyles and Evans). How do we see the continuity among the parts? What are the streams of tradition, the metaphors, the images that are woven within the units? Has chapter 55 been placed at the end of Second Isaiah to form a fitting and powerful conclusion to the 1—55 unit? Have chapters 65 and 66 been editorially placed at the end of the Isaiah to bring the images of chapter 1 full circle and thus to closure? Did the writer of Second Isaiah have First Isaiah in hand? Are YHWH's ethical concerns (for example, that the people are oppressing the poor) consistent among all the Isaiahs? Is it an accident that the metaphor of light finds its way into all three parts of Isaiah? Water? Natural imagery of bush and shrub? Blindness and insight? Glory? How did the primary metaphor of female Daughter Zion take her shape, and why was she brought forth to create pathos and then hope among the readers? How does each unit read when put in the context of the sixty-six chapters of a whole? What new understandings can we glean from that endeavor?

Each study, of course, is colored by the interests and persuasions of its author; such is the nature of interpretation. But together their questions help us see the interplay between the parts of Isaiah. The reinterpretations of tradition between the parts of Isaiah provide a model for contemporary readers who are, as a result, invited to make new interpretations for their own times and places.

Resources

Craig C. Broyles and Craig A. Evans. *Writing and Reading the Scroll of Isaiah: Studies of an Interpretive Tradition*. Leiden, N.Y.: Brill, 1997.

Richard Clifford. "Isaiah, Book of (Second Isaiah)." In *The Anchor Bible Dictionary*. Vol. 3. Garden City, N.Y.: Bantam, 1992.

J. Severino Croatto. "Exegesis of Second Isaiah from the Perspective of the Oppressed: Paths for Reflection." In *Reading from this Place: Social*

Location and Biblical Interpretation in Global Perspective, edited by Fernando Segovia and Mary Ann Tolbert. Vol. 2. Minneapolis: Fortress Press, 1995.

George Lakoff and Mark Johnson. *Metaphors We Live By*. Chicago: University of Chicago Press, 1980.

Christopher Seitz. "Isaiah, Book of (First Isaiah)," and "Isaiah, Book of (Third Isaiah)." In *The Anchor Bible Dictionary*. Vol. 3. Garden City, N.Y.: Bantam, 1992.

10

Jeremiah and Ezekiel

JON L. BERQUIST

The prophetic books of Jeremiah and Ezekiel reflect the concerns of Judah at the end of the 600s and the beginning of the 500s B.C.E. Over these years, Judah faced political uncertainty and conflict. The great powers of Babylonia and Egypt struggled against each other for control of the land between them, and Judah was repeatedly caught in the middle. Eventually, Babylonia conquered Judah and sacked Jerusalem. In 597 and in 586 B.C.E., the empire took a number of Judeans into exile, where they experienced a different kind of life in Mesopotamia in the core of the Babylonian Empire. Most Judeans, especially those not in leadership roles or among the social elite, remained near Jerusalem. Others fled to Egypt. The result was a dispersion (or diaspora) of Jews in Egypt, Judah, and Babylon. These communities, uncertain about their future, mined their earlier traditions for insights to interpret their situations. The books of Jeremiah and Ezekiel offer theological interpretation of Judah's exilic era, shaped in hindsight.

Jeremiah

Historical Context

The book of Jeremiah sets itself within the reigns of King Josiah of Judah and subsequent rulers (Jer. 1:2–3), or approximately 627–586 B.C.E., the forty years up to and including the Babylonian army's destruction of Jerusalem. During this time, the monarchy of Judah experienced great distress as the international empire of Babylonia exerted increasing pressure on the societies of the eastern Mediterranean seaboard. Babylonia's chief enemy in the region, Egypt, sometimes created puppet governments in the area as a defense zone against Babylonia. At other times, the region became a staging ground for military skirmishes with the Babylonian army. The repeated incursions of Babylonian and Egyptian military force and political control rendered small in-between nations, such as Judah, tenuous and highly vulnerable. A quick succession of kings and a breakdown of Judah's internal social structures marked the years attributed to Jeremiah's prophetic career.

Reading through Jeremiah

The book of Jeremiah, as it has been transmitted in Hebrew in the Masoretic tradition and then divided into chapters in Christian tradition, contains fifty-two chapters. However, the Septuagint (a translation of the books of the Hebrew Bible into Greek, undertaken about 2,200 years ago) reflects a shorter text, and most scholars have assumed that the Masoretic Hebrew tradition contains material added in a manuscript tradition different than the one from which the Greek translation was made. Almost all English translations at the start of the twenty-first century render this longer Hebrew text, and references in this chapter will be to the English translations of the Hebrew edition.

The divergence of Greek and Hebrew editions indicates that the book of Jeremiah had already been copied and transmitted in different formats even before 2,200 years ago. Even then, readers disagreed about what to include in the book. However, the two editions share the same basic structure. The book moves from a concern with the future of Judah and Jerusalem to an examination of the wider political world, with a segment in between about the activity of the prophet. The longer version contains the following parts:

> Prologue: the call of the prophet (Jer. 1)
> Proclamations against Judah and Jerusalem (2—25)
> Jeremiah's prophetic activity (26—36)
> Flight to Egypt and destruction of Jerusalem (37—45)
> Oracles against the nations (46—51)
> Epilogue: the historical context (52)

This structure spirals outward, in at least two different senses: It moves from the individual life of the prophet to the corporate life of peoples, and it moves from a focus on Judah and Jerusalem to a consideration of Judah's near neighbors, such as Egypt, and eventually to an overview of more distant geographical regions. These two outward spirals shape the general outlines of the book's content.

Prologue: The Call of the Prophet (Jeremiah 1). The book's prologue offers a story about how God called Jeremiah to be a prophet. It introduces several themes, which are discussed further under Theological Perspectives, below.

Proclamations against Judah and Jerusalem (Jeremiah 2—25). Chapters 2 to 25, the largest block of material in the book of Jeremiah, contain oracles and proclamations against Judah and Jerusalem. Jeremiah attributes the nation's dire trouble to its politics, religion, and lack of social justice. Early on, the prophet announces the main points of condemnation: Judah has erred religiously by forsaking God for other gods (2:11), and Judah has failed politically by looking to allegiances with Egypt (2:18). These themes of forsaking God and political autonomy for other political and religious centers become entwined throughout these chapters, often in images of faithlessness and abandonment in a sexual relationship (3:6–11; 4:30; 5:7; 7:9; 9:12–14; 11:13; 13:26; 16:11; 23:10). Social justice also appears throughout these chapters, as the prophet condemns Judah for its horrendous treatment of its own poor and needy (5:28; 6:13; 7:6; 11:14). Jeremiah argues against the worship of idols (10:3–11; 14:22; 18:15; 19:5) but is also critical of the religious practices of Yahweh worshipers, including the temple priests (Jer. 7), prophets (14:13–16), scribes who teach the law (8:8), and persons who fail to observe correctly the Sabbath (17:22).

In Jeremiah's prophetic logic, the people failed by relying on Egypt militarily and by depending on other gods, so divine punishment is inevitable. Babylonia will come from the north and lay waste to Judah and Jerusalem, leaving only desolation. The inhabitants of Judah should accept this punishment (25:28–29) and not seek ways to avoid the coming disaster, whether through political allegiances or any practices of religion. God will give to the Babylonian army those Judeans who go along with this scenario and do not resist the destruction. Captive, they will at least be alive, in contrast to the many persons whose lives God will end (21:7–9). Jeremiah also indicates that these survivors, exiled to Babylonia, will eventually return after Babylonia's defeat in seventy-five years (23:3–8; 25:12). The only path to restoration for this remnant, according to Jeremiah, is in accepting the punishment, facing the exile, and surviving by the grace of God until their descendants can return to Jerusalem.

Jeremiah's Prophetic Activity (Jeremiah 26—36). The book next offers stories and anecdotes, selected or written by a later editor, about Jeremiah's prophetic ministry. According to the stories, many of the leaders of Judean society opposed Jeremiah. The first of these stories portrays Jeremiah standing in the temple court and proclaiming that those inhabitants and worshipers who do not repent will face disaster. As a result of this proclamation, "the priests and the prophets and all the people" respond to Jeremiah, "You shall die!" and they attempt to kill him (26:8). Jeremiah survives, but whenever he speaks, his message causes opposition. For instance, in chapter 28, another prophet, Hananiah, confronts Jeremiah and offers a competing prophecy, claiming that God will end Babylonia's power and defeat their army within two years. In chapter 29, Jeremiah writes a letter to the Jews who are already living in Babylonia as a result of exile. He tells them to settle down and make plans to stay in Babylonia permanently, for they will not return within their own lifetimes. Throughout these chapters, the book of Jeremiah depicts the prophet in interaction with those people who would have heard his messages and speeches. By showing opposition to Jeremiah, the writer of the book places the reader in a position that requires a decision: Will the reader be like Jeremiah, or like the audience that made the mistake of not listening to this prophet?

Flight to Egypt and Destruction of Jerusalem (Jeremiah 37—45). The tale of Jeremiah's opposition to the reigning government of Jerusalem continues. In chapter 37, the royal court imprisons Jeremiah, accusing him of trying to defect to the Babylonians. In chapter 38, Jeremiah confronts one of his detractors, a priest named Pashhur. The two prophets argue over the content of God's true message to the people, and Jeremiah condemns Pashhur and other governmental leaders. Jeremiah says that God plans to send the people of Jerusalem (especially the elites and upper classes) into Babylonian exile, an experience that they will find humbling and demeaning.

Jeremiah 39 narrates the Babylonian army's attack on Jerusalem. Although the king, Zedekiah, attempts to flee, the Babylonian army captures him and those with him. The king of Babylon sentences Zedekiah to the punishment of watching his sons and nobles be killed; then Zedekiah's eyes are removed, so that his last images are those of the deaths of his relatives and friends, and he is taken into exile in Babylon. However, the king of Babylon does not have Jeremiah killed. Instead, Jeremiah's imprisonment continues.

After the invading army leaves the Jerusalem area, some of the remaining Jewish nobles conspire to kill the governor, whom the Babylonian king has appointed to rule over the area on behalf of the empire. After the assassination, they are afraid that the Babylonian forces will attack again. The conspirators ask Jeremiah's prophetic advice, and Jeremiah receives a word from God that these nobles should stay in Jerusalem without fear, and that God will build them up if they have the courage to stay (42:10–11). However, the men do not obey Jeremiah's prophecy. They flee to Egypt, and they take Jeremiah with them. Jeremiah prophesies again that God will punish them for their faithless departure from Jerusalem. Jeremiah 45 notes how Baruch, Jeremiah's scribe, wrote all these things into a scroll at Jeremiah's instruction. (Some scholars believe that this was an early but incomplete edition of the present book of Jeremiah.)

Oracles against the Nations (Jeremiah 46—51). Prophetic books of the Hebrew Bible typically include denunciations of other nations, focusing on their political activity and social life. Egypt is the first nation denounced in the book of Jeremiah, followed by Philistia, Moab, Ammon, and Babylon. Later editors probably collected these prophetic announcements of doom here near the end of the book for thematic rather than chronological reasons (they are not necessarily from the end of the prophet's career).

Epilogue: The Historical Context (Jeremiah 52). The book concludes with a historical narrative that repeats some of the information from Jeremiah 44. Jeremiah 52 is very similar to 2 Kings 24:18—25:30, although there are some differences in wording. This probably indicates that it is the work of an editor, shaping the book into a historical framework compatible with 1 and 2 Kings. The passage emphasizes that the Babylonian government and military was thoroughly in control of Jerusalem and able to appoint governors at will for Judah. However, after some time of imprisonment, King Jehoiachin of Judah (taken captive in 597, one of the recipients of the letter in Jer. 29) is released from captivity and allowed to live as an honored guest within the Babylonian king's palace. The exile was not necessarily a time of suffering; many people lived comfortable lives in the empire.

Theological Perspectives and the Book of Jeremiah

The main point of the book of Jeremiah is that God will punish God's own chosen people of Judah and Jerusalem, and that the people should accept this punishment of Babylonian conquest from God. God will allow a future restoration of those people who stay in Jerusalem or who are taken into captivity in Babylon. However, pain and death result for most of those who depend on their own might and refuse to accept God's punishment. Those who flee to Egypt (including the prophet Jeremiah) vanish from the book. It ends with a slight hint of pending restoration as an imprisoned Judean king begins to find favor in the Babylonian court.

Themes of punishment and restoration permeate the book and create a sense of theological coherence. However, an editor shaped the book of Jeremiah to fit the overall pattern of the other prophetic books, with an outwardly moving spiral from the prophet's life to the life of the community to the wider aspects of God's involvement in the world at large. This leaves room for other theological ideas to present themselves throughout the book.

The Prophetic Call Narrative. The first chapter of the book of Jeremiah begins to develop the themes of God's coming punishment and the possibility of restoration for those who accept the punishment. Jeremiah 1 contains a story about how the prophet first received the word of God and began to prophesy:

> Now the word of YHWH came to me saying, "Before I formed you in the womb I knew you, and before you were born I consecrated you; I appointed you a prophet to the nations."
>
> Then I said, "Ah, Lord YHWH! Truly I do not know how to speak, for I am only a boy."
>
> But YHWH said to me, "Do not say, 'I am only a boy'; for you shall go to all to whom I send you, and you shall speak whatever I command you. Do not be afraid of them, for I am with you to deliver you, says YHWH." Then YHWH put out his hand and touched my mouth; and YHWH said to me, "Now I have put my words in your mouth. See, today I appoint you over nations and over kingdoms, to pluck up and to pull down, to destroy and to overthrow, to build and to plant." (Jer. 1:4–10)

Thus, Jeremiah's prophetic career represents the sending forth of God's own words from Jeremiah to other people, even beyond Judah's borders. Many other prophetic books tell stylized call stories (see Isa. 6:1–8, Ezek. 3:1–11, and Am. 7:10–17) explaining how past experiences had prepared the prophets for prophecy. These stories provided reasons why people should listen to the prophets, and now, in the text, they explain why readers should pay attention to the prophet's words. Although there may be psychological and historical roots behind the narrative, the prophetic call has been presented to persuade the reader to believe.

The political role of prophet to the nations is at the core of Jeremiah's message, and it provides a context for interpreting all Jeremiah's words that follow. Jeremiah's message does not focus on the individual or on the inner life of faith, nor is Jeremiah particularly concerned with the moral character of Judah's own activities.

The purpose of Jeremiah's prophecies is "to pluck up and to pull down, to destroy and to overthrow, to build and to plant" (Jer. 1:10). The first four of these purposes are negative and destructive. The book portrays Jeremiah's work primarily as the proclamation of doom and destruction, even though that devastation would lead to a new foundation for society. Many interpreters speak of this as a pattern of punishment followed by restoration. Such a view usually depends on a theology in which God removes blessings from a failed generation, in order to reinstate those same blessings to a later generation that is either innocent or forgiven. However, the theme of punishment does not appear in this opening chapter of Jeremiah, and the last two steps of Jeremiah's task, building and planting, seem to involve more than restoring a previous status quo. They will introduce something new, built on fresh foundations and nourished in rejuvenated soil. God plans to reconstruct the people's life on both national and international levels. The suffering and the devastation will take away the evil habits from the people and establish the foundation for a new kind of life together that will be better than they have ever known.

The Book of Comfort. Jeremiah 30—31, sometimes called the Book of Comfort, tells of a new day coming for Jerusalem. That new day will be a time of great distress, but it will result in a reversal of fortunes for God's people. This passage is strongly theological in its interests. God proclaims this new day in a new scroll to the prophet Jeremiah, who announces, explains, and celebrates the new day and all its ramifications. This passage likely derives from the postexilic period (539 B.C.E. or afterward), when the people of Jerusalem questioned what kind of new life would be possible for them as a colony in the Persian Empire.

This section of the book of Jeremiah presents the Babylonian exile of 586 B.C.E. as God's punishment and the later political events of the early Persian Period as God's restoration of favor to the people. However, the verb *shuv,* usually translated as "to restore" (the people and/or their fortunes) in these chapters (30:3, 17, 18; 31:23), is better understood as "reversing" the people's fortunes (rather than returning them to a previous condition). Note that later in the book God also reverses the fortunes of other peoples, including some of Judah's enemies (Jer. 48:47; 49:6; 49:39; 50:19). God keeps moving Judah and all the world forward to a new reality; although there are many reversals along this path, these twists and turns are part of God's way of bringing all people into closer relationship.

God's new day for the people changes the conditions of external social life for Judah, as well as its neighbors, as the first part of this passage explains (chap. 30). Great social evils such as slavery meet their end. Even though God's rearrangement of society has been very destructive for all those who have held fast to the old ways of life, now compassion will spring forth from God in unexpected ways. The people will never again experience God's anger, but instead will find healing for the incurable wounds that God has inflicted on them.

In chapter 31, Jeremiah details further how this new day will appear to God's people. The physical and political elements of God's new compassion are plain: There will be a repopulation of the land of Judah, gathering people dispersed throughout the known world, as well as bringing orphaned children and separated families together (31:4–17). The repopulation is the result of God's long-standing activity to create a place where humans and animals will live together in harmony. This new life together is the goal to which God has been working all along and toward which all of Jeremiah's prophecy has pointed.

> The days are surely coming, says YHWH, when I will sow the house of Israel and the house of Judah with the seed of humans and the seed of animals. And just as I have watched over them to pluck up and break down, to overthrow, destroy, and bring evil, so I will watch over them to build and to plant, says YHWH. In those days they shall no longer say: "The parents have eaten sour grapes, and the children's teeth are set on edge." But all shall die for their own sins; the teeth of everyone who eats sour grapes shall be set on edge. (Jer. 31:27–30)

The six verbs from Jeremiah's call (1:10) are repeated here and claimed as God's activity (along with a seventh: bringing evil upon the people). Furthermore, God reverses an old proverb about grapes, which stressed how each individual's actions had far-reaching effects on loved ones and future generations. In the new future that is arriving, God says, such old proverbs will no longer be useful. The old cause-and-effect patterns of life will begin to break down, because each person will be held responsible for that person's own actions. New responsibility is a crucial part of God's new activity for the people. No more will the sins and failures of some bring death to countless others; instead, God will insist on direct responsibility and will work to limit the spread of sin's disruption throughout the world. God continues to explain this new reality in terms of a new covenant. Once more, this is not a return to or a restoration of what came before the exile, but instead it is a new thing that God is doing. Furthermore, this prophecy reflects a vision of life with God that still waits in the future.

> But this is the covenant that I will make with the house of Israel after those days, says YHWH: I will put my law within them, and I will write it on their hearts; and I will be their God, and they shall be my people. No longer shall they teach one another, or say to each other, "Know YHWH," for they shall all know me, from the least of them to the greatest, says YHWH; for I will forgive their iniquity, and remember their sin no more. (Jer. 31:33–34)

In this new covenant, unlike all those before in Israel's and Judah's experience, God will write the divine law within the hearts of God's own people. Just as God will break the systems of human cause and effect through a new ethic of responsibility, God will remove the systems of ethical teaching and religious instruction from the people. (This responds to Jeremiah's concern, expressed, for example, in 23:1–4, that the people's leaders have been bad and dangerous "shepherds.") Instead, everyone will know God. The hierarchies of religious practice shatter in the face of God's presence with all God's people. No more will secondhand knowledge of God be the goal of human faith, but direct experience of God will infuse the lives of all. Again, Jeremiah's vision of the future reflects realities that did not occur in the prophet's own time and have not yet occurred even in our time. In this new covenant, all will know God. This will change human society forever, and the faithful Judeans together will build a peaceful city in Jerusalem (31:38–40).

Early Christians may well have had this section of Jeremiah in mind when referring to their own religious experience as a new covenant, such as that established at Jesus' last supper (Lk. 22:20; but other similar passages may well reflect the phrase "blood of my covenant" in Zech. 9:11–17) and in the early Christian practices of communion or eucharist (1 Cor. 11:25; see also 2 Cor. 3:6 and Heb. 8—9). Certainly, Jeremiah 30—31 provides one of the Bible's great reflections on the newness of God's activity and so is suitable for reflection at any point when God's people encounter the surprising power of such newness. But Jeremiah's vision here is specific in several elements: the end to social injustices on international levels, the instigation of personal responsibility, universality of the experience of God, the end to religious hierarchies and the impulse to conversion, and the building of a peaceful city. In these ways, Jeremiah's vision stands as a unique contribution to the biblical witness and remains beyond our own experiences of history.

Ezekiel

Historical Context

The book of Ezekiel also begins with a historical framework, stating that Ezekiel received these words while he was in exile in Babylonia. Whereas Jeremiah prophesied in Jerusalem shortly before the Babylonian conquest of Judah (and during some of the initial defeats and deportations), Ezekiel already experienced exile when his prophecy began.

> In the thirtieth year, in the fourth month, on the fifth day of the month, as I was among the exiles by the river Chebar, the heavens were opened, and I saw visions of God. On the fifth day of the month (it was the fifth year of the exile of King Jehoiachin), the word of YHWH came to the priest Ezekiel son of Buzi, in the land of the Chaldeans by the river Chebar; and the hand of YHWH was on him there. (Ezek. 1:1–3)

Because Jehoiachin was taken into exile in Babylon in 597 B.C.E., Ezekiel's prophecy began in 592 B.C.E. and continued for slightly more than twenty years. This places the book of Ezekiel within the body of literature produced by the Jewish exiles while living in Babylonia. During this time, the exiles' life was strongly influenced by the Babylonian Empire. Many of the exiles had been wealthy or powerful urban residents of Jerusalem, and now they lived in more rural areas, such as along river banks. At the same time, this exile meant moving from a small region on the fringes of the empire into the center of imperial might and civilization. The cultural shock of this move may well have been dramatic and long-lasting in its effects.

Old Testament scholarship has long maintained that the exile was a crucial period within Israel's historical development. Many scholars assume that the exile gave the Israelites a chance to reflect on their past experience and to perceive a pattern: When they were faithful to God, God rewarded them, but in their times of rebellion against God, God used other nations to punish Israel and Judah. This interpretation of history is certainly present in several parts of the Old Testament, although scholars today are less certain that it reflects a theological or hermeneutical principle for the Old Testament as a whole. The book of Ezekiel challenges this interpretation of history and offers a different view of life in exile. Although many Old Testament texts (including Jeremiah, as well as much of the Pentateuch, the Deuteronomistic History, and the prophets) may have been written or revised during the exile, Ezekiel is rare in that it explicitly describes the exile.

Reading through Ezekiel

Ezekiel's forty-eight chapters follow some of the same structural principles that we observed in the book of Jeremiah. The material has been arranged to present a portrait of the prophet at the start of the book, and then to move into larger frameworks. Similarly, the book's interests shift from a consideration of Judah and its fall to a wider concern with the surrounding nations. However, this structure extends only through chapter 32. The book of Ezekiel then returns its focus to Judah and its future, including prophecies of hope and an emphasis on God's reconstruction of the land around a new temple.

Prophetic call (Ezek. 1—3)
The fall of Judah (4—24)
Oracles against the nations (25—32)
The fall of Jerusalem and the rise of hope (33—39)
Vision of the new temple (40—48)

Prophetic Call (Ezekiel 1—3). Ezekiel's first three chapters narrate a prophetic call in order to explain how Ezekiel became a prophet and why readers should pay attention to the book's words. In chapters 1 to 3, Ezekiel recounts a vision that he saw while along a river near Babylon. In this vision, God drives an angel-powered chariot through the sky, moving from Jerusalem to Babylonia. God departs the Jerusalem temple, where God has lived for centuries, and follows the path of the exiles. God no longer lives in any one place, but is mobile. This is a radical and unexpected theological move within the Hebrew Scriptures. God's freedom of motion may have been part of Israel's early tabernacle traditions, but for most of the Old Testament, this theological idea was overshadowed by the insistence on God's stable and secure dwelling in the temple. Ezekiel depicts a God who moves, who is self-motivated, and who is self-sufficient, without need of temple or anything other than God's own being. (The chariot appears again in 10:15–22 to reinforce the idea of the independence of God's glory.)

Not only does God approach Ezekiel and choose him as a prophet, but God commands him to speak and provides him with a scroll to eat (2:8—3:3)—a dramatic illustration of the concept of having God's words in one's mouth! Ezekiel receives the exact words that he is to say to the people of Israel, but this does not mean that God's words as spoken by the prophet will be effective. Ezekiel's rebellious audience is too stubborn to hear his words, even when Ezekiel proclaims them as directly from God (3:8–12; compare Isa. 6:9).

The Fall of Judah (Ezekiel 4—24). The largest section of the book of Ezekiel, chapters 4 through 24, deals with Judah's collapse and destruction. Ezekiel's prophetic message includes passages of poetry and oratory, as found in prophets such as Isaiah and Jeremiah, but Ezekiel also makes frequent and significance use of prophetic sign-acts. The present section opens with the report of such a sign-act, in which Ezekiel makes a model of Jerusalem and lies in front of it for more than a year (Ezek. 4). The prophetic act (as well as the speech that goes with it) would have been performed in some public area, so that passersby could see it and learn from it. Texts about prophetic sign-acts are difficult to evaluate as historical records; perhaps the prophet performed this for the whole span of time without any breaks or departures, perhaps he enacted it daily, or at least regularly, in one place or in a variety of places, or perhaps the reporting is more of an idealized interpretation. Within the original context, news of the sign-act would have traveled by word of mouth, and the audience would have shifted over time, allowing Ezekiel multiple opportunities to explain the act's significance. We are most likely reading a standardized report of a sign enacted repeatedly over a significant period of time and with numerous variations, like prophetic speeches, which also were likely delivered several times and recorded only in some normative form. Ezekiel used a variety of different sign-acts, such as shaving (Ezek. 5) and packing to leave (Ezek. 12).

Through both sign-acts and prophetic oracles, Ezekiel 4—24 reiterates the proclamation of Judah's fall. Previously, the nation of Judah had suffered significant defeats, but it had not been dissolved and Jerusalem had not yet been completely destroyed. Ezekiel avers that the situation will only deteriorate, leading to the destruction of the city and nation. Because of the people's idolatry and rebelliousness against God, God will abandon them to devastation by the surrounding nations. Ezekiel's prophecy contains a variety of striking images toward this end.

Oracles against the Nations (Ezekiel 25—32). Ezekiel, like some other prophetic books, gathers oracles against several nations—Ammon, Moab, Edom, Philistia, Tyre, and Egypt—into one sequence. The first three of these nations receive relatively few comments from the prophet, but Tyre (26—28) and Egypt (29—32) are each the subjects of several chapters, the tone and style of which are reminiscent of Ezekiel's prophecies about the impending fall of Judah. Ezekiel sees connections between the way God treats Judah and the way God treats other nations.

The Fall of Jerusalem and the Rise of Hope (Ezekiel 33—39). Ezekiel now finds ways to offer hope even in the face of Judah's defeat and Jerusalem's sure destruction. Sentries and sentinels will not prevent the devastation (33:1–9), but God does promise to spare those who turn away from their sins and live in righteousness (33:10–20). Ezekiel 34 declares that God opposes the leaders who have led others astray; these leaders will be punished because they should have been responsible for others. God will eventually bring renewal to the people by cleansing them and setting them right from the inside (36:16–38). God declares to the people,

> A new heart I will give you, and a new spirit I will put within you; and I will remove from your body the heart of stone and give you a heart of flesh. I will put my spirit within you, and make you follow my statutes and be careful to observe my ordinances. Then you shall live in the land that I gave to your ancestors; and you shall be my people, and I will be your God. (36:26–28)

Ezekiel 37's vision of the dry bones also proclaims that there will be new life for the people (see below). After this, a vision tells of destruction coming against Israel from Gog (king of an unknown land, Magog), who will annihilate the people of Judah but will in the end be severely punished by God (38—39). Once more, a prophecy of destruction leads to hope, even if only after great suffering. Eventually, God will end the people's exile, bring them back to their land, pour divine spirit into them, and be with them forever (39:25–29).

Vision of the New Temple (Ezekiel 40—48). The ending chapters of the book of Ezekiel, dated in the text to 573 B.C.E., describe a vision in which Ezekiel is transported to Jerusalem to stand in the area where the old temple once stood. In that place, Ezekiel sees a new temple. The vision explains the details of this new temple's construction and elaborates its furnishings, servants, practices, and environs. This temple is an act of imagination, existing only in the vision and in the text of these chapters. It is an idealized building with perfect dimensions that are described to express ideas of perfection. Even the surrounding territories are measured in round numbers, and each of Israel's twelve tribes receives an equal apportionment (Ezek. 47—48). Ezekiel envisions a temple in which everything runs smoothly to produce a nation of equity and justice. There shall be no king, but only a prince who shall not oppress anyone (45:8).

Theological Perspectives and the Book of Ezekiel

The Two Sisters. In Ezekiel 16 and 23, the prophet tells two separate but related stories that are violent metaphors of God's relationships with Israel and Judah. Chapter 16's story revolves around a woman whom God had discovered as an orphaned infant, abandoned alongside a road. God rescued the girl, who then grew into a woman. When God saw her again, God married her. God gave her many expensive gifts, but she became sexually involved with others. She murdered her own children by sacrificing them to other gods. In reaction, God gathers her sexual partners and has them torture her to death. The vision explains that this is due punishment for Judah's sins and that God will forgive Judah but only in such a way that Judah bears shame and disgrace forever.

Ezekiel 23 tells of two sisters, Oholah (Samaria/Israel) and Oholibah (Jerusalem/Judah), who were prostitutes in Egypt in their youth. God married both of the sisters and had children with each of them. Oholah was unfaithful with the Assyrians, and so God gave her over to them, and they killed her. Oholibah has been even more promiscuous with the Babylonians, and so God will have her killed as well.

These chapters are horrific in their imagery and misogynist in their vision of evil women whose husbands justifiably kill them for relational brokenness. These striking images increase the impact of the prophecies about Judah's destruction, but they do so in a lascivious way that borders on pornographic fantasy. Ezekiel continues a prophetic tradition (see Hos. 1—3) of comparing the relationship of God and people to that of a dysfunctional husband and wife, with marital unfaithfulness a metaphor for human idolatry. These metaphors devolve into violence and degradation; Ezekiel's messages of hope seem far distant from passages such as this.

The Dry Bones Come to Life. The best-known passage in Ezekiel is chapter 37. It begins with a vision of Ezekiel transported into a valley that is filled with human bones. These bones have been shattered, shriveled, and strewn across the valley floor. Perhaps they are the bones of a Judean army defeated and slaughtered by the Babylonians. The bones are not joined in corpses or even skeletons; they lie in piles of broken fragments. God asks Ezekiel if it is possible for those bones to come to life again, and Ezekiel admits that only God knows. God tells Ezekiel to prophesy to the bones that they will live again. When Ezekiel speaks, a wind (in Hebrew, *ruah*) comes forth and begins to stir the bones. As the wind grows, the bones begin to shudder and then to jump into the air. Lifted by the wind, the bones spin in flight and strike each other, sticking together to form whole bones and eventually skeletons. Then muscle and tissue begin to grow on the skeletons of the dead soldiers, to form whole bodies. With another word of prophecy, the wind becomes breath (also *ruah*) and enters into the army, bringing the bodies to life.

> Then he said to me, "Mortal, these bones are the whole house of Israel. They say, 'Our bones are dried up, and our hope is lost; we are cut off completely.' Therefore prophesy, and say to them, Thus says the Lord YHWH: I am going to open your graves, and bring you up from your graves, O my people; and I will bring you back to the land of Israel. And you shall know that I am YHWH, when I open your graves, and bring you up from your graves, O my people. I will put my spirit [*ruah*] within you, and you shall live, and I will place you on your own soil; then you shall know that I, YHWH, have spoken and will act," says YHWH. (Ezek. 37:11–14)

The point of the prophetic story is that God intends to bring the Judeans back to life. Despite the deaths of individuals and of their society, deaths that the Judeans have experienced and are prophesied to experience further, God's last word for them will be a word of hope. God's spirit will be in the people, and they will know God's activity on their behalf.

Resources

Joseph Blenkinsopp. *Ezekiel.* Interpretation. Louisville, Ky.: John Knox Press, 1990.

Ronald E. Clements. *Jeremiah.* Interpretation. Atlanta: John Knox Press, 1988.

Moshe Greenberg. *Ezekiel 1–20,* and *Ezekiel 21–37.* Anchor Bible, vols. 21 and 22A. Garden City, N.Y.: Doubleday, 1983 and 1997.

William L. Holladay. *Jeremiah. Hermeneia.* 2 vols. Philadelphia: Fortress Press, 1986 and 1989.

Renita J. Weems. *Battered Love: Marriage, Sex, and Violence in the Hebrew Prophets.* Overtures to Biblical Theology. Minneapolis: Fortress Press, 1995.

11

The Book of the Twelve

RAYMOND F. PERSON, JR.

The book of the Twelve (also known as the Minor Prophets) consists of the following twelve smaller books of prophetic literature: Hosea, Joel, Amos, Obadiah, Jonah, Micah, Nahum, Habakkuk, Zephaniah, Haggai, Zechariah, and Malachi. From at least the time of Ben Sira (a teacher in Jerusalem between 200 and 180 B.C.E.; see p. 254), these twelve smaller "books" were understood together as one collection rather than twelve individual books, probably because they were written on one scroll. In other words, just as the prophetic material associated with Isaiah, Jeremiah, and Ezekiel was written on one scroll each, the prophetic material concerning the Twelve was written on one scroll. This is the origin of the name the book of the Twelve.

Not only were these twelve smaller books understood as one collection, but they were also understood to have a common message. A closer look at the reference by Ben Sira demonstrates this:

> May the bones of the Twelve Prophets send forth new life from where they lie, for they comforted the people of Jacob and delivered them with confident hope. (Sir. 49:10)

Ben Sira refers to "the Twelve Prophets" as a whole and suggests that this collection's message is one of comfort and "confident hope." This chapter will follow Ben Sira's lead in focusing on the book of the Twelve rather than analyzing each individual book independently.

The Literary History of the Book of the Twelve

The literary history behind the book of the Twelve begins, just as the literary histories of the Major Prophets did, with orally delivered prophetic messages that were eventually written down. This part of the process alone must have covered many centuries, because Hosea, Amos, and Micah prophesied in the eighth century B.C.E. and Haggai and Zechariah prophesied in the sixth century B.C.E. However, even once the messages of a specific prophet were recorded, the literary process continued as new readers edited and added to the texts to apply the message of the prophets of earlier generations to their present situation (we have already seen such processes at work in the formation of the books of Isaiah, Jeremiah, and Ezekiel). Amos' original prophecy of doom against the Northern Kingdom of Israel and its sanctuaries (3:1—6:14), for instance, was reinterpreted by later readers to include the Southern Kingdom of Judah (see 2:4–5, which most scholars believe is a later addition).

One of the clearest examples of a prophet's message being reinterpreted later is found in the book of Zechariah. There is a striking difference in content, style, and vocabulary between Zechariah 1—8, which includes the original message of the prophet Zechariah, and Zechariah 9—14, which most scholars believe was added later. Some of the ways that Zechariah 1—8 and Zechariah 9—14 differ in content include the following: (1) The name of the prophet Zechariah is found only in Zechariah 1—8 (1:1, 7; 7:1, 8). (2) There are no date formulas in Zechariah 9—14, even though date formulas are important in Zechariah 1—8 (1:1, 7; 7:1). (3) In Zechariah 1—8, the governor Zerubbabel and the high priest Joshua are important figures (3:1–10; 4:1–10; 6:9–15); however, no specific leaders are mentioned in Zechariah 9—14. Yet the later writer(s) of Zechariah 9—14 used themes from Zechariah 1—8, so that there is some thematic connection between these two parts of this book. The writer(s) of Zechariah 9—14 reinterpreted Zechariah 1—8 for a new time. Hope was gone that the now-deceased governor Zerubbabel, a descendant of King David, would become king (see 4:1–10); therefore, the later writer places his hope in God: "And YHWH will become king over all the earth; on that day YHWH will be one and his name one" (14:9).

The following chart will help you remember some of the distinctive features of each individual book. Given what has just been said, however, the chart's generalizations about each book's date and message will have to be taken with a grain of salt. We simply cannot assume that everything in a given prophetic book comes from the prophet for whom the book is named.

The Twelve at a Glance

Hosea: Set in the Northern Kingdom as Assyria approaches (late 700s B.C.E.). Compares Hosea's experience with an unfaithful wife to God's feelings about a religiously pluralistic Israel. Final form prophesies both doom (at Assyria's hands) and restoration.

Joel: Probably composed in the Persian Period (539–331 B.C.E.). Calls for Judah to repent so that the imminent "day of YHWH" will be a time of rejoicing rather than grief.

Amos: A Southern Kingdom shepherd declares that God will destroy the prosperous Northern Kingdom for its social injustices during the reign of Jeroboam II (786–746 B.C.E.). Final form concludes with God's promise to restore Judah and the house of David.

Obadiah: Seems to be set early in the Babylonian exile (500s B.C.E.). Declares judgment against Edom for its aggressive stance toward defeated Judah.

Jonah: Probably written in the Persian Period but set in the time of Jeroboam II (786–746 B.C.E.). A prophet flees God's command to proclaim judgment against Nineveh (capital of the Assyrian empire). A storm and a big fish carry him back in the right direction. Jonah sulks because God has compassion for the Ninevites.

Micah: Set in Judah after Assyria's 722–721 B.C.E. defeat of Israel. Condemns exploitation of common people by the Jerusalem elite. The elite believe that God will protect Jerusalem no matter what, but Micah says that because they have defied God, Judah will fall to Assyria as Israel already has.

Nahum: From around the time of Nineveh's fall (612 B.C.E.). Celebrates the decline of the Assyrian empire, declaring its fall a divine judgment. Anticipates peace and prosperity for Judah.

Habakkuk: Late 600s B.C.E. Declares that the rising Babylonian empire is God's instrument of punishment against a violent and disobedient Judah.

Zephaniah: Set early in the reign of Josiah (640–609 B.C.E.), as Babylon becomes a threat. Condemns Judah's leaders for corruption and oppression. Says God will punish the elite, but a righteous remnant will survive.

Haggai: Set during the late 500s B.C.E. Calls for those who have returned from exile to assist in rebuilding the temple and to live according to God's will, so that God will allow Judah to prosper.

Zechariah: Chapters 1 to 8 share Haggai's setting and message. Chapters 9 to 14, added later, express disillusionment with returnee leaders and declare that God will soon come in judgment to purify and restore the community.

Malachi: Set during the Persian Period (539–331 B.C.E.). Condemns corrupt and improper worship in the rebuilt temple and intermarriage of God's people with foreign women. God will bring judgment in a "great and terrible day of YHWH" (4:5).

Just as the individual books of the twelve Minor Prophets underwent long, complicated processes of change from the original words of the prophets to the current books, the collective book of the Twelve grew and changed over time. Evidence for this comes from different manuscript versions, because the order of the twelve individual books is not the same in every manuscript. The most important manuscript traditions for the book of the Twelve are the traditional Hebrew text (referred to by scholars as the Masoretic Text, or MT), the ancient Greek translation (which scholars call the Septuagint, or LXX), and a Dead Sea Scroll from Qumran's Cave 4 (the scholarly reference code for this scroll is 4QXII[a]). Based on his careful study of these manuscript traditions, Barry Alan Jones (pp. 221–34) reconstructs the literary history of the book of the Twelve in five layers. His reconstruction is summarized in the following chart. The first two columns represent his reconstructions of collections before the existing manuscript traditions but closely related to them. The third, fourth, and fifth columns represent the Dead Sea Scroll (4QXII[a]), the LXX, and the MT respectively. Later collections appear to the right of their predecessors. Brackets mean that an individual book is not found in known manuscripts of that tradition. (4QXII[a] is fragmentary and only contains Zechariah, Malachi, and Jonah, in that order. The first two collections are known only hypothetically, so all their books are in brackets.) Bold print indicates a change from the previous collection. Underlining denotes additions. Capital letters denote rearrangements.

Notice that in the three existing manuscript traditions, Joel, Obadiah, and Jonah occur in different locations. Different sequences of texts suggest to scholars that the differing texts were probably added to an earlier text or collection. When these three are removed, we end up with a book of the Nine, containing the nine books that all the manuscripts contain in the exact same order. This book of Nine has the obvious structure of three groups of three individual books, according to chronology. Hosea, Amos, and Micah are prophets of the eight century (700s B.C.E.), all of whom emphasize the threat of the Assyrian empire. Nahum, Habakkuk, and Zephaniah are prophets of the seventh century (600s). Haggai, Zechariah, *known hypothetically*

Dead Sea Scrolls

Book of IX	Book of XI	4QXII^a	LXX–XII	MT–XII
[Hosea]	[Hosea]	[Hosea]	Hosea	Hosea
[Amos]	[Amos]	[Amos]	Amos	**JOEL**
[Micah]	[Micah]	[Micah]	Micah	Amos
	[Joel]	[Joel]	Joel	**OBADIAH**
	[Obadiah]	[Obadiah]	Obadiah	**JONAH**
			JONAH	Micah
[Nahum]	[Nahum]	[Nahum]	Nahum	Nahum
[Habakkuk]	[Habakkuk]	[Habakkuk]	Habakkuk	Habakkuk
[Zeph]	[Zeph]	[Zeph]	Zeph	Zeph
[Haggai]	[Haggai]	[Haggai]	Haggai	Haggai
[Zech]	[Zech]	Zech	Zech	Zech
[Malachi]	[Malachi]	Malachi	Malachi	Malachi
		Jonah		

and Malachi are prophets of the sixth and fifth centuries (500s and 400s), all prophesying during the Persian Empire's control of Israel.

The next collection is a book of the Eleven with Joel and Obadiah added between the eighth-century prophets and the seventh-century prophets because of their thematic connections. Both Joel and Obadiah refer to the future day of YHWH, the judgment day. Joel 1—2 relates well to the themes of judgment against Israel and Judah found in Hosea, Amos, and Micah. Joel 3—4 and Obadiah relate well to the theme of judgment against the foreign nations found in Nahum and Zephaniah. Therefore, Joel and Obadiah provide a thematic transition from the judgment against Israel and Judah in Hosea, Amos, and Micah to the judgment of the foreign nations in Nahum and Zephaniah.

The first book of the Twelve was the book of the Eleven with Jonah added to the end of the collection, as is preserved in 4QXIIa. Jonah differs from all other books of the Latter Prophets in that it is primarily a narrative *about* a prophet rather than a collection of prophetic speeches. Although some other prophetic books contain narratives (see especially Isa. 36—39 and Jer. 26—29), Jonah is the only book included among the prophets that is not primarily prophetic speeches. Jonah's prophetic speech (Jon. 3:4) is only five Hebrew words! The book's satirical narrative critiques nationalistic tendencies in other prophetic literature. By placing Jonah at the end of the prophetic collection, the 4QXIIa manuscript uses it to reflect on prophecy in general.

The next book of the Twelve takes the order preserved in the LXX. This collection understands Jonah as prophetic literature itself—that is, as another judgment oracle against a foreign nation. Thus it appears in roughly chronological order following Obadiah and preceding Nahum, both of which also contain judgment oracles against foreign nations. Jonah's prophetic preaching in Nineveh led to the Ninevites' repentance and YHWH's withholding of their destruction (Jon. 3—4). This story line suggests that Jonah should precede Nahum, which prophesies Nineveh's destruction. Therefore, Jonah was moved from its original position at the end of the collection to the position between Obadiah and Nahum.

The final book of the Twelve has the order preserved in the MT and used in most English translations. In this collection, the chronological order is further revised by placing Joel, Obadiah, and Jonah within the original collection of the three eighth-century prophets.

With each of these additions and reorderings, some of the content of the individual books may also have been revised. For example, the LXX of Amos 9:12 reads (emphasis added),

> In order that the remnant of *humanity* might *seek* me, and all the nations who are called by my name, says the Lord God who does this.

But the MT of Amos 9:12 reads (emphasis again added),

> In order that they may *possess* the remnant of *Edom* and all the nations who are called by my name, says YHWH who does this.

How might we explain this difference? In the MT, Obadiah follows Amos. Because Obadiah includes a judgment oracle against Edom and uses the verb "possess" (1–14), the obvious explanation is that the MT of Amos 9:12 was changed to provide a transition from Amos to Obadiah by using the catchword "Edom." The use of this catchword was already suggested in the LXX, where Obadiah is immediately preceded by Joel, which includes judgment against Edom in its ending (3:19). Hence, this connection was simply added in a revision of the end of Amos to provide a transition to Obadiah. This one example demonstrates how the literary history of the book of the Twelve as a collection may have contributed to changes within the individual books themselves and further demonstrates that the book of the Twelve was understood as a unity.

The Theological Messages of the Book of the Twelve

As with the other books in the Latter Prophets (Isaiah, Jeremiah, and Ezekiel), the messages found in the book of the Twelve move from judgment to promise, from destruction to restoration, from doom to hope. This movement is evident in the order of the individual books in the collection.

The book of the Twelve begins with prophecies from the eighth-century prophets who proclaim judgment against Israel during the Assyrian empire (Hosea, Amos, Micah) and ends with prophecies from the Persian Period prophets who are concerned with the nature of the restoration of Israel (Haggai, Zechariah, Malachi). This movement is also evident within many of the individual books, as the following three examples demonstrate. The book of Amos begins with judgment oracles against Israel, Judah, and surrounding nations (1:1—9:10) and ends with God's promise to restore Israel (9:11–15): "I will restore the fortunes of my people Israel, and they shall rebuild the ruined cities and inhabit them" (9:14). The book of Zephaniah begins with judgment oracles against Judah and surrounding nations (1:1—3:13) and ends with a call to the people of Israel to rejoice, because YHWH will restore Israel (3:14–20). The book of Haggai begins with YHWH's judgment against the returned exiles because they have not yet rebuilt YHWH's temple (1:3–11), but ends with a promise to restore the institution of the Davidic monarchy after the temple is rebuilt (2:20–23). Thus, we can see that this theological theme of judgment to restoration influenced the literary history of the book of the Twelve both as a unified collection and within its individual books, once again reminding us that we cannot assume that all the prophetic material in these books goes back to the prophets for whom the books are named.

To better understand the theme of judgment followed by restoration, we need to look at its different parts and how other themes operate within it. Let's begin with the underlying theme of covenant, then look at the themes of judgment and restoration individually.

Covenant in the Book of the Twelve

A covenant is an agreement between two parties, one of which is usually in a superior position. The subordinate party agrees to remain loyal to the superior party by obeying certain laws and commandments established by the superior party. The superior party generally agrees to protect the subordinate from political and military foes. This political model is used to describe YHWH's relationship with Israel. The people agree to remain loyal by obeying YHWH's commandments, and YHWH agrees to defend Israel from its enemies. Of course, if there is a breach in the contract in that the people of Israel disobey, then YHWH's obligation to protect Israel no longer remains. Often YHWH will turn against the rebellious subjects in order to coerce them back into obedience.

Although what is required of Israel in its covenant with YHWH is spelled out in more detail in the legal materials in the Pentateuch, the book of the Twelve occasionally refers to the "law" (*Torah*) of YHWH. For example, in the book of Hosea, YHWH commands that the trumpet of judgment be blown against Israel because it has broken the covenant:

> Set the trumpet to your lips!
> One like a vulture is over the house of YHWH,
> because they have broken my covenant,
> and transgressed my law. (Hosea 8:1)

Because many of the historical prophets behind the book of the Twelve prophesied before the legal material reached its final form, we cannot assume that all these prophets have the same thing in mind when they refer to "law." In some places, their understanding seems to agree with legal material in the Pentateuch, but in other places tensions exist. Therefore, we need to ask what the prophetic understanding of the covenant and its obligations on Israel was.

The most basic commandment, which is also found in the Ten Commandments (Ex. 20:2–6; Deut. 5:6–10), is absolute allegiance to YHWH and YHWH alone. Idolatry is strictly forbidden. Judgment is proclaimed against Israel for its worship of "idols" (for instance, Mic. 1:7), "other gods" (for instance, Hos. 3:1), and the "Baals" (for instance, Hos. 11:2). The reasons for YHWH's judgment against Israel proclaimed through Hosea included idol worship.

> They [Israel] made kings, but not through me;
> they set up princes, but without my knowledge.
> With their silver and gold they made idols
> for their own destruction.
> Your calf is rejected, O Samaria.
> My anger burns against them.
> How long will they be incapable of innocence?
> For it is from Israel,
> an artisan made it;
> it is not God.
> The calf of Samaria
> shall be broken to pieces. (8:4–6)

Here, Hosea condemns the people of the Northern Kingdom of Israel for anointing kings and princes in the name of other gods and worshiping idols, including the calf of Samaria, which was placed in the sanctuary in Bethel by King Jeroboam I (see 1 Kings 12:26–33). Hosea proclaims that this calf "is not God" (8:6). The adulterous relationship with other gods is symbolized by Hosea's marriage to Gomer, "a wife of whoredom," and by their "children of whoredom," named "Not Pitied" and "Not My People" (Hosea 1:2–9). For this religious adultery, Hosea prophesies destruction of the northern kingdom of Israel.

Certain cultic practices are sometimes assumed, such as "sacrifices" and "offerings." However, these are deemphasized relative to other legal materials of the Pentateuch and, in fact, are almost rejected in the angry rhetoric of YHWH when the people of Israel have broken the other basic commandment of the covenant, the commandment to maintain social justice.

> I [YHWH] hate, I despise your festivals,
> and I take no delight in your solemn assemblies.
> Even though you offer me your burnt offerings and grain
>   offerings,
> I will not accept them;
> and the offerings of well-being of your fatted animals
> I will not look upon.
> Take away from me the noise of your songs;
> I will not listen to the melody of your harps.
> But let justice roll down like waters,
> and righteousness like an everflowing stream. (Am. 5:21–24)

> "With what shall I come before YHWH,
> and bow myself before God on high?
> Shall I come before him with burnt offerings,
> with calves a year old?
> Will YHWH be pleased with thousands of rams,
> with ten thousands of rivers of oil?
> Shall I give my firstborn for my transgression,
> the fruit of my body for the sin of my soul?"
> He has told you, O mortal, what is good;
> and what does YHWH require of you
> but to do justice, and to love kindness,
> and to walk humbly with your God? (Mic. 6:6–8)

In both these passages, certain requirements of the Mosaic law—sacrifices, offerings, festivals—are judged as completely ineffective if injustice and unrighteousness remain. Economic exploitation and the brutality of war are strongly condemned and lead to YHWH's wrathful, but just, judgment of Israel.

In summary, the covenant stipulations presupposed by the prophetic rhetoric in the book of the Twelve include strict monotheism and a radical vision of social justice. When Israel and Judah do not meet these stipulations, the prophets proclaim divine wrath that will bring doom and destruction.

Judgment in the Book of the Twelve

In 722 B.C.E., the Assyrians destroyed the Northern Kingdom of Israel and took many of the people into exile. In 587 B.C.E., the Babylonians destroyed the Southern Kingdom of Judah and took some of the people into exile. These two historical events certainly lie behind the message of many of the prophets. Hosea and Amos clearly understand the threat of the expanding Assyrian empire as the means by which YHWH will punish the Northern Kingdom of Israel. Micah warns the Southern Kingdom of Judah that it risks the same fate at the hands of the Assyrians. Habakkuk and Zephaniah clearly understand the threat of the expanding Babylonian empire as the means by which YHWH will judge Judah. Haggai and Zechariah reflect on the temple destroyed by the Babylonians and how those who have returned from the Babylonian exile must rebuild the temple and its institutions.

The influence of these two catastrophic events reaches beyond the historical messages of the prophets to shape the overall literary character of some of the individual books in the book of the Twelve. For example, the historical prophet Amos clearly prophesied that YHWH would punish the *Northern* Kingdom of Israel with destruction at the hands of the Assyrians (3:1—9:10). But what meaning might these judgment oracles have for the *Southern* Kingdom of Judah generations later? Because the punishment of the Northern Kingdom of Israel was seen as a warning about what might befall the Southern Kingdom of Judah, a later editor of the book of Amos placed words of judgment against Judah within the mouth of the character of Amos:

> Because they [people of Judah] have rejected the law of YHWH,
> and have not kept his statues...
> I will send fire on Judah,
> and it shall devour the strongholds of Jerusalem. (2:4–5)

In this way, Amos' words of judgment to Israel in the eighth century were applied also to Judah in the sixth century. Disobedience to the stipulations of the covenant with YHWH leads to destruction and exile for both kingdoms.

These same covenantal stipulations were applied to Israel's neighbors in judgment oracles against the nations (Am. 1:3—2:3; Ob. 1–14; Nahum; Zeph. 2:4–15). The foreign nations, of course, had their own religions and their own gods; therefore, they could not be said to worship YHWH alone. However, this is seldom mentioned in the oracles against them, occurring infrequently and only indirectly (Nah. 1:2, 14; Zeph. 2:11). Because these nations did not have Israel's special revelation concerning God, nor any direct commandments on how they were to worship, they were not understood as directly disobedient in this regard. The prophets do, however, assume that all nations of the world may be held to the same high standards with regard to social justice. This is illustrated well in the book of Amos.

The book of Amos begins with a prophetic superscription and a poetic introduction to the main theme of judgment:

> The words of Amos, who was among the shepherds of Tekoa, which he saw concerning Israel in the days of King Uzziah of Judah and in the days of King Jeroboam son of Joash of Israel, two years before the earthquake. And he said:
>
> YHWH roars from Zion,
> and utters his voice from Jerusalem;
> the pastures of the shepherds wither,
> and the top of Carmel dries up. (Am. 1:1–2)

These verses suggest that Amos' words were words of judgment against the Northern Kingdom of Israel within a short period. This is also suggested in Amos' report of his call when he summarizes that call with "YHWH said to me, 'Go, prophesy to my people Israel'" (7:15). Although the majority of the book of Amos is judgment oracles against the Northern Kingdom of Israel (2:6—9:10), two sections do not fit this pattern: the passages concerning restoration (9:11–15, discussed previously) and the oracles against the nations and Judah (1:3—2:5).

Immediately following the superscription and poetic summary of judgment are judgment oracles against Damascus (1:3–5), Gaza (1:6–8), Tyre (1:9–10), Edom (1:11–12), the Ammonites (1:13–15), Moab (2:1–3), Judah (2:4–5), and Israel (2:6–16), all of which have the same form. Each oracle begins with the formulaic phrase "Thus says YHWH: For three transgressions of [name], and for four, I will not revoke the punishment; because [list of transgressions]" and ends with a predicted punishment of destruction. The transgressions listed for the foreign nations all concern violations of YHWH's standards for social justice, especially brutality in war. For example, the judgment against the Ammonites is "because they have ripped open pregnant women in Gilead in order to enlarge their territory" (1:13). After the foreign nations are condemned, Judah is also condemned "because they have rejected the law of YHWH and have not kept his statutes" (2:4). The judgment against these seven nations (three plus four) prepares for what is clearly the most important oracle in this group, the oracle against the Northern Kingdom of Israel (2:6–16). Its importance is not only suggested in that the oracle against Israel is the last one in this series, but also because it is the longest, with the most detailed description of transgressions and resulting destruction. This is consistent with the overall theme of Amos' prophecy concerning judgment against Israel. In this oracle Israel is condemned for both violations of social justice (for instance, "because they sell the righteous for silver"; 2:6) and cultic practices influenced by pagan worship (for instance, "they lay themselves down beside every altar"; 2:8).

If Amos' prophetic ministry was to the Northern Kingdom of Israel, it may be that he did not proclaim these oracles against the nations, but that they were added by later editors. Such an addition would not only connect the book of Amos to other prophetic books with added oracles against nations (see, for example, Jer. 46—51 and Ezek. 25—32) but would also make the theological claim that YHWH is God over all the nations, over all of creation. YHWH not only controls history affecting Israel, but controls all history, bringing judgment on all peoples who violate YHWH's standards for social justice. Thus, the oracles against the foreign nations in the book of Amos remind us once again that we cannot assume that all the material in a book is from the prophet whose name is associated with that book. Concerns beyond a specific book may have influenced its development as part of a unified book of the Twelve.

Restoration in the Book of the Twelve

The understanding of covenant behind the messages of the prophets not only implies judgment against a disobedient Israel but also implies that once Israel has been punished and then repents and returns to YHWH, YHWH desires to restore Israel and renew the covenant. YHWH has made a promise to Israel, especially King David, that will continue into the future. In this way, judgment leads to restoration of a righteous remnant of Israel.

Although this theme may have been proclaimed before the destruction of Judah by Babylon, it clearly becomes a dominant prophetic theme in the exilic and postexilic periods. The vision of restoration can be understood to take two different forms, historical and eschatological. The historical understanding envisions a restoration that is somehow continuous with present history. The eschatological understanding envisions restoration only after a dramatic intervention by YHWH that brings an end to history as we know it, dramatically changing all of creation.

A good example of a historical vision of restoration is found in the book of Haggai. The book ends with a prophecy concerning Zerubbabel, the descendant of King David who has been appointed governor of Judah by the Persian emperor Darius I.

Speak to Zerubbabel, governor of Judah, saying, I am about to shake the heavens and the earth, and to overthrow the throne of kingdoms; I am about to destroy the strength of the kingdoms of nations, and overthrow the chariots and their riders; and the horses and their riders shall fall, every one by the sword of a comrade. On that day, says YHWH of hosts, I will take you, O Zerubbabel my servant, son of Shealtiel, says YHWH, and make you like a signet ring; for I have chosen you, says YHWH of hosts. (2:21–23)

Haggai assumes that the return of the Jews to Jerusalem and the rebuilding of the temple under Zerubbabel is not simply a Persian strategy to control conquered peoples and their land for the sake of the Persian empire. Haggai assumes that YHWH who punished Judah by destruction and exile at the hands of the Babylonians has now punished the Babylonians at the hands of the Persians to begin to restore Israel. In other words, YHWH is controlling history so as to bring about a restored Israel and a renewed covenant. YHWH promised King David that one of his descendants would forever sit on the throne in Jerusalem (see 2 Sam. 7:16), and YHWH is fulfilling that promise. Zerubbabel may only be governor now, but Haggai believes he will soon be king.

As more and more such historically limited visions fail to become true, the vision of Israel's restoration becomes more eschatological. Restoration is no longer understood to be something that YHWH will bring about through regular political history. Instead, YHWH will end history and start over. Although many of those who are alive when YHWH ends history will continue into the new reality, according to this vision, the new reality will be radically different from the present one. This is illustrated well in Zechariah 14:1—21.

On that day there shall not be either cold or frost. And there shall be continuous day...not day and not night, for at evening time there shall be light...YHWH will become king over all the earth; on that day YHWH will be one and his name one. The whole land shall be turned into a plain from Geba to Rimmon south of Jerusalem. But Jerusalem shall remain aloft on its site....And it [Jerusalem] shall be inhabited, for never again shall it be doomed to destruction; Jerusalem shall abide in security. (Zech. 14:6–7, 9–11)

Creation will be dramatically changed, so that there will be "continuous day" and the mountains around Jerusalem will be flattened. The political order will be changed, so that no human being will reign as king. Only the true King, YHWH, will reign—reign over all the earth, over all the nations. Jerusalem will no longer be a victim of conflict between the ancient superpowers of Mesopotamia and Egypt, but will be secure forever under YHWH's reign.

Note that both Haggai 2:23 and Zechariah 14:6 refer to "that day"— "the day of YHWH." Originally, this language probably referred to a future day of judgment within history against Israel's enemies, a tradition continued in the oracles against the nations. Later, some prophets unexpectedly change its meaning, so that it refers to a day of judgment against disobedient Israel (Am. 5:18–20; Joel 1:13—2:11; Hag. 2:21–23). Finally, "the day of YHWH" acquires an eschatological meaning, referring to the day in which YHWH will end history, judge the unrighteous, and restore Israel and creation.

Thus in Zechariah 12—14, the day of YHWH includes judgment against the nations, leading to the restoration of Israel with an end to former institutions (such as kingship, prophecy, and priesthood) and a new creation with a continuous day. Although the nations will be judged, some among the nations will survive and will come to Jerusalem every year for the festival of booths, when they will worship YHWH (Zech. 14:16). Thus, the theme of judgment to restoration, doom to hope, not only applies to Israel but to all the nations of the world. The nations are judged by YHWH now on the basis of YHWH's standard of social justice. In the future, they will be included in the restoration of Israel, which will be a blessing to all the nations as they come to share its special revelation.

Resources

Elizabeth Achtemeier and Frederick J. Murphy. The Twelve Prophets. Vol. 7 of *The New Interpreter's Bible,* edited by Leander Keck. Nashville: Abingdon Press, 1996.

Barry Alan Jones. *The Formation of the Book of the Twelve: A Study in Text and Canon.* Society of Biblical Literature Dissertation Series 149. Atlanta: Scholars Press, 1995.

12

Psalms

Marti J. Steussy

Psalms is one of the most beloved books of the Bible. Of all the books of the First Testament, it is Psalms that accompanies the Second Testament books in the tiny abridged "pocket Bibles" carried by many Christians. Believers turn to the psalms for comfort ("YHWH is my shepherd, I shall not want"; Ps. 23:1) and lofty words of praise ("YHWH, our Sovereign, how majestic is your name in all the earth!" Ps. 8:1). Yet the psalms also express less comforting emotions. "You [God] have made us like sheep for slaughter," accuses Psalm 44:11. "YHWH, why do you cast me off? Why do you hide your face from me?" asks Psalm 88:14. The speaker of Psalm 58:8 calls for God's curse against the wicked: "Let them be like the snail that dissolves into slime; like the untimely birth that never sees the sun." "Happy shall they be," says Psalm137:9 to Babylon, "who take your little ones and dash them against the rock!" Although few would contest that humans are capable of such sentiments, Bible readers sometimes wonder about how to understand them as the word of God.

We begin our study of the vibrantly expressive poems in Psalms by identifying the most common types of psalm. Next, we look at the headings of the psalms and consider the ancient tradition associating King David with the psalms. After that, we inquire into the large-scale structure of the Psalter (another name for the book of Psalms). At the end of the chapter, we return to the question of the theological significance of the psalms.

Types (Genres) of Psalms

Although the individual psalms in the Psalter are quite diverse in length and style, they all share a few core characteristics. First, they are poetry: densely written, packed with striking images, often alluding rather than spelling things out plainly. Often one line will echo the idea of the previous one, forming a thought-rhyme, as it were: "Why do the nations conspire, / and the peoples plot in vain?" (Ps. 2:1). At other times, the second line will provide a counterpoint to the first: "For YHWH watches over the way of the righteous, / but the way of the wicked will perish" (Ps. 1:6). Although Hebrew poetry does not exhibit the strict patterns of rhythm, rhyme, and stanza division that characterize much English poetry, the lines are usually approximately balanced in length, and the Hebrew text often contains sound-plays, such as in Psalm 122:6: "Pray for the peace of Jerusalem" = *sha'alu shalom yerushalayim.* Many psalms seem to have a stanza structure, although the stanzas may not be equal in length. Sometimes one finds a refrain, such as, "Why are you cast down, O my soul, / and why are you disquieted within me? / Hope in God; for I shall again praise him, / my help and my God" (Ps. 42:5–6a, 11; 43:5).

The word *psalm* is Greek for "song," and in ancient times many or most of the psalms were probably sung. A number of the psalms have musical instructions at the top. For instance, Psalm 45's heading tells us it is "a love song," to be performed "according to Lilies" (probably the name of a tune). Another probable musical marker is the word *Selah,* which sometimes appears at the ends of lines within psalms (see, for instance, Ps. 3:2, 4, 8). *Selah* may signal a pause in which instrumental music would have been played. In general, however, we know little about how the psalms might have been performed musically.

The final feature that all the psalms have in common is that they are worship literature. The majority are prayers, addressed directly to God ("Give ear to my words, YHWH"; Ps. 5:1). The rest are praises and meditations that speak about God ("The heavens are telling the glory of God," Ps. 19:1; "The earth is YHWH's and all that is in it," Ps. 24:1). Many of the psalms are structured for communal use. For example, Psalm 100 ("enter his gates with thanksgiving, and his courts with praise"; v. 4) was probably used as a call to worship in ancient times, just as it often is today. The speaker of Psalm 119, however, says, "I live as an alien in the land" (v. 19) and throughout the psalm refers to "I" and "me," never "we." This suggests that Psalm 119 may have been used in individual meditation and study outside the temple. Although scholars debate the original settings of individual psalms, ultimately all the psalms in the collection found employment both within temple worship (while the temple still stood) and outside it.

Individual Laments

"I will bless YHWH at all times," says the speaker of Psalm 34:1, "his praise shall continually be in my mouth." Although such continual praise remains an ideal for many Jewish and Christian believers today, individuals are most likely to pray when they are in trouble and want help. This was probably just as true in ancient times, for the single most common type of psalm is the individual prayer for help from God. Scholars refer to such psalms as *individual laments*. The components usually found in a lament psalm are:

Invocation: direct address to God, calling for God's attention
Complaint: description of the psalmist's trouble
Plea: request for divine action
Motivation: reasons why God might want to act
Conclusion: statement of trust and/or intent to praise

We see all these components in Psalm 13. It begins with a direct address to God (invocation) in verse 1: "How long, O YHWH?" The difficulty (complaint) is then developed in a series of questions: "Will you forget me forever?...How long must I bear pain in my soul?"(vv. 1–2). The plea comes in verse 3: "Consider and answer me...Give light to my eyes." In this psalm, the motivations, expressed in verses 3 and 4, are first that the psalmist will die if not helped and second that the psalmist's enemies will rejoice if this happens. Notice the assumption, in the first motivation, that God cares whether the psalmist lives or dies. The second motivation seems to assume that the psalmist's enemies are also God's enemies and God therefore doesn't want them rejoicing, or that God is concerned about the divine reputation, which will suffer if the enemies see God failing to protect someone who appeals for help.

The beginning of verse 5 can be translated "but I trusted in your steadfast love" (as in the *New Revised Standard Version* [NRSV]), in which case this is another motivation, or "I trust" (as in the *New American Bible* [NAB]), in which case the verse declares confidence that the prayer will be heard and acted on. In verse 6, the psalmist shifts to a note of confident praise ("I will sing to YHWH, because he has dealt bountifully with me"), sounding almost as if this verse is spoken at a later time, after the trouble has ended. Alternatively, we might suppose that the speaker is still in trouble, but so confident of help that he or she feels as if future help has already taken effect.

You can see from the previous paragraph that analyzing the structure of a psalm—even a short and relatively simple one—is not an exact science. Sometimes our categorization of a given line will depend on our interpretation of its words and underlying assumptions. Also, most lament psalms do not follow the ideal pattern of the genre as clearly as Psalm 13 does. One or more components of the pattern may be missing. For example, Psalm 88, one of the most desperate of the individual laments, lingers in complaint and motivation and never quite arrives at a plea, let alone statements of trust or promises of praise. (Verse 2 does have the form of a request but should probably be considered part of the opening call for divine attention, rather than a separate plea.) Parts of the basic pattern may be repeated, as in Psalm 86, which speaks thanks and praise in verses 12–13, then returns to lament and motivation in verses 14–17. Even though the basic pattern is seldom followed exactly, understanding its components can help us interpret the variety of kinds of statements we find in lament prayers, and knowing the basic sequence can help us see the distinctiveness of the changes that individual laments bring to the basic pattern.

The language of an individual lament is typically intense and highly emotional: "My bones are shaking with terror"; "I flood my bed with tears" (Ps. 6:2; 6). Such language strikes most readers as highly "personal," and we quickly find ourselves speculating about the speaker's life and circumstances. What can we know about the life situations from which the individual laments come?

One striking feature is the frequency with which these prayers mention enemies. Often these seem to be military enemies, prompting the suspicion (reinforced by the "David" headings, to which we will return later) that we may be dealing with royal prayers. Other psalms speak of enemies who use words as weapons (see, for instance, Ps. 5:9–10: "There is no truth in their mouths...let them fall by their own counsels"). These, too, may come from royal contexts rife with intrigue. Judean theology spoke of a special covenant relationship between king and God, in which God pledged to protect the king against his enemies ("I [God] will crush his [the king's] foes before him"; Ps. 89:23). Later, ordinary readers adopted this imagery of special personal relationship, applying the "enemy" language to their own problems, whether in the form of outside enemies or personal issues such as depression and alcoholism. In this way, the psalms came to speak for new generations in new contexts.

Enemy talk receives particular stress in laments that protest the psalmist's innocence (for instance, Psalms 4, 7, 17, 26, 35, 109, and 139). Scholars are not certain how these psalms functioned in the religious life of ancient Judah and Israel. Psalm 26 ("I wash my hands in innocence, / and go around your altar, O YHWH"; v. 6) looks like it might be a priest's affirmation of worthiness to perform his duties (compare Ps. 15 and 24, which speak of the requirements for entering into God's presence). Psalm 35, by contrast, appears to protest false accusations: "Malicious witnesses rise up; / they ask me about things I do not know...they say, 'Aha, Aha, / our eyes have seen it'" (35:11, 21). Possibly this psalm presents the king's protest against accusations that he has violated his covenant responsibilities toward YHWH. Psalm 109 contains a long and disturbing section of ill wishes ("may his children wander about and beg") in verses 6 through 19. The NRSV translation presents this section as a quote of the accusers' words against the psalmist (109:6, "they say," not present in the Hebrew text), whereas other translations present this section as the psalmist's curse on an accuser (compare the curses in Ps. 58). Even if 109:6–19 cites the accusers rather than the psalmist's own desires, it is clear that the psalmist wants God to turn those ill wishes on the enemy or enemies: "May that be the reward of my accusers from YHWH" (109:20). As we ponder these psalms, it may help us to remember that the psalmists do not appear to have expected any meaningful afterlife ("in death there is no remembrance of you"; Ps. 6:5). In their thinking, if God was going to do justice, God needed to do it in worldly ways. We should also remember that under a covenant theology that stressed God's patron relationship to the client worshiper, the question of God's possible responsibilities toward other persons may not have gotten much consideration. In Psalm 18:30, the king praises YHWH as "a shield for all who take refuge in him," and then says in verse 41 that his (the king's) enemies "cried to YHWH, but he did not answer them." The speaker seems unaware of the tension between these two depictions: If God shields all who take refuge, why didn't God shield the king's enemies when they called on God's name? These psalms provide a sobering lesson about the ease with which people through history have assumed that being loved by God entails God's partisanship on one's own behalf.

A few of the lament psalms use terminology that might indicate sickness on the part of the psalmist (for example, 38:3–11: "My loins are filled with burning, / and there is no soundness in my flesh"; see also 31:9–10 and 41:3–4). These same psalms also speak of enemies: "I hear the whispering of many—/ terror all around!—/ as they scheme together against me, / as they plot to take my life" (31:13). "When they come to see me, they utter empty words, / while their hearts gather mischief" (41:6). It may be that the psalmist is simply worried about enemies taking advantage of the sickness, but perhaps more is being implied: The psalmist may believe that the enemies are "whispering" curses and evil charms that *cause* the sickness. Psalm 41:6 says that the enemy "speaks *shawe*." Although NRSV translates *shawe* as "empty words," the psalmist's concern may be not that the words are empty but that they have power for mischief (note the second half of the verse). The enemies may be doing exactly what Exodus 20:7 forbids when it says, "you must not use the name of YHWH your God for *shawe*" (author's translation). Yet the psalmists also speak of their sickness as divine punishment: "Do not rebuke me in your anger" (6:1). "There is no soundness in my flesh / because of your indignation; / there is no health in my bones / because of my sin" (38:3). "YHWH, be gracious to me; / heal me, for I have sinned against you" (41:4).

In the ancient world, the causes of illness (bacteria and viruses too small to be seen, or malfunctions in even tinier chemical structures within our own cells) were largely unknown, and one's chances of surviving an illness were far less than in modern Western society. What were ancient folk to make of plagues that could decimate a city within days? They concluded that the gods, or God, must be angry, and they often seem to have reasoned backward from the fact of illness to the assumption of offense against God. (For biblical attacks on this assumption, see the book of Job and also Jn. 9:2–3. These texts share the ancient assumption that God causes or at least authorizes illness, but both deny that one can reason backward from illness to sin.)

We tend to assume that a psalmist who says "heal me, for I have sinned against you" knows exactly what he or she has done wrong and is confessing the justice of God's action (although he or she also assumes that God can be persuaded to heal). But given the ancient assumptions, the psalmist may simply be assuaging an arbitrary deity's inscrutable anger with a generic confession—"all right, I can see that I must have offended you, so whatever it was, I'm sorry, and please, *please* forgive me and make me healthy again!" Certainly these ancient prayers ought not be taken today as theological proof that the sick must deserve their suffering.

We have seen now that many of the individual laments may have been intended for royal use. The problems for which they seek God's help seem to include enemy machinations, false accusations, and sickness. This said, we should also acknowledge the highly figurative character of their poetic language. Take a look, for instance, at Psalm 22. Verses 7 and 8 speak of people who "mock" the psalmist, even quoting some of their words, but we are not told what situation provokes their scorn or whether the scorn itself might be the primary problem. The following stanza (vv. 9–11) speaks to God as the one "who took me from the womb; / you kept me on my mother's breast." The Hebrew words here are full of soft *m* and *b* sounds and gutturals that remind us of a baby suckling: *ki 'attah gochi mibbaten, mavtichi 'al shedey 'immi* (pronounce the *ch* sounds as in Scottish "loch"). But for all their intimacy, these lines tell us nothing about the psalmist's identity except that the speaker has a sense of long-standing relationship with God. The psalm mentions several dangerous animals (bulls, dogs, lions, and wild oxen, in vv. 12–13, 16, and 20–21). Are these literal descriptions of the psalmist's danger or, as most interpreters suppose, symbolic references? Images in verses 14 and 15, such as the dried-up mouth, could point to any of several illnesses, but others read these lines, too, as figurative and regard verse 16's band of evildoers as the "real" problem. Although some scholars seek the psalm's life setting on a battlefield or sickbed, others envision an annual ritual of royal humiliation after which the king would be reinstated as God's ruling representative.

In the end, we can say practically nothing definitive about the circumstances of the original speaker of Psalm 22, except that the situation was so bad as to suggest that God had abandoned the psalmist. Although this lack of clarity frustrates our desire to know the psalmist as an individual, it is also a strength, for it means that the psalm's vivid lament can be appropriated by other persons suffering a variety of problems. Jesus is said to have quoted this psalm while on the cross (compare Ps. 22:1 with Mt. 27:46 and Mk. 15:34; this association may then have prompted the gospel writers to use the psalm as a source of information about what happened to Jesus during the hours that he was separated from his disciples before the crucifixion). The language of other individual laments functions similarly. As personal as these prayers seem, they are not simply an author's private prayers. They are prayers recorded for use and reuse, valuable less as records of their composers' feelings than as vehicles for the articulation of subsequent prayer. In each psalm, the prayers of many persons across many centuries converge.

Psalms of Trust

Given the model of God as a powerful royal patron who would protect "all who take refuge in him" (Ps. 18:30), it should come as no surprise to find a category of psalms that seem primarily devoted to asserting the psalmist's loyalty and trust. Such psalms usually imply some situation creating a need for, or potentially giving rise to doubt about, God's protection. For instance, Psalm 23 mentions a "darkest valley" and "enemies." Structurally, one can think of trust psalms as a lament type in which a concluding assertion of trust has become the dominant feature.

The Psalter contains relatively few individual psalms of trust (Psalms 11, 16, 23, 27, 62, 63, and 131). All these psalms bear David headings (which appear on only about half the psalms overall). We will say more later about these headings, but they may suggest that the trust psalms, like so many of the individual laments, are rooted in the covenant relationship between Judah's king and YHWH. The enemies might say, "There is no help for you in God" (Ps. 3:2), but the king would counter to God with his own declaration: "My soul clings to you; / your right hand upholds me" (Ps. 63:8). The royal theology declared, after all, that a king who trusted in YHWH would "not be moved" (Ps. 21:7).

To locate the trust psalms in a royal covenant relationship is not, however, to limit them to that relationship. Like the laments, the trust psalms use language appropriable by Jewish and Christian believers in a variety of situations. Even today, the trust psalms' protestations of calm confidence help people face their difficulties with a sense of quiet assurance that God will see them through. For this reason, the trust psalms, especially Psalm 23, are among the Psalter's most beloved and best-known poems.

Individual Thanksgivings

In our discussion of individual laments, we saw that such prayers typically conclude with statements of trust or declarations that the psalmist will praise God for deliverance accomplished. We commented that the trust psalms could be viewed as a form of lament in which the statement of confidence became the dominant element. In individual psalms of thanksgiving (Psalms 30, 32, 66, 92, 116, and 138; see also the king's thanksgiving in Psalm 18), the other concluding element of lament, praise for deliverance, takes center stage. The close relationship between thanksgivings and laments is shown by the fact that in some intermediate cases, such as Psalm 22, interpreters do not agree whether they are looking at a lament ("my God, why have you forsaken me?"; 22:1) with an unusually well-developed conclusion or a thanksgiving ("[God] did not hide his face from me, / but heard when I cried to him"; 22:24) preceded by an unusually strong recollection of distress.

Psalm 66:15 mentions "burnt offerings of fatlings," "smoke of the sacrifice of rams," and "an offering of bulls and goats." Psalm 116:17–18 mentions "a thanksgiving sacrifice" and payment of vows. These allusions may tell us something about the original life setting of the thanksgiving psalms. Like people today, when ancient folk found themselves hard pressed, they had a tendency to say, "God, if you get me out of this one, I will…" Because they believed that animal sacrifices were particularly pleasing to God, such vows often took the form of pledging to bring an animal for sacrifice. One might also express gratitude with an animal offering without having made a prior vow. Instructions regarding such offerings appear in Leviticus 3; 7:11–18; and 22:17–30. Part of the animal would go to the officiating priests. Part would be burned on the altar. The rest would be cooked and eaten by the offerer and his or her guests (any meat not consumed within a prescribed time had to be burned). Psalm 22:25–26 gives a vivid picture of the resulting community celebration:

From you comes my praise in the great congregation;
my vows I will pay before those who fear him.
The poor shall eat and be satisfied;
those who seek him shall praise YHWH.
May your hearts live forever!

People today sometimes stereotype vow taking and thanksgiving sacrifices as primitive religious behavior. However, even in biblical times, priests were anxious to stress that God's help was not simply "bought" by promises of sacrifice. Psalm 50, which presents a sort of warning sermon about such matters, urges that vows be paid (50:14). Yet in it God also says to the worshipers, "If I were hungry, I would not tell you, / for the world and all that is in it is mine" (50:12). God emphasizes the need for righteous behavior and seems to suggest (the wording is not completely clear) that public acknowledgement of what God has done for the worshipers is more important than the sacrifices per se (50:12–15). The following psalm similarly denies that God can be manipulated, yet continues to see animal sacrifices as part of healthy worship life (51:15–19). The lament and thanksgiving psalms stress the importance of testimony. "I will tell of your name to my brothers and sisters…future generations will be told" (22:22, 30). "Come and hear, all you who fear God, / and I will tell what he has done for me" (66:16).

Community Prayers

Corresponding to the individual laments and thanksgivings we find community laments (Psalms 44, 74, 80, and 137), songs of trust (Psalm 90), and thanksgivings (Psalms 65, 124, and 136). The line between such community psalms and their individual counterparts is not always cleanly drawn, for sometimes a psalmic "I" seems to be the community (later we will see this happening in Psalm 51), and sometimes an individual articulates a prayer for "us." Psalm 44 has an interesting alternation of first-person plural ("we," 44:1–3, 5, 7–14, 17–26) and an "I" voice (44:4, 6, 15–16) that is probably the king's.

Reading these psalms in light of the historical and prophetic books, which clearly interpret national defeats as divine punishment, it is easy to read statements such as "you have been angry" (Ps. 60:1) as implicit admissions of guilt. A few psalms do explicitly confess communal sin: "Do not remember against us the iniquities of our ancestors" (79:8); "You forgave the iniquity of your people" (85:2); "You have set our iniquities before you" (90:8); "Both we and our ancestors have sinned; / we have committed iniquity, have done wickedly" (106:6). Most, however, sound puzzled that the nation's patron God has abandoned it to defeat. "Why does your anger smoke against the sheep of your pasture?" (74:1). "How long will you be angry with your people's prayers?" (80:4). "How long shall the wicked exult?" (94:3). Some explicitly protest innocence: "We have not forgotten you, / or been false to your covenant" (44:17). We even see the covenant breaking explicitly attributed to God rather than the nation: "You have renounced the covenant with your servant"; "where is your steadfast love of old, / which by your faithfulness you swore to David?" (89:39, 49).

Like the pleas for personal healing, then, communal laments seem to assume God's responsibility for whatever happens. More strongly than the psalms of illness, however, these laments protest that what happens is sometimes undeserved by those to whom it happens. On this point the communal laments agree with Job and John. We might also note concurrence with the apocalyptic texts of Daniel and the Second Testament, which depict great suffering coming, at least initially, to those who are *most* faithful. Like those apocalyptic texts, although on a more worldly and historical level, the communal laments display a confidence that ultimately God will punish the enemies and grant victory and restoration to God's own people.

Hymns of Praise

Of all the psalm genres, it is the hymns of praise that have been most eagerly embraced for ongoing use by worshiping congregations through the centuries. Thousands of musical settings have been provided for them, along with a variety of rhymed English versifications. Psalmic hymns underlie such modern favorites as "A Mighty Fortress" (Ps. 46), "Joy to the World" (Ps. 98), "All People that on Earth do Dwell" (Ps. 100), "Praise to the Lord, the Almighty" (Ps. 103, 104), and "All Creatures of our God and King" (Ps. 148).

Like other genre distinctions, the line between hymns of praise and thanksgivings blurs at times. In general, psalms that refer to past distress and give thanks for historical deliverance (see, for instance, Ps. 124) are classified as thanksgivings, whereas psalms that praise God's power and goodness in more general terms are categorized as hymns (Ps. 8 and 104 are good examples).

The praise psalms often speak of God's power as creator. Psalm 8, for instance, marvels at "your heavens, the work of your fingers, / the moon and the stars that you have established" (8:3). It then speaks of God's grant of dominion to human beings (or possibly "a human being"; 8:4–6), in terms reminiscent of Genesis 1. Psalm 33 also reminds us of Genesis 1 as it asserts, "He spoke, and it came to be; he commanded, and it stood firm" (Ps. 33:9). Beneath others of these psalms, however, we can discern the logic of an ancient Near Eastern paradigm in which the earth is understood to have been created in the wake of a high god's victory over the watery powers of chaos and death. Because of this victory, the god has dominion over the heavens and earth, which are then shaped into their present habitable form:

> You rule the raging of the sea;
> when its waves rise, you still them.
> You crushed Rahab [a name for the primeval sea monster] like a
> carcass;
> you scattered your enemies with your mighty arm.
> The heavens are yours, the earth also is yours;
> the world and all that is in it—you have founded them.
> The north and the south—you created them. (Ps. 89:9–12)

According to the paradigm, the conquering god then builds a palace/ temple and rules as king—which means, according to the ancient Near Eastern ideology of kingship, that the creator god is now responsible for maintaining justice and protecting the weak. "Righteousness and justice are the foundation of your throne; / steadfast love and faithfulness go before you" (89:14).

These themes of kingship, creation, and divine justice receive particular emphasis in a subgroup of hymns called the *enthronement psalms* (Ps. 93, 96—99, and perhaps 47). Many scholars have speculated that these psalms originally arose in connection with a First Temple festival celebrating God's victorious creation battle with the forces of chaos, along with God's associated royal dominion and just rule. "The floods lift up their roaring" (93:3); "the earth sees and trembles" (97:4); "say among the nations, 'YHWH is king! / The world is firmly established; it shall never be moved. / He will judge the peoples with equity'" (96:10).

Another subset of praise psalms, often referred to as *Zion psalms* (46, 48, 76, 84, 87, and 122) call our attention to the chosen place of YHWH's throne, Zion. "Zion" is a name used for Jerusalem, and especially its Temple Mount, in contexts that emphasize the city's spiritual status as God's chosen place. These psalms tend to speak of Jerusalem in highly mythologized terms: "Beautiful in elevation...the joy of all the earth" (48:2). Indeed, phrases about "a river whose streams make glad the city of God" (46:4) and "Mount Zion, in the far north" (48:2) hardly seem to apply to earthly Jerusalem at all—instead, they come from a general Canaanite stock of descriptive terms pertaining to the high god's dwelling place on a holy mountain from which gush life-giving rivers. "They feast on the abundance of your house, / and you give them drink from the river of your delights [in

Hebrew, "the river of your *edens*"]. / For with you is the fountain of life" (Ps. 36:8–9; compare Gen. 2:10–14; Ezek. 47:1–12; Dan. 7:9–10; and Rev. 22:1–5). In the Zion psalms, God's dwelling is not only a place of justice but a place of peace: "He makes wars cease to the end of the earth; / he breaks the bow, and shatters the spear; / he burns the shields with fire. / 'Be still, and know that I am God!'" (Ps. 46:9–10).

As we move into the later sections of the Psalter, we find praise psalms with more explicitly historical references. Psalm 99 refers to Moses, Aaron, and Samuel. Psalm 105:9–10 contains the Psalter's only reference to the trio of patriarchs, Abraham, Isaac, and Jacob. Psalm 114 employs the language of fleeing sea and skipping mountains with reference to the exodus rather than creation. Psalm 135 describes YHWH as both the one who "brings out the wind from his storehouses" and the one "who struck down the firstborn of Egypt" (135:7–8). Furthermore, as the basic lament form moves from complaint to praise, so the Psalter itself moves from a lament-heavy genre mix to a praise-dominated one: The final third contains a greater percentage of praise psalms than do the first two thirds. The changing nature of the praise psalms in the later part of the Psalter probably reflects the development from Judah's First Temple religion, which was very much like that of other ancient Near Eastern nations, to Second Temple faith, recognizable as the precursor of Judaism and Christianity today.

Liturgical Psalms

The liturgical psalms (for instance, Psalms 15, 24, 81, and 118) are a somewhat miscellaneous group, but all are clearly designed for use in public worship. We have already mentioned that Psalm 50 seems to be a sort of teaching sermon regarding proper sacrifice. Most of the liturgical psalms involve several voices. Psalm 24, for instance, begins with a statement about YHWH's founding of the earth on the waters (see earlier for the mythological background). Someone then asks who may enter the temple: "Who shall ascend the hill of YHWH? / And who shall stand in his holy place?" (24:3; compare Ps. 15). An answer is given in verses 4 and 5: "Those who have clean hands and pure hearts, / who do not lift up their souls to what is false, / and do not swear deceitfully. / They will receive blessing from YHWH, / and vindication from the God of their salvation." Verse 6 ("such is the company of those who seek him") may be affirmation from the entering group that they meet the qualifications. In verses 7 and 9, an approaching group (perhaps carrying the ark signifying YHWH's presence) addresses the gatekeepers: "Lift up your heads, O gates! / and be lifted up, O ancient doors! / that the King of glory may come in." A challenge comes back in verses 8 and 10: "Who is this King of glory?" The answers list off YHWH's qualifications in ascending sequence: YHWH, strong and mighty, mighty in battle, YHWH of hosts, the King of glory!

Several of the liturgical psalms (50, 75, 81, 82, 95, and 132) apparently call for a prophet or priest to speak directly, in first person, on YHWH's behalf. Sometimes the message is a warning: "Hear, O my people, while I admonish you" (81:8). Overall, however, the tone is that of a God who yearns to bless. "O that my people would listen to me…with honey from the rock I would satisfy you" (81:13, 16). "I will abundantly bless its [Zion's] provisions; / I will satisfy its poor with bread" (132:15).

Wisdom Psalms

The psalm genres we have discussed so far tend to be addressed directly to God, and we can easily imagine their role in private or public worship, even if some of the associated customs (such as carrying the ark about, or offering animals for sacrifice) are strange to us. The wisdom psalms (for instance, Psalms 37, 49, 73, 112, 127, and 133) read less as prayers or hymns than as reflections on human life in the presence of God. A number of them are written in acrostic format (successive units begin with successive letters of the Hebrew alphabet). Many present a strikingly optimistic view of the relationship between faith and worldly happiness: "Happy is everyone who fears YHWH, / who walks in his ways. / You shall eat the fruit of the labor of your hands; / you shall be happy, and it shall go well with you" (128:1–2). Others, notably Psalm 73, take grim note of the exceptions: "I was envious of the arrogant; / I saw the prosperity of the wicked. / For they have no pain; / their bodies are sound and sleek" (73:3–4).

The Torah psalms (1, 19, and 119) are a special subset of wisdom psalms that especially praise the beauty and goodness of God's *torah,* or teaching. The massive Psalm 119 can function as a kind of meditative exercise to induce a mood of love for God's word, whereas Psalm 1's commendation of Torah meditation may be meant as instruction for reading the Psalter itself.

The Headings and Authorship of the Psalms

Modern and Ancient Headings

Many English Bibles give each psalm a descriptive title. For instance, Psalm 45 may be headed "A Royal Love Song" or "Ode for a Royal Wedding." These titles have been provided by modern translators and editors to help readers understand what each psalm is about. The problem with these clarifying titles is that they may function to limit our understandings of the psalms to which they are attached. For instance, Psalm 54 can easily be understood as a prayer for deliverance from enemies. But it can also be understood as a thank-you from someone who has already been delivered (see the last two verses). A heading that points us toward one of these possibilities may keep us from noticing the other. Because modern descriptive titles are *not* part of the original Hebrew text of the psalms, we should be careful about allowing them dictate our interpretations. They suggest reasonable ways of reading the psalms but should not rule out other reasonable possibilities.

Ancient editors also attached headings to most of the psalms. In English translations, these ancient headings typically appear in a special typeface just before the first verses of their psalms. The ancient heading of Psalm 102, for instance, reads, "a prayer of one afflicted, when faint and pleading before YHWH." Unlike the modern descriptive titles, these ancient headings *do* appear in the Hebrew text, where they are numbered among the verses. Thus, the verse of Psalm 102 that begins "Hear my prayer" is verse 1 in most English translations but verse 2 in the Hebrew text. (Two major translations, the NAB and the Jewish Publication Society's *Tanakh,* use the Hebrew numbering. Scholarly writers also tend to cite psalm verses by their Hebrew numbering, which means that the verse numbers given in advanced commentaries and articles may be higher than the numbering in most English Bibles by one or two psalm verses.) We noted earlier that many of the ancient headings contain musical instructions. For instance, Psalm 4's heading notes that the song is to be performed "with stringed instruments."

Often the ancient headings mention people or groups of people. Psalm 66 is marked "to the leader"; Psalm 25's heading says "of David"; and Psalm 42's heading says that it is "of the Korahites" (probably a guild of temple musicians). All these headings use the Hebrew preposition *le* plus the name of a person or group. Unfortunately, *le* is a very ambiguous term: It can mean "to," "for," "belonging to," or "in the style of." Interpreters have traditionally assumed that the person named is the author of the psalm, but *leDavid* could easily mean "in a style like David's" or "dedicated to David" rather than "written by David." Note that a psalm may be *le* more than one person. For instance, Psalm 39 is *le* the leader, *le* Jeduthun, and *le* David.

Did David Write the Psalms?

Both Jews and Christians have tended to read the *leDavid* notations as statements about authorship. This assumption has been reinforced by the fact that the headings of a few David psalms (3, 7, 18, 34, 51, 52, 54, 56, 57, 59, 60, 63, and 142) associate them with specific situations in David's life. Most biblical scholars today, however, doubt the historicity of these headings. To see why, let's look more closely at two situationally associated psalms.

Psalm 3's heading associates the psalm with David's flight from his son Absalom (described in 2 Sam. 14–16). Looking at the psalm itself, we can easily imagine that the speaker is a king. Who else would have so many enemies? This is furthermore a king in trouble. The enemies' line about "no help for you in God" (3:2) reminds us of Shimei's accusations in 2 Samuel 16:7–8: "YHWH has given the kingdom into the hand of your son Absalom...for you are a man of blood." We might suppose that the plea for deliverance in Psalm 3:7 was answered by God's subversion of Absalom's plans (2 Sam. 17:14). So far, things seem to fit.

The psalm, however, assumes that God stands firmly on the psalmist's side (enemy accusations not withstanding). The psalmist shows complete confidence that God will deliver and sustain him. In rising against the king, the enemies are effectively rising against God (in accord with the scenario of Ps. 2). In 2 Samuel, by contrast, Absalom's rebellion is instigated *by God* in response to David's abuses of power: "Thus says YHWH: I will raise up trouble against you from within your own house" (2 Sam. 12:11; notice the connection between the full text of this verse and 2 Sam. 16:22). This means that the psalm and 2 Samuel give us quite different depictions of YHWH's role.

Even more strikingly, in 2 Samuel David *knows* that God is involved in the rebellion, which is why David meekly flees rather than turning to fight. When Shimei hurls his accusations at the fleeing king in 2 Samuel 16, David says, "Let him alone, and let him curse; for YHWH has bidden him" (16:11). The psalm's speaker, by contrast, asks God to hit the enemies on the jaw and break their teeth (Ps. 3:7). This contrast between David's narratively reported responses during his flight from Absalom and the attitude displayed by the psalmist makes it difficult to combine the accounts as if both were accurate historical reports.

Now let's look at Psalm 51, attributed in the heading to David on the occasion of Nathan's confrontation with him over his adultery with Bathsheba (2 Sam. 11—12). This time, the psalmist's attitude fits well with David's repentance as reported in 2 Samuel. "Have mercy on me, O God...for I know my transgression" (Ps. 51:1, 3). But questions rise when we look carefully at the details of the psalm. "Against you [God], you alone, have I sinned," says the psalmist (51:4), but what about Uriah? Commentaries often explain that in biblical thought, a sin against the neighbor is a sin against God. True enough, but nowhere are we told that it thereby ceases to be a sin against the neighbor! For that matter, why does the heading mention Bathsheba and adultery but not Uriah and the more serious sin of murder? Why does the psalmist say, "I was born guilty"? Quite aside from whether the Israelites had any concept of original sin during the monarchic period (most interpreters believe they did not), the guilt at stake in the confrontation with Nathan was not one incurred at birth. The "crushed bones" of 51:8 have no referent in the Samuel account, and there is no indication that Jerusalem's walls or sacrificial services were compromised by David's sin (over against the implications of 51:18–19).

The language of the psalm raises further questions. Psalm 51 uses expressions and vocabulary that have far more in common with prophetic writings from the time of Jerusalem's fall and afterward than with older poems in the Bible (contrast Ps. 18, which might conceivably come from David's time). For instance, the plea for a clean heart and new spirit in 51:10 reminds us of the post-586 promise for a new covenant written on the heart (Jer. 31:31–33) and Ezekiel 36:26's promise, "A new heart I will give you, and a new spirit I will put within you" (see also Ezek. 11:19 and 18:31). We might similarly relate the crushed bones of Psalm 51:8 to Ezekiel 37's dry bones. The sinful mother and guilty baby of 51:5 may be linked to Ezekiel 16:3–4's accusations about Jerusalem's parentage and Jeremiah 3:25's statement about the people's collective sinfulness from youth. The cleansing of Psalm 51:7 recollects Ezekiel 36:25's promise, "I will sprinkle clean water upon you." All these prophetic images (broken bones, guilt from youth, cleansing, new heart and new spirit) are communal ones, related to the fall of Judah and its eventual restoration. If we use them as our key to interpretation, then the "I" of Psalm 51 becomes the community, and the final two verses make perfect sense: God's acceptance of the people's repentance will be signaled by the rebuilding of Jerusalem and God's glad receipt of its offerings.

Furthermore, if the psalm is "really" about exile and restoration, the heading's focus on adultery becomes understandable: Adultery had become the favorite prophetic metaphor for unfaithfulness to God ("against you, you alone..."). Therefore adultery, not murder, provides the point of contact with David's story. The implicit hope in the heading is that just as David eventually survived and prospered, so will the praying community.

To sum up, the details of Psalm 3 raise grave questions about whether it was really composed for the situation mentioned in its heading. Psalm 51's language and resonances point toward a historical situation centuries beyond David's time. Similar issues arise with other "Davidic" psalms, both those with situational headings and those with simple *leDavid* attributions. All this suggests that the simple *leDavid* headings should probably be understood as dedications of some sort, rather than statements about authorship. The more detailed situational headings (the ones that say, "of David, when...") may have been added at fairly late stage in the editing of the Psalter, perhaps in the Hellenistic Period (after 331 B.C.E.), when Jews became particularly interested in attributing their scriptures to ancient religious leaders. In a time of increasing interest in individual spirituality and prayer, when there was no longer any Davidic king (during most of the Second Temple period there was no Judean king of any kind), the situational headings helped make royal psalms relevant to all individuals by directing the reader's imagination from the royal speaker's special office to his human vulnerability. For instance, Psalm 3's heading shifts attention from the situation of an anonymous besieged king (the simplest reading of the psalm itself) to a David who has been betrayed by someone near and dear (a much more familiar situation for most readers). Even though only a minority of psalms have these situational headings, they suggest a personalizing interpretative approach that could be, and has been, adopted for virtually all the psalms.

The *leDavid* headings, then, do not provide solid ground for supposing that David actually wrote all the psalms that have them (although a few David psalms, such as Psalm 18, do seem to be very old). The more detailed situational headings tell us even less about when and why particular psalms were *written*. Instead, they suggest a way of *reading* David psalms as prayers of an individual in close relationship to God.

If David Didn't Write the Psalms, Who Did?

Who did write the psalms, then? The short answer is, "We don't know." A better answer might be, "Hymn writers, or their ancient equivalents." This cuts against our habit of trying to imagine an intensely personal context for each psalm, a habit encouraged by the Davidic situational headings (see above). But it fits with the contents of the psalms themselves. Many contain clear indications that they were meant for use in worship. Psalm 100, for instance, calls worshipers to "enter his gates with thanksgiving, /and his courts with praise" (v. 4) and is still used as a call to worship by many congregations today. Even psalms that use large amounts of personal "I" language describe matters in terms that can be appropriated by a variety of different people. Particular psalms may have been prompted by particular circumstances in a writer's life, as are many hymns today. But we don't preserve hymns as records of their writers' circumstances. Instead, we embrace them because we can read our own circumstances into them: They give us a language for expressing our own experiences and sentiments. In the same way, psalms do not seem to have been collected for their value as historical witnesses, but for their usefulness to the present and future. Sometimes this involved a change in application: A psalm originally written as propaganda in praise of a reigning king could later be understood to describe the virtues of God's own kingship; or Psalm 51, with its strong overtones of national repentance, could become a standard text for individual confession.

When were the psalms written? If we cannot depend on the heading to tell us who wrote a particular psalm, then we must date it primarily on internal evidence, asking about its linguistic and theological affinities and the situations to which it seems to refer. Applying these criteria to Psalm 51 suggests a date sometime after the fall of Jerusalem. As a very, *very* rough rule of thumb, many of the psalms in the first three-fifths of the Psalter (Ps. 1—89) may have come from the Monarchic Period (about 1000–586 B.C.E.), whereas most psalms in the latter part (Ps. 90—150) seem to be Second Temple psalms. This is not an absolute rule, however, because some Psalms early in the book (such as Ps. 51) seem to show later influence, and some psalms that come later (such as Ps. 110) may be "leftovers" from the Monarchic Period. Each individual psalm must be dated on its own evidence. The book as a whole seems to have reached its present form very late, in the last one or two centuries B.C.E., because Psalms manuscripts have been found at Qumran with psalms arranged in a different order from that of the present Hebrew Psalter.

The Organization of the Book of Psalms

Like the songs in our own hymnals, the Psalter's psalms seem to have been collected over time. Traces of earlier stages in the process are still visible—for instance, a note in Psalm 72:20 that says, "The prayers of David son of Jesse are ended." This comment must be a leftover from some earlier edition of Psalms, because in the present Psalter, some psalms before 72 are not David psalms, and some David psalms appear after 72.

At four points in the book of Psalms (Ps. 41:13; 72:18–19; 89:52; 106:48), we find blessing formulas that begin "Blessed be YHWH" and conclude with the word "Amen." Each of these blessings seems to occur at a break point in the Psalter. For instance, the blessing in 41:13 comes at the end of a long string of David psalms. In Psalm 42, something new begins: a long string of psalms attributed to "the Korahites" (probably a guild of singers). Tradition has interpreted the four blessing formulas as dividers that separate the Psalter into five parts or "books."

Possibly this five-part division was meant to correspond to the five parts of the Torah. If so, Psalm 1's reflection on the happy fortunes of the one who delights in Torah and meditates on it day and night may be meant to suggest the proper approach to Psalms, as well as to the so-called books of Moses.

Explicitly royal psalms occur at three key junctures in this five-part arrangement. Immediately following Psalm 1, and paired with it by lack of a heading (unusual in a Book 1 psalm) and the opening/closing formula "happy is/are," comes Psalm 2, which seems to be a coronation psalm. The psalm begins with a stereotyped scenario of earth's political powers plotting a rebellion against YHWH. Verse 3 quotes their rebellious words. But YHWH, verses 4 and 5 tell us, just laughs at their puny threats. In verse 6, YHWH speaks, announcing God's own action: "I have set my king on Zion, my holy hill." In verses 7 to 9, we hear the king's voice, telling how God has chosen him. Embedded in the king's words we find another quote of what YHWH has said, beginning with "you are my son; today I have begotten you." This quote tells us two things. First, it suggests that the king in Jerusalem was thought of as having a special son/father relationship with YHWH. (This idea is also articulated in 2 Sam. 7:14; 1 Chron. 17:13; and Ps. 89:26.) Second, because the decree is reported by a grown man (or at least one old enough to proclaim the words), we must think of the "begetting" in symbolic or heavenly terms rather than as a literal report. This fits well with the extravagant promise reported: "Ask of me, and I will make the nations your heritage" (v. 8).

The translation of the final verses (10–12) is a little uncertain, but clearly they are addressed mostly to the rebellious kings, who are warned that they will perish if they do not submit to YHWH (or his anointed king). The closing line, "Happy are all who take refuge in him" (is "him" YHWH or the king?), serves to reassure the congregation that their national future is secure.

The promises of Psalm 2—especially coming to us, as they do, from a long-fallen kingdom—are clearly extravagant. They express a longing and an ideal for how God was supposed to relate to the king, rather than a literal reality. Realizing the distance between these promises and the realm of any normal king, early Christians supposed that the words must "really" apply to Jesus, whom Christians proclaimed as God's literally begotten son (Mt. 1:20) and "anointed one" (Hebrew, *messiah;* Greek, *christos*). As we will see, many other parts of the ancient royal ideal were also applied to Jesus. But there is no evidence that the original composer or hearers of Psalm 2 would have understood the words as describing a far-future messiah whose kingdom was "not from this world" (Jn. 18:36). Instead, they would have heard the psalm as affirmation that their nation's government was divinely instituted, approved, and upheld.

Psalm 72, the final psalm of Book 2, also articulates a royal ideal. Like Psalm 2, it imagines Jerusalem's king as ruler of the known world ("all nations give him service"; Ps. 72:11), but it also pictures him as a bringer of righteousness and prosperity within the nation. He will deliver the needy and administer justice. Even the agricultural economy will prosper under his care (72:4, 6, 16). His reign will be long lasting, so that the people need not fear the dangerous turmoil associated with changes of royal administration.

Book	Psalms included	Imaginative time frame
Book 1	Psalms 1—41	Ideal monarchy (David)
Book 2	Psalms 42—72	Ideal monarchy (David)
Book 3	Psalms 73—89	Fall of monarchy
Book 4	Psalms 90—106	Exile
Book 5	Psalms 107—150	Second Temple Period

Although the psalm ends with a note about "the prayers of David son of Jesse" (72:20), Psalm 72's heading refers to Solomon (*leShelomoh*) rather than David. Because its opening verse mentions a king's son, one possibility is to read it as a prayer of David *for (le)* Solomon. If this is the case, then Books 1 and 2 of the Psalter *imaginatively* span the period of David's active rule, from his coronation to his handing over of power to his son Solomon. This imaginative picture is enhanced by the fact that most of the Psalter's David psalms occur in Books 1 and 2. In about half these David psalms, an individual "I" voice, who could easily be a king, appeals to God for help on the basis of a strong personal relationship such as the one suggested in Psalm 2. Nonetheless, the identification of Books 1 and 2 as "Davidic" is an imaginative construct, for we have seen that not all the David psalms fit the reported circumstances of David's life, and some of the psalms in Books 1 and 2, such as Psalm 51, show signs of having been composed around or after the fall of Jerusalem (about half a millennium later than David's time).

Book 3 begins with a meditation on the contrast between God's promised goodness to the people (in Hebrew, Ps. 73 begins, "Truly God is good to Israel," rather than "good to the upright") and the observed prosperity of the wicked. It closes, in another strategically located royal psalm, with an anguished accusation that God is "full of wrath against your anointed" and with the question, "Will you [God] hide yourself forever?" (Ps. 89:38, 46). In between, we find many psalms lamenting military defeat and pleading for God's help for the nation (Ps. 74, 79, 80, 82, 83, 85). Imaginatively, this book then represents the long downhill slide recorded in 1 and 2 Kings, culminating in the fall of Judah and the Babylonian captivity of its king and other national leaders.

Book 4 begins, surprisingly, with a *le* Moses psalm—the only such psalm in the entire collection. In fact, seven of the Psalter's eight mentions of Moses come in Book 4. (This is, by the way, a startlingly small number of times to mention someone who figures so prominently in the Torah. It raises questions about just how central the exodus/Sinai/wilderness experiences really were for temple worship, especially in the First Temple Period.) Yet, imaginatively, Book 4 is the exilic book. In its opening psalm, the people wail that "we are consumed by your [YHWH's] anger" (Ps. 90:7), and in its closing psalm they plead, "Gather us from among the nations" (Ps. 106:47). Why, then, the emphasis on Moses? We can distinguish three reasons.

First, as we saw in Psalm 2, appeals to Davidic covenant theology all too naturally tended to emphasize God's promises, without saying too much about God's demands. As the royal covenant is presented in Psalm 89, God did reserve the right to punish the Davidic kings (vv. 30–32), but the bottom line was that their throne would be secure (vv. 33–37). Mosaic covenant theology, by contrast, placed more emphasis on the obedience that God expected from the people. Its clear threats of punishment for disobedience made it easier to explain how Jerusalem could have fallen.

Second, even though Moses was associated with God's commands, he was also remembered as a leader who had interceded successfully for the people when God became angry with them (recall especially the golden calf incident in Ex. 32—34). "[YHWH] said he would destroy them," proclaims Psalm 106:23, "had not Moses, his chosen one, / stood in the breach before him, / to turn away his wrath from destroying them." Book 4 dedicates its opening prayer to this Moses in the hope that God's wrath will once again be turned away.

Finally, Moses was associated with the wilderness wanderings (between exodus and entry into the land), an experience that became the dominant theological symbol for Babylonian exile. (We have already seen wilderness imagery used for the exile in the prophetic writings, particularly Isa. 40—55.) Remembering Moses' wilderness leadership gave the exiles hope that even if they were weak and fell prey to murmuring and complaining (Ps. 106), they too would eventually travel from their wilderness to Judah.

Book 4 is noteworthy not only for its emphasis on Moses, but also for its string of enthronement psalms (93; 95—99). Their proclamation that "YHWH is king!" provides another part of the book's response to the Davidic dynasty's fall: The people still have their real king, who is God, still very much in charge. Some of the Book 4 psalms may have come from the First Temple Period, before Jerusalem's fall, and some may have been composed later in the Second Temple Period, but imaginatively, they are now arranged to speak from and about the period between Jerusalem's fall and the return of its ruling class under Cyrus.

Given the imaginative "historical" framework emerging in our survey of the books of the Psalter, it will come as no surprise that Book 5, which we can by now expect to be the Second Temple book, begins with a call for thanks from "the redeemed of YHWH," those who have been "gathered in from the lands" (Ps. 107:2–3). Book 5 does still contain some *leDavid* (108—110; 122; 124; 131; 138—145) and royal (110; 118; 132; 144) psalms, but unlike the first three books, it is not dominated by prayers for help. Instead, it contains the Psalter's greatest concentration of praise and thanksgiving psalms. Note especially its closing run of psalms (146—150), each beginning and ending with a call to "Praise YHWH"—in Hebrew, *Hallelujah!*

Book 5 has a roughly concentric shape. The runs of David psalms near the beginning and end (Ps. 108—110; 138—145) are each bracketed by "give thanks" and "praise YHWH" psalms. In the middle, Book 5 has two "hearts." The first is the massive Psalm 119, with eight verses (sixteen lines) for each of the twenty-two letters of the Hebrew alphabet. Every stanza praises God's word (or law, commandment, ordinances, etc.) and proclaims the psalmist's faithfulness. Not a single one of the 176 verses mentions "us" or "we," making Psalm 119 a fitting capstone to Psalm 1's theme of individual meditation on God's word. Reading Psalm 119 aloud (which is how all writing seems to have been read in ancient times) becomes a kind of meditative exercise that induces precisely the mode of awe and love of God's word of which the psalm speaks.

Book 5's other "heart" is the collection of fifteen "songs of Ascents" (Ps. 120—134). Different theories exist about the meaning of the "Ascents" heading on each of these psalms, but most agree that these psalms were somehow linked with pilgrimage to Jerusalem. All the Ascents psalms are fairly short, with lovely lyrical images, and are good candidates for memorization (Psalms 121, 122, 130, and 131 are especially popular memory psalms). Although the collection contains a variety of prayers, reflections, and calls to praise, it seems overall to point toward the joy of communal worship in the (Second) Temple. Perhaps the king who reported such extravagant divine promises in Psalm 2 is gone now, but the Ascents collection suggests that God still oversees the collective life and well-being of the people.

The Theology of the Psalms

A great deal about the theology of the Psalms has already been said in this chapter. In closing, we attend to just two central points: the royal theology of the psalms and their human honesty.

Royal Visions

The book of Psalms directs our attention to two kings: the human Davidic king and God. The divine king, YHWH, rules over both earth and heaven (including the other heavenly powers; Ps. 89:7; 95:3). YHWH does so by right of creation (sometimes pictured as a victory over chaos forces embodied in the waters). As high king, YHWH is now responsible for maintaining justice and caring for society's least powerful members (Ps. 10:14, 18; 146:9). Psalm 82 (see also 58) suggests that other gods have forfeited their divine rights by failing to carry out these responsibilities of justice and protection.

The human Davidic king rules only as an agent of YHWH: "I have found my servant David; /with my holy oil I have anointed him" (89:20). As YHWH's agent, he too is responsible for justice and care of the weak. "In your majesty ride on victoriously / for the cause of truth and to defend the right" (45:4). "He delivers the needy when they call, /the poor and those who have no helper" (72:12). He is even supposed to bring fertility to the land: "May he be like rain that falls on the mown grass," "may there be abundance of grain in the land" (72:6, 16). God's assistance will make him victorious in war: "YHWH will help his anointed;/ he will answer him from his holy heaven / with mighty victories by his right hand" (20:6).

With respect to the people (and the kings of other nations), the Davidic king is godlike: "I will make him the firstborn, the highest [or "most high"; *'Elyon*] of the kings of the earth" (89:27). With respect to YHWH, of course, he is a servant (89:20), but also a son (2:7; 89:26). The language of the covenant between king and God emphasizes not the legal details of their transactions (what we might call "contractual" language) but the love, trust, and mutual loyalty that should exist between them (18:1–3, 50, the language of household relationships).

What happened to such ideals after the Davidic dynasty fell in 587–586 B.C.E.? One answer is that Judaism and eventually Christianity came to view this highly personal relationship with God as the model and norm for all believers, not just the king. This has allowed ordinary believers through the subsequent centuries to appropriate originally royal psalms as their own prayers. Meanwhile, people continued to long for government that would fulfill the royal tradition's ideals of prosperity, safety, justice, and compassionate care for the weak. Some hoped that God would anoint a new king ("*messiah*") to bring about such a reign. The Christian writers of the Second Testament applied royal terms such as "king," "Lord," "anointed," "son" (of God and of David), and "servant" to Jesus. However, they also saw that the world was not yet operating according to the standards of the longed-for messianic kingdom, which is why they continued to look for a fulfillment to come in the future.

The traditional application of royal language to Jesus makes it look, in Christian hindsight, as if many of the royal psalms are "prophecies" of Jesus. It would be more honest for Christians to acknowledge the connection between royal ideals and Jesus without trying to assert that such psalms were originally intended to speak of Jesus. Believers might also do well to reflect that in the democratization of royal theology, ordinary Christians and Jews fall heir to the responsibilities (justice and care for the weak) of the king, as well as to his privilege of personal relationship with God.

Honesty in Prayer

The diverse genres of psalms cover a wide range of human experience and emotions and display a variety of viewpoints regarding God (for instance, the psalms articulate a range of opinions on whether righteousness reliably leads to prosperity in this life). In many places, particularly when the psalmists speak of their enemies, we see them all too blithely assuming their own righteousness and a corresponding Godforsakenness for their enemies. When a psalmist asks for enemies to be "like the untimely birth that never sees the sun" (58:8) or declares a blessing on those who dash "little ones" against the rock (137:9), we need to remind ourselves that these are very human words *to* God. We must not confuse the psalmists' beliefs and desires with God's own.

Often, however, the *process* of the psalms testifies to something slightly different than their *content*. Psalm 88:14, for instance, asks, "Why do you hide your face from me?" Focusing only on the content, as Bible readers are often wont to do, we would come away from this with some very troubling questions about God's hiddenness. If we take time to explore the context of the statement (always a good idea when studying the Bible), we might become even more troubled, as we encounter statements such as, "You [God] have put me in the depths of the Pit" and "You have caused friend and neighbor to shun me" (88:6, 18).

But although the *content* of this psalmist's words testifies that he or she feels isolated and in mortal danger and considers God directly responsible for the situation, the *process* of the prayer says something different. Clearly, the psalmist has not given up on the conviction that God cares and may yet be persuaded to reverse the situation. The next psalm, 89, exhibits a similar disparity between content and process. After a hopeful beginning declaring that "your [God's] steadfast love is established forever; / your faithfulness is as firm as the heavens" (v. 2) the psalmist boldly accuses, "You have renounced the covenant" (v. 39). Yet despair does not lead the psalmist to turn away from God. Instead, we get a call for God to return to faithfulness: *Remember,* the psalmist pleads in 89:47 and 50. Surely the "steadfast love of old" (89:49) can be recovered!

We noted earlier in this chapter that although the standard lament template ends in statements of trust or praise, not every lament psalm closes in this fashion. The two psalms just mentioned, 88 and 89, are among those that close without such "resolution." This leads to yet another observation about their process: Not only does the psalmist continue to call on God, but the psalmist does not feel obliged to supply an answer on God's behalf. Unlike Job's friends (see chap. 14), these psalmists are willing to leave the ball in God's court. They make their plea and then stop, in faith that God may actually answer.

The psalms thus testify to a God who meets humans in the messy concreteness of personal and political life. They testify to a God who cares about human feelings and problems. They testify to a God who attends not only to praise and confessions of trust but also to human confusion, anger, questions, and accusations. Psalms offers a model for spirituality that begins with honesty about who we are, how we feel, and what we want. The Psalter ends with praise—but it does not begin there.

Resources

Leslie C. Allen. *Psalms 101–150.* Vol. 21 of *Word Biblical Commentary.* Rev. ed. Nashville: Thomas Nelson Publishers, 2002.

William H. Bellinger, Jr. *Psalms: Reading and Studying the Book of Praises.* Peabody, Mass.: Hendrickson Publishers, 1990.

Peter C. Craigie. *Psalms 1–50.* Vol. 19 of *Word Biblical Commentary.* Waco, Tex.: Word Publishing, 1983.

Carroll Stuhlmueller. "Psalms." In *The HarperCollins Bible Commentary,* edited by James L. Mays. Rev. ed. San Francisco: Harper San Francisco, 2000.

Marvin E. Tate. *Psalms 51–100.* Vol. 20 of *Word Biblical Commentary.* Waco, Tex.: Word Publishing, 1991.

13

Proverbs and Ecclesiastes

LEO G. PERDUE

Proverbs and Ecclesiastes belong to a body of writings that scholars refer to as wisdom literature. Job (discussed in chap. 14) and the apocryphal books of Sirach and the Wisdom of Solomon (discussed in chap. 16) also fall into this category. Similar literature was produced in Egypt and Mesopotamia, and these other ancient Near Eastern wisdom writings provide a helpful context for understanding the biblical wisdom books. This chapter begins by highlighting some features of biblical wisdom literature in general. We then turn to the specific books of Proverbs and Ecclesiastes.

Wisdom Literature

The term *wisdom* can be used in more than one sense with respect to First Testament writings. In the first, narrower sense, it refers to the wisdom books mentioned above, which employ distinctive literary forms associated with wisdom. These forms include characteristic types of sayings (such as those that designate one thing "better than" something else or identify a category of person that is "happy" or "blessed"), direct instructions about how to live, and philosophical dialogue.

Within the wisdom literature itself, however, *wisdom* refers less to knowledge of the scientific variety than to practical and moral knowledge and virtues such as piety ("the fear of God/YHWH"), discipline, moderation, diplomatic and appealing use of language, respect for wise ancestors, and the obtaining of righteousness (the cosmic order that resides at the basis of communal and individual life). These virtues are to be cultivated and actualized in the life of the sage. The Hebrew and Greek nouns for "wisdom" (*hokma* and *sophia*) are feminine, and "Wisdom" is sometimes personified as a woman with features of a goddess.

Finally, scholars sometimes use the term *wisdom* in a broad sense to describe the worldview expressed in a variety of writings that share vocabulary and values with the wisdom literature and might be supposed to come from similar social circles. It is in this broader sense, for instance, that Moshe Weinfeld argues for a "wisdom" connection in Deuteronomy (see p. 73) and that the stories of Daniel 1—6 are described as "wisdom tales" (see pp. 245–46). Although the wisdom books proper are found in the Writings division of the Hebrew canon, the occurrence of wisdom language and themes in the Torah and Prophets (for instance, Jer. 17:5–11) suggests that the sages who compiled the wisdom literature were also among the final editors of the Hebrew Bible.

An interesting aspect of Proverbs, Ecclesiastes, and Job is that their writers do not ground their work in the election traditions of ancient Israel. (By contrast, the apocryphal wisdom books discussed in chapter 16 do appeal to special covenant traditions.) Instead, the sages of the Hebrew Bible point to creation as the theological key to religious and moral understanding. They think that reason, experience, and astute observation of creation are the means by which to come to a knowledge of God and reality. This suggests that the God who originated and continues to sustain the cosmic order is open to all peoples. Thus, the sages of Israel recognize the authenticity of wisdom in other nations, even though Israelite wisdom may be deemed superior (1 Kings 4:29–34).

During the 1900s C.E., most Christian biblical scholars and theologians identified God's special acts for Israel and God's special covenants with that people as the heart of First Testament biblical theology. The Hebrew Bible's wisdom books, which have almost nothing to say about salvation history and covenants, were accordingly ignored or even denigrated. Today, interest in the wisdom books is increasing, in part because wisdom theology offers a helpful basis for Christian dialogue with other religions and the natural sciences.

Proverbs

In Proverbs, wisdom is both the ability to observe a righteous order (*tsedaqa*) in the cosmos and the incorporation of this righteousness (*tsedeq*) in the everyday speech and action of the community and the individual. One who does this successfully is "righteous" (*tsaddiq*). Thus, wisdom is strongly associated with justice or righteousness, centered in the defining character of God the creator.

Social Settings

The book of Proverbs reflects a variety of social settings, including the family household, in which father and mother instructed their children in moral behavior, and the royal school, in which the children of the ruling house, nobles, and future scribes and officials were instructed in proper behavior. The education of scribes and bureaucrats in the postmonarchic period likewise covered a variety of areas, including morality (see the essays in Gammie and Perdue).

Sages in these settings were largely conservatives who sought to undergird and maintain the social orders of the household, royal court, and (in the postexilic period) ruling empires that incorporated Judah/Judea into their political system as a small colony. Thus, sages included parents, teachers in royal and colonial schools, and scribes who transmitted their knowledge to their children in the form of household guilds. The most complete description of the postexilic sage is found in an apocryphal text, Sirach 38:34–39:11 (probably written in the 100s B.C.E.).

The Genres of Proverbs

Most of the genres of wisdom literature are found in Proverbs. These include the wisdom sayings: the proverb, the comparison, the beatitude, the numerical saying, and the better saying. The sayings provided a detailed study of life, with special attention to moral virtues. The sage who committed these brief sayings to memory would savor not only their content but also their rhetorical craft. Form and content entwined to shape a world of beauty and order, in which knowledgeable sages might expect to enjoy longevity, happiness, honor, harmony, and a family with children.

The Hebrew word for these sayings, *mashal,* comes from a verb meaning "to be like" or "to compare" and also "to master or rule." On the one hand, the term suggests an understanding of reality as a well-integrated order in which meaningful relationships exist between diverse things. On the other, it hints at how the sages sought through their sayings to master life—to know how and when to act in various circumstances.

The *mashal* usually consists of two parallel lines. The second line may develop the thought and language of the first (synonymous parallelism, found for instance in Prov. 21:12 and 22:7, 8, 14), contrast with the first in language or thought (antithetical parallelism, found in 10:4, 5, 12), or extend the language or thought of the first (synthetic parallelism, found in 15:3 and 21:6, 7, 21). In a comparison, two objects, not immediately similar, are said to resemble each other in one or more ways (for instance, 10:26 and 11:2). A numerical saying lists two or more things that are held together by a common feature (30:15–16, 18–19, 21–23, 24–28, 29–31). In the "better" saying, one item is identified as more valued than another, although the latter may also possess desirable features (see 15:16, 17). A "happy" saying refers to a state of joy or blessing of one who practices a virtue or possesses a valued thing (for instance, 3:13 and 14:21). An "abomination" saying identifies unethical actions that adversely affect both the doer and the larger community (for instance, 3:32 and 6:16). On occasion, sages might make their points with rhetorical, catechetical, or impossible questions (see 20:9, 24 and 22:27).

Proverbs also contains at least two longer wisdom forms. The instruction on the moral life consists of an introduction exhorting the audience to listen and obey, a list of admonitions and prohibitions coupled with a dependent clause, and a conclusion that points to the results of following or ignoring the teaching (for instance, 1:8–19). A wisdom poem is an artistically shaped form of two or more strophes such as the texts about Woman Wisdom (1:20–33, 8–9 and 31:10–31).

Literary Structure

Superscriptions (the first of which introduces both the first section and the entire book) divide Proverbs into seven collections. An eighth division, the concluding poem, has no superscription. (Note: Translations in this chapter are by the author.)

"The Proverbs of Solomon, Son of David, King of Israel" (Prov. 1—9)
"The Proverbs of Solomon" (10:1—22:16)
"The Sayings of the Wise" (22:17—24:22)
"These Also Are Sayings of the Wise" (24:23–34)
"These Are Other Proverbs of Solomon That the Officials of King Hezekiah of Judah Copied" (25—29)
"The Words of Agur" (30)
"The Words of King Lemuel of Massa, Which His Mother Taught Him" (31:1–9)
An acrostic poem on the ideal Wise Woman (31:10–31)

The superscriptions of Proverbs, like those of several other wisdom texts, were provided by editors who collected the sections. The superscriptions contain little, if any, directly reliable historical information, but they do suggest that sages originated the original collections by drawing on sayings and other genres of wisdom texts from the school traditions and perhaps also by composing sayings. The references to Solomon and Hezekiah imply royal patronage of the work of the scribes. (Israelite and Jewish legend also associates Solomon with Ecclesiastes, the Wisdom of Solomon, and the Song of Songs, perhaps because Solomon is so closely associated with wisdom in 1 Kings 3—11.) It is helpful to note that wisdom texts of other ancient Near Eastern cultures also tie wisdom to royal courts (see, for example, the Egyptian instructions of Ptah-hotep, Meri-ka-Re, and Amenemhet [Pritchard, 414–425]). The symbolization of wisdom in the form of Solomon and the royal court suggests a new way of viewing the world as Israel moved from a more mythic understanding of reality to the analytical way of knowing grounded in empirical observation and reasoned thought. This allowed for openness to knowledge that resided in creation and was encapsulated in wisdom texts not only in Israel but also in the other various cultures of the ancient Near East with whom Israel and later Judah/Judea came into direct contact.

Major Themes

Proverbs covers a multitude of topics, which may be divided into five major categories: the household, kingship and the court, the path to sagehood, the personification of wisdom, and creation theology.

The Household. Because of its economic value and central importance in communal order (24:3–4 and 24:27), the household was one of the social locations for the teaching of wisdom and also served as a major topic of reflection. The possessions of a household, including its material property, people, and livestock, were of great value and came as a blessing to the wise. Loss of them was one of the great afflictions overwhelming the wicked and foolish (24:30–34. The tradition of the sages may have been formed and transmitted, at least in part, in households in which parents educated their children in virtues associated with the family (6:20–23). The household was multigenerational and extended laterally to include unmarried aunts, uncles, and more distant relatives. In addition, day laborers, bond servants, and slaves were marginal members of the household unit (17:2). Most households consisted of two or more houses, often sharing one or more walls and a common courtyard for household tasks and cooking. The large majority were rural, and even city dwellers likely owned nearby farms. Central to the value of the household was the patrimony, which included the land and its buildings, livestock, utensils, and tools. When the household's head died, the larger share of the property would go to a descendant, normally the firstborn son, and other portions to the remaining children (13:22). A household's wealth and means of existence depended largely on the produce and livestock of the patrimony. If a household's property was lost, the family's surviving members would enter into marginal status as slaves, bond servants, and day laborers to other families (27:10). Sages taught that to lose land was one of the worst possible punishments for foolish or wicked behavior, and its continued possession was one of the greatest blessings (2:21–22; 3:33; 11:29; 14:11).

Male sages were blessed by having one wife (marriage was usually monogamous) who was virtuous, industrious, wise, and the mother of numerous offspring (2:17; 18:22; 19:13; 31:10–31). Having a foolish or contentious wife was considered a great misfortune (25:24; 27:15–16). Adultery and fornication with the "strange woman" was a threat to the integrity of the household (5:1–23; 6:24–35; 7:1–27). Virtuous and wise children were valued, and foolish and wicked offspring brought great sorrow to their parents (10:1; 15:20; 17:6, 25; 19:13, 26; 23:24; 28:7, 24; 29:3; 30:11, 17). Wise and obedient children were supposed to follow their elders' teaching, accept the chastening of their punishment, work diligently, and care for aged parents (1:8; 15:5; 19:26; 20:20; 22:6; 23:13–16, 22; 29:3, 15, 17). The sages upheld a strong household work ethic, warning that laziness led to impoverishment and disaster (6:4–11; 10:3–5; 12:11; 19:15).

Kingship and the Court. Also central to Israelite community life, at least during the period of the monarchy, was kingship (see the discussion of superscriptions earlier). Rulers were mainstays of order for the larger community (28:2), and the court served as one social location for the cultivation and transmission of wisdom. Without the legitimate order of righteous kings, even foreign ones, chosen by God through Woman Wisdom (8:15–16), disruption and chaos threatened (14:28; 29:2, 16). Therefore, slaves should not rule over kings (19:10), nor maidens over their mistresses (30:23). Ideally, kings possessed wisdom and were to rule justly (8:15–16), so that many would seek their favor (29:26). Kings, above all, were to incorporate the virtues of wisdom (31:2–9), including defending the rights of the poor and more generally engaging in righteous rule (31:8–9). For kings to rule wickedly was an abomination to God (16:12; see 28:15), for they were a major instrument of divine decisions (21:1). They were responsible for punishing the wicked (20:26) and depended on the wise righteous for counsel (29:12). Although the kings possessed great power and wisdom, enabling them to rule justly (28:16; 29:4, 14) and for a long time (29:14), even their reigns did not last forever (27:24).

For those in the presence of kings, the sages counseled proper decorum (23:1–3). They taught that wisdom and righteous behavior would bring royal favor (19:12; 22:11) and avert royal wrath (14:35; 16:12; 20:2).

The Path to Sagehood. Proverbs stresses that wisdom is not simply a matter of understanding, but also of action, a "way" of life (1:15; 2:8–15, 20; 4:10–16, 26–27; 5:6; 8:20; 10:17; 12:28). The divine gift of wisdom comes only to those willing to walk the path to sagehood—a lifelong journey continued even by aged sages (1:2–7). It begins with piety ("fear of YHWH/ God," 1:7; 2:5; 3:7; 8:13; 9:10; 31:30) and includes the pursuit and study of wisdom, proper speech, reason and experience, control of the passions, and retribution. It leads to insight and fullness of life (4:1–9).

This emphasis on "walk" includes a concern for proper "talk." A sage knows what to say and when, avoids loquaciousness, and coins wise sayings, whereas the fool lies, flatters, and deceives (10:11, 18–19, 21, 31–32; 11:9, 13; 12:6; 13:3; 14:25; 15:1–2, 23, 26; 16:27–28, 32; 17:4, 7; 19:1, 9, 19; 25:11–22; 28:23; 29:5). The rhetoric of language is as important as the content (10:20; 26:9).

We have noted that the sages were not secular humanists who avoided religious faith, but rather were religious men and women who believed that their wisdom originated with God (2:6–7; 3:5–10). The sages used their reason—attributed to God—to draw conclusions about the nature of the cosmos, the community, and individual life. Experience was the arena for testing those conclusions. A teaching that did not coincide with experience was disputed or repudiated.

Sages were especially concerned about controlling their passions, from sexual desire to anger (5:7–23; 7; 10:12; 14:17, 29–30; 15:18; 17:27–28; 18:6–8, 21; 25:23). They described the fool as one led astray by lust, pride, and anger (5:7–23; 16:18; 21:24; 22:24).

The sages generally adhered to a doctrine of retribution, believing that God rewards the virtuous and punishes wicked fools (3:33–34; 5:7–23; 12:7, 19, 21; 20:22). Blessings for the wise included long and prosperous lives, wise and virtuous wives and obedient children, happiness and contentment, and harmony with the cosmos and the community (2:21–22; 3:1–2, 13–18, 22, 33; 8:18–21). Fools who rejected wisdom's invitation to life (1:22–33) were likely to die young, suffering pain, ostracism, and poverty (1:19). Yet the sages recognized that at times even the wise could experience poverty, and the foolish wicked could gain power and wealth (10:3). Even wise action could not abrogate YHWH's judgments (20:24; 25:2; 27:1; Koch 1983).

The Personification of Wisdom. Proverbs personifies Woman Wisdom as the medium of creation (Prov. 8:22–31). She is the Queen of Heaven who selects kings to rule and who, as God's instrument, maintains the creation of the world (8:12–21). She is also a teacher who exhorts the unlearned to take up wisdom and thereby avoid destruction (1:20–33). She instructs the simple in wisdom (8:1–11) and gives abundant life to the wise and righteous (8:32–36). Taken as a whole, she becomes the voice of God who is heard in the wisdom tradition that she personifies and in the teachings of the sages. In the concluding poem (31:10–31), she becomes incarnate in the "Woman of Worth" who embodies wisdom ideals for the household.

Creation Theology. The central theological theme of Proverbs is that God creates and sustains the cosmos, the righteous community, and individual human lives. The sages, through their teachings and actions, participate in sustaining the divinely shaped reality (Perdue, 1994).

Creation of the cosmos is first articulated in a poetic fragment in 3:19–20 that uses architectural metaphors to describe God's establishment of the earth through wisdom and securing or sustaining of the heavens by means of understanding (see also 8:27, 29; 24:3). Wisdom continues to maintain order in world, community, and individual life. Echoes of a creation battle with chaos are found in 3:20 (compare Ex. 14:16; Isa. 51:9–11; Neh. 9:11; and Ps. 78:13). Last of all, YHWH brings life-giving moisture in the form of dew that sustains life (3:20; compare Job 28:25–26 and 36:27–28).

In Proverbs 8:22–31, Wisdom—having called potential students in 8:1–21—describes her own role in creation. She uses metaphors of engendering and birth ("I was brought forth" and "I was poured out") to speak of herself as YHWH's firstborn, "the little child" who becomes mediator between God and the inhabited world (8:22, 24) in which she delights. This is not creation *ex nihilo* ("out of nothing"), but rather shaping from a formless void. YHWH's divine decrees form a three–part universe that is secured by mountain pillars and imposes limits on the waters of the sea (which was often viewed in ancient Near Eastern myth as a chaos monster).

Wisdom and creation are also present elsewhere in Proverbs. In 10:1—22:16, creation theology is taken up in the issue of justice for the helpless and needy. Although the sages greatly value wealth (10:15; 13:8) as a divine reward for wisdom, righteous action, and individual industry, they also recognize that wealth can come from evil behavior (11:16; 28:15–16). The poor, regardless of the reasons for their lot in life, deserve charity from the wise and well-to-do (14:31). Care for the poor is grounded in YHWH's role as creator and defender of the poor and desolate. Although the sages' sphere of responsibility for fellow humans does not seem to extend beyond ethnic boundaries, it does include all Israel. One honors YHWH not simply in giving offerings but also in acts of charity on behalf of the poor (19:17; 28:8). Acts of oppression, by contrast, insult the creator, and the perpetrator will not be held innocent (17:5). YHWH, creator of the organs of knowing and perceiving, gives light to the eyes of the poor, as well as to their oppressors (20:12; 29:13).

The topic of rich and poor reappears in 22:2, 7, 9. The generous who share their bread with the poor are blessed, though the wealthy are often those in power who govern the poor. When rich and poor meet in social processes of intercession, negotiation, and litigation, they should remember that YHWH is creator of them both. The wealthy are to remember their origins in dealing justly with the needy.

Ecclesiastes

Date and Context

The form of Hebrew used in Ecclesiastes (sometimes referred to by its Hebrew title, Qoheleth) indicates that the book most likely dates from the late 300s B.C.E. In the first verse, the anonymous author refers to himself as "the Teacher [Hebrew *Qoheleth*], son of David, king in Jerusalem." The term translated "teacher" is a feminine participle of the verb *qahal,* meaning "to gather, or assemble" (from whence the Greek *ecclesiastes,* "assemblyman," derives). It probably refers either to a teacher who gathers students or to a wise editor who assembles sayings and other literary forms. The words "son of David, king in Jerusalem" gave rise to the legend that the book was written by Solomon, the supposed author of several wisdom writings. However, the phrase simply means a descendant of David, a Davidic ruler, not necessarily an immediate son. The "teacher," who presumably is the author of the text, seeks to give added weight to the authority of what he teaches by assuming a royal role. The epilogue (12:9–10) abandons this pose of royalty and describes Qoheleth as one who was "wise," "taught knowledge to the people," and "weighed," "studied," and "arranged" numerous sayings.

The Genre of Ecclesiastes

An imaginary instruction attributed to a long-deceased king is a form with many parallels in the Bible and elsewhere. The book is not simply an anecdotal collection of sayings but a first-person narrative that depicts a teacher instructing an audience. Two "righteous sufferer poems" from Mesopotamia ("A Man and His God" and "I Will Praise the Lord of Wisdom" [Pritchard, 589–91 and 596–600]) have important similarities to Qoheleth, including first-person narrative by a fictional aristocratic narrator and the questioning of divine judgment, but are not presented as the words of dead kings.

Closer parallels may be found in Egypt. For instance, in a song found in a royal tomb dating from the First Intermediate Period (2160–2040 B.C.E.), a harper instructs visitors in the importance of celebrating the deceased's life and in skepticism about any future existence (Pritchard, 467).

Similar to the "song of the harper" are the grave biographies common in ancient Egypt from the Old Kingdom through Hellenistic times. These tomb inscriptions are presented as words of the deceased that provide instruction for righteous living. These biographies seek not only to teach wisdom to the living but also to summarize the deceased persons' lives in order that they may make their way into the afterlife. However, later examples begin to emphasize the caprice of gods whose sovereign will and work are beyond human knowledge. These texts also begin to express skepticism about the efficacy of mortuary religion in leading to the afterlife. Some even wonder if the grave is the eternal home of the dead.

The most important parallels to Qoheleth are Egyptian and biblical royal instructions (Pritchard, 414–25). Egyptian royal instructions appeared during the Old Kingdom and continued well into the Hellenistic Age. The earliest form includes a title that indicates that the teaching is an "instruction" and provides the rank and name of the teacher. This introduction is followed by a series of admonitions and prohibitions that comprise the teaching proper. Sometimes the teaching concludes with a note telling of the sage who sets forth the teaching or the scribe who makes the copy. A more developed form of the instruction includes a legendary narrative between the introduction and the teaching proper. The legend sets forth an imaginary setting for the issuance of the teaching. Two royal instructions that are presented as teachings from the lips of deceased kings are "The Instruction for King Merikare" (from the First Intermediate Period, 2160–2040 B.C.E.) and "The Instruction of Amenemhet" (from the Middle Kingdom, 2040–1558 B.C.E.). The "Instruction for King Merikare" is portrayed as coming from the ruler's deceased father, who utters an instruction to his son, Merikare, on matters of just rule that leads to success. "The Instruction of Amenemhet" comes from the founder of the twelfth dynasty of the Middle Kingdom. In this instruction, the ruler speaks not only of his successes but also of his failures leading to his assassination.

Biblical royal instructions include "David's Instruction of Solomon" (1 Kings 2:1–12) and "The Words of King Lemuel of Massa, Which His Mother Taught Him" (Prov. 31:1–9). In the first biblical text, an aged David, approaching death, instructs his son Solomon in the specifics of just rule and eliminating potential threats to his power. In the second biblical text, the Queen Mother instructs her son in a more general way, advising him at the beginning of his reign to practice justice and to avoid adultery and strong drink. What these royal instructions appear to have in common is that they occur during rites of passage when new rulers assume the throne. In Solomon's case, his co-regency with David is coming to an end because of the latter's approaching death. One may conclude, then, that Qoheleth fits the literary fiction of a dead or dying king who instructs his audience of students, not a successor, in wise decorum and offers his reflections on the limits of wisdom, the human condition, and divine sovereignty.

Literary Structure

At first glance, Qoheleth may appear to be a random grouping of sayings about a variety of topics. However, closer examination reveals a careful literary structure.

Introduction (Eccl. 1:1–11; note the parallels in the conclusion)
    Opening scribal note (1:1)
    Theme: breath of breaths (1:2)
    Question: what profit from toil? (1:3)
    Two-stanza poem: cosmology (1:4–11)
Body (1:12—11:8)
    Introduction to Parts 1 and 2 (1:12–18)
    Part 1: cosmology, anthropology, and moral order: human action
        (1:12—5:19)
            (refrain: "breath")
        Solomon's accomplishments (2:1–26)
            Carpe diem ("seize the day," 2:24–26)
        Time: human toil and divine action (3:1–13)
            Carpe diem (3:12–13)
        Judgment and human nature (3:14–22)
            Carpe diem (3:22)
        Royal rule and the cult (4:1—5:20)
            Carpe diem (5:18–20)
    Interlude: joy, appetite, and desire (6:1–9)
    Part 2: the sovereignty of God and moral order: human knowing
        (6:10—11:8)
            (refrain: "cannot find out/who can find out," 7—8)
        Divine sovereignty and human wisdom (6:10—8:15)
        Divine sovereignty and human wisdom (8:16—9:10)
        Divine sovereignty and human wisdom (9:11—11:8)
Conclusion (11:9—12:14)
    Two-stanza poem: anthropology (11:9—12:7)
    Theme: breath of breaths (12:8)
    Closing scribal note (12:9–14)

Major Themes

The book's literary frame highlights two comparable themes. The first, "breath of breaths" ("vanity of vanities" in the *New Revised Standard Version* [NRSV]) is used in contexts of the significance of human action and knowing and the transitory nature of human life and accomplishments. All human life is filtered through this literary lens. The statement that "all is breath/

vanity" is often followed by the words, "and a desire for the life-giving spirit" (author's translation; NRSV: "and a chasing after wind"). Humans find themselves in an impossible situation. We seek to transcend ephemerality and retain the spirit. But the spirit, originating with God, returns to the creator at death. No one escapes the fleeting quality of existence. What we accomplish in life soon disappears and is lost to human memory. According to Qoheleth, life is not absurd (as later existentialists claimed), but fleeting, leaving no lasting gain. This leaves the second theme, *carpe diem* ("enjoy the day"), as the meaning of life. Nothing accomplished by human beings endures beyond death, so we should enjoy life while we have it.

These two themes have given rise to widely varying perceptions about the overall tone of Qoheleth. Some, focusing on the "breath" theme, see the book as dark and despairing. Others, focusing on the *carpe diem* theme, regard it as a joyful work. The fact that it can support such widely varying interpretations is itself a witness to the work's complexity.

The two-part internal structure of the book highlights two other related themes: first, the relation of creation, the moral order, and human action; and second, the relation of divine sovereignty, the moral order, and human knowing. In Part 1, the first-person narrator assumes the role of the long-dead Solomon in addressing the theme of human action. Linking his activities with those of Solomon, Qoheleth concludes that all human deeds are ephemeral. One may enjoy and treasure them in the moment, but they quickly pass from view. Humans cannot achieve immortality through their deeds. Even wisdom, although much to be desired, cannot ensure success. The only result of life that makes it worthwhile is the joy that one may derive from human labor. Even this sense of satisfaction and celebration, if experienced, quickly passes.

The theme of Part 2 underscores both divine sovereignty and human inability to find out or to discover what God is doing (Murphy 1991). In contrast to other sages, who assume that God is known through wisdom teachings and creation, Qoheleth takes the role of cynical sage and suggests that the Creator and Sustainer of life resides beyond human knowing. Agreeing with other sages that God determines all that occurs in reality and human life, Qoheleth argues that God's decisions and actions cannot be understood even by sages, much less by fools. This being the case, wisdom has no true value in knowing the will and action of God.

Conclusion

Wisdom originates and continues to thrive within a socially conservative, often aristocratic milieu. When royal rule, whether Israelite or foreign, is benign, wisdom makes its bed with the appropriate political partners and seeks to legitimate and maintain the existing social structure. Proverbs is an example of such conservative wisdom. In periods of despair, when major social transitions have occurred that do not fit the tradition's teachings, the sages reflect increasing pessimism about wisdom and mastering life. In these darker times, God seems hidden. Ecclesiastes is a prime example of such questioning wisdom literature. In it, God's judgment is still understood to be determinative, but access to divine decrees is denied even to the sages. (Job, to be discussed in chap. 14, is another example of questioning wisdom.) However, the period of cynicism seems to have been relatively short-lived. The teachings of Ben Sira and the Wisdom of Solomon (see chap. 16) return to a more conventional wisdom view of knowing and doing.

Resources

James L. Crenshaw. *Old Testament Wisdom. An Introduction.* Rev. and enl. ed. Louisville, Ky.: Westminster John Knox Press, 1998.

John G. Gammie and Leo G. Perdue, eds. *The Sage in Israel and the Ancient Near East.* Winona Lake, Ind.: Eisenbrauns, 1990.

Klaus Koch. "Is There a Doctrine of Retribution in the Old Testament?" In *Theodicy in the Old Testament,* edited by James L. Crenshaw. Issues in Religion and Theology 4. Philadelphia: Fortress Press, 1983.

Roland E. Murphy. *Wisdom Literature: Job, Proverbs, Ruth, Canticles, Ecclesiastes, Esther.* Forms of the Old Testament Literature 13. Grand Rapids, Mich.: Eerdmans, 1981.

Leo G. Perdue. *Wisdom and Creation: The Theology of Wisdom Literature.* Nashville: Abingdon Press, 1994.

J. B. Pritchard, ed. *ANET = Ancient Near Eastern Texts.* 3d ed. Princeton, N.J.: Princeton University Press, 1968.

14

Job

CLAUDIA V. CAMP

The book of Job is a conundrum. It raises questions it does not answer. It answers questions it does not raise, and then it turns the answers into questions again. There can be no simple summary of the "meaning" of the book. There are a number of points scholars often make about the book's form and its place within comparative ancient Near Eastern literature. We shall save these for the end of the chapter, and begin inductively, reading closely through different parts of the book of Job itself.

There is one important preliminary point, however: We must always remember that the book of Job is a piece of literature and not a report of history. Most of the book is in the form of speeches written in highly stylized poetry (you will notice the typical Hebrew poetic form of "parallelism": two, or sometimes three, lines will create a "thought rhyme"). This was not the way real people talked, even way back when! Thus, when we think about the characterizations of people, or even God, in the book, we must recognize that an author (or authors) has chosen to present these characters in a certain way. Although the later Jewish and Christian communities (rather remarkably) incorporated the book of Job into their respective canons of sacred scripture, the book itself retains the unsettled character of great art wrestling with the depths of intractable human experience. It does not present itself as "the voice of God." Rather, God's voice mixes with those of the other characters, adding to rather than resolving complex issues.

Reading through Job

The book of Job contains a large poetic section (3:1—42:6) sandwiched between the introduction and conclusion, which are both written in prose (1:1—2:13 and 42:7–17). The poetic section may be further broken into three parts: an opening monologue by Job followed by discussion between Job and his three friends (3—31), a long speech by a fourth friend (32—37), and God's speeches and Job's response (38:1—42:6). For reasons of space, the following discussion skips over the second of these three poetic sections.

The Prose Prologue (Job 1—2)

Although most of the book of Job is written in poetry, our first encounter with the book is with prose. These first two chapters contain folktale-like characterizations, but also a formal repetitiousness of style. The scene opens on Job (his name means "enemy"), who lives in the land of Uz, a location unknown to us. He is, then, non-Israelite, already a fascinating suggestion of the universalizing focus of wisdom literature (see pp. 209–10). Job is "blameless and upright, one who feared God and turned away from evil" (1:1). The narrator's characterization of the hero in the first verse is repeated twice more by God (1:8; 2:3). As readers, we can never forget this clear indication of Job's righteousness and thus the undeservedness of his subsequent suffering. The conventional morality of the time (clearly evident, for example, in the book of Proverbs) subscribed to the theory of retribution, that the good are rewarded and the evil punished. Job's moral status would in this view lead naturally to the next facts we learn, namely, that Job is very wealthy, highly honored, and has many sons and daughters. Job offers sacrifices on their behalf, just in case any of them might sin in some way.

In 1:6, the scene shifts to heaven. YHWH is presented, again in a manner typical of the time, as a potentate surrounded by minions (compare 1 Kings 22:19). These heavenly beings (NRSV; literally, "sons of god [or the gods]") come before YHWH, and among them is the satan. Now who is this character? The satan appears only three times in the Hebrew Bible (outside Job 1—2, we find him in Zech. 3:1–2 and 1 Chron. 21:1). It is thus a mistake to think of him as important to Israelite religious thought.

Also incorrect is the usual assumption that the satan is identical with the later Jewish and Christian personification of evil known as Satan. Although you would not know it from most English translations, a definite article ("the") appears before this word in all but one of its Hebrew Bible usages. This suggests that it should not be capitalized: It seems to be a common noun rather than a proper name. The satan is one of YHWH's servants with a special role. The term means "adversary," and it appears that the satan's task is to bring charges, like a prosecutor in a court case. When YHWH points to Job's exemplary character, the satan raises the question of Job's motivation: "Does Job fear God for nothing?" (Job 1:19). YHWH accepts the question as a legitimate one and hands Job over into the satan's power, with the limitation set against any affliction of his person.

The scene returns to earth (1:13). Four messengers come in quick succession to Job, each the lone escapee of a disaster: The Sabeans have stolen Job's oxen and killed his servants; "the fire of God" has fallen and burned up his sheep and yet more servants; Chaldeans have stolen Job's camels and killed his servants; a wind has collapsed the house of Job's eldest son, killing all his children who were dining there. Job's response is the one usually associated with the proverbial "patience of Job" (see Jas. 5:11):

Naked I came from my mother's womb,
and naked shall I return there;
YHWH gave, and YHWH has taken away;
blessed be the name of YHWH. (1:21)

Notice already here in the "prose" prologue that Job's utterance is in the form of poetic parallelism.

Back in heaven (2:1), with heavy repetition, YHWH and the satan resume their interchange. This time YHWH offers up Job's body to the satan's challenge, restricting only the taking of his life. On earth, Job, now covered with loathsome sores, sits on an ash heap where his bodily impurity will not infect the community. His wife proposes that he curse God. He calls her foolish, acknowledging that those who receive good from God will also receive bad. The narrator assures us that "Job did not sin with his lips." His three friends—Eliphaz, Bildad, and Zophar—arrive and sit silently with him for seven days and seven nights.

Chapter 3 brings us a new literary form—poetry—and a new Job, a Job of protest rather than compliance. Before we turn to this, let us think back on what the prose prologue has offered in the way of questions and answers and more questions. *The great challenge to modern interpreters here is to set aside our long-taught beliefs about what the Bible teaches and to consider what this text actually says.* There are two narrative assertions in these chapters that are important for the larger story. One we have already noted: Job is righteous and undeserving of suffering. The other is that YHWH is in control of the situation. Although the satan is the "hit man," textual repetition stresses the need for God's permission before the satan acts, as well as God's unquestioned ability to put whatever limitations on those actions that God wishes to put. Indeed, after chapter 2, the character of the satan will never again appear or be referred to in the book of Job. His narrative role as foil to YHWH's confidence in Job is complete.

Here, then, is the rub: How could God do this to a person? Why, we must ask, is Job turned over, by the God he so faithfully serves, to the severest imaginable emotional and physical torture? The most common answer is that Job is being "tested." But what is this a test *of*? It seems that Job's faith is being tested to see if it can withstand misfortune. But why is such a test necessary? The text allows two possible answers. Perhaps God allows this test to prove to the satan that God can really pick the winners. The idea of God in a bit of manly competition with an underling is not dear to the modern heart, but it cannot be dismissed as a way of reading these chapters. The other alternative is that God truly does not know what the answer is to the satan's question about Job's motivation, and that God feels a need to know. This is, in a sense, a "nicer" view of God, but it challenges the modern notion of an omniscient God. Although I do not have the space here to make the case for a nonomniscient God, this is in fact the typical if not universal view in the Hebrew Bible. The idea that God did not know the measure of Job's faith would certainly have been a live possibility for ancient readers.

Job's Opening Monologue and the Dialogue with His Friends (Job 3—31)

Chapter 3. Both form and content change dramatically in chapter 3, Job's opening monologue: from prose to poetry, and from resignation to protest. Job does not "curse God," as the satan had predicted, but he does curse the foundational gift from God, the day of his birth. He wishes for death or, better, to have never been born. The speech is laden with irony when compared with earlier and later portions of the book. Whereas the satan had challenged God for the protective hedge or fence God had put around Job (1:10), Job reacts with dread to being "fenced in" by the deity (3:23). At the same time, his despairing call for clouds and darkness to settle on the day of his birth foreshadows the rhetoric of YHWH's speeches, as do his references to the sea, to Leviathan, and to his wish that the doors of his mother's womb had been shut (38:8–9; 41:1–34; compare 7:12).

Chapters 4—27. Now comes a highly stylized dialogue between Job and his three friends Eliphaz, Bildad, and Zophar. There are two complete cycles in which Job alternates speeches with each of the friends. There appears to have been a third cycle, but it has been broken, either intentionally or accidentally. Eliphaz's third speech (chap. 22) is followed, as expected, by one of Job's (chaps. 23—24). Bildad's third speech, however, is unusually short (chap. 25), and there is none for Zophar. Job's last speech of the dialogue (chaps. 26—27) contains some conventional ideas that, unless they are ironic, seem to reflect more the views of the friends. There is also, surprisingly, a fourth friend, Elihu, who suddenly appears for a long speech in chapters 32 to 37, after Job and the other three have finished. Both the literary merit and the presence of any really new ideas in Elihu's speech are debated by scholars. Although I will not discuss the speech, I encourage you to read it and see for yourself what you think of it.

Recognizing the interpretive problem created by the third cycle and by the entrance of Elihu, we can still, I believe, characterize the basic ideas of the friends and Job. There is not enough space here to work through all the literary richness of the dialogue. I shall focus on just a few chapters to try and give a sense of the whole.

Eliphaz's first speech (chaps. 4—5) suggests the range of responses the friends offer to Job's plight. As if to remind readers of the word-crafter behind the words, Eliphaz's speech begins, as most of the dialogue speeches do, with a reference to language itself, here couched in conciliatory terms: "If one ventures a word with you, will you be offended? / But who can keep from speaking?" (4:2). Eliphaz at first credits Job with supportive behavior toward others in need, and commends to him the same fear of God and integrity acknowledged in chapters 1 and 2 (4:3–6). The ground suddenly shifts in 4:7, however, when Eliphaz asks, in the conventional terms of retributive justice, "who that was innocent ever perished?" and answers himself, "those who plow iniquity and sow trouble reap the same." In spite of his initial affirmation of Job's righteousness, then, Eliphaz quickly shifts to the kind of moral reasoning that is the hallmark of the friends' speeches: Not only do the wicked get what they deserve, but one can know the wicked by their suffering. Eliphaz and the other two "miserable comforters" (16:2) seem not to notice the contradiction between their empirical observation of Job's good character and their theory of reward and punishment. Indeed, by the conclusion of the speeches, Eliphaz has forgotten Job's goodness altogether, accusing him of the most reprehensible crimes (22:5–9).

But Eliphaz's analysis of Job's situation does not end with this inhumane inversion of the theory of retribution. He offers no less than three further "answers" explaining Job's fate. He relates, first, a hair-raising description of a night vision, when a ghostly spirit challenged, "Can mortals be righteous before God? / Can human beings be pure before their Maker?" (4:17). The rhetorical questions demand the answer "no!" Bildad takes the idea that worthless humans deserve even worse than they get to high art in his equation of human beings with maggots and worms (25:6; compare 11:4–6; 15:14–16). But notice how this extreme view of human worthlessness removes what justice theoretically lies in the theory of retribution. If there is no hope for human goodness, of what use is reward and punishment? The friends' "humans as scumbags" argument obviates their other ideas about just deserts for the individual. Eliphaz's repertoire of answers does not end here. Perhaps it's not a matter of punishment at all, but merely divine discipline (5:17–27): God wounds, but binds up; strikes, but heals. And the one who has been through the training will earn the best of God's protection and blessings in the end. Curiously, although this rationale seems to echo the prologue, it is the least developed option in the poetry. More prominent in the friends' speeches, and coming to the fore in God's own, is a final possibility: the idea that divine motivations are simply a mystery. God does "great things and unsearchable, marvelous things without number" (5:9; compare 11:7–8; 15:7–8). But this is no explanation at all and indeed undercuts the possible relevance of any explanation. If God's deeds are truly inexplicable from a human point of view, then even those that appear to make sense do so only by coincidence. So much for divine justice!

The friends do not come out looking too good, either as friends or as logicians. Has the poet's art failed in creating these shrill, cardboard characters? I do not think so. As characters in a drama, they do not need to be likeable, or even realistic, to portray a real aspect of the human condition. What, then, do they represent? Is it perhaps the human longing to find a comfort zone where our questions about life cease to trouble us? Is it the tendency we all share on some level to let our hunger for answers—right answers—close our eyes to real undeserved suffering and close our minds to the illogic with which we patch together our explanations and nonexplanations? When faced with suffering like Job's, would we resist the urge to respond like his "friends," finding sin where there is no sin or offering the pablum of divine mystery to a starving child? Perhaps these characters provide a necessary mirror for us all.

Like the friends, Job moves from one position to another as he seeks solace, if not answers, for his plight. Although his lament in chapter 3 focuses on his own misery and search for respite, it hints already at larger issues of injustice and fate. Job evokes images of the powerful rich and the lowly slave, all of whom meet in death. The motif of the hard service of the slave as a metaphor of all human life, as well as Job's own misery, appears again in 7:1–10 and 14:1–17, again associated with the brevity of life.

The barest suggestion in chapter 3 of God's responsibility for human suffering—especially Job's—gains momentum as the dialogue moves along. Indeed, in his overwhelming sense of life's transience, Job finds the freedom to speak against God's affliction of humankind (7:11; 9:22; 10:1). How can God make him beg for death any harder than God already has done (compare 10:18–22)?

Although the war of words between Job and his friends escalates rapidly, they do share certain premises, among them the importance of the theory of retribution. Just as the breakdown of the theory in Job's case leads the friends to wilder and wilder accusations, it leads Job himself on a journey of introspection regarding his own worth and his relationship with God. In early speeches, Job acknowledges the possibility that he could have sinned, yet he is from the outset uncomprehending of the degree of punishment he is receiving and why pardon is unavailable (7:20–21; 14:16–17). (The contemporary Christian reader, who is often taught about the "wrathful" God of the Old Testament, might note Job's expectation of divine mercy.) Indeed, he raises the obvious point that, if God kills him, the relationship will be over altogether. (This raises another point at odds with much Christian belief: The ancient Israelites had no belief in an afterlife.)

Like the friends, Job acknowledges the overwhelming power of God (chaps. 9; 12), but his emphasis increasingly falls on the chaotic nature of this power rather than, as in Eliphaz's chapter 5 speech, for example, on its just beneficence. Indeed, Job asserts that justice cannot stand before divine power. Now claiming his own innocence, Job says God would nonetheless prove him perverse, plunge him into filth (9:20, 31). More sweepingly,

> When disaster brings sudden death,
> he mocks at the calamity of the innocent.
> The earth is given into the hand of the wicked;
> he covers the eyes of its judges—if it is not he, who then is it?
> (9:23–24)

Job has come to the perception that God dispenses life and blessing one minute and affliction the next, taking no notice of righteousness or wickedness (10:8–17). He claims the right of protest.

Job's anger at God expressed in chapters 9 and 10 is righteous anger, but this is a difficult emotional space for a sufferer to maintain. It is not surprising, then, that by the end of chapter 10, he has succumbed once more to a simple wish for death. More surprising, perhaps, is that out of Job's anger and despair new possibilities for relating to himself, his situation, and perhaps his God gradually emerge. J. Gerald Janzen (p. 94 and elsewhere in his Job commentary) refers to a sequence of what he calls moments of "imaginative outreach" in Job's speeches. The first of these occurs already in 9:32–35, though the insight is expressed negatively. Job's very condemnation of God for making evil out of innocence paradoxically produces for him the idea of going to trial with God. The possibility is here dismissed: God would need to quit terrorizing Job; an "umpire," unavailable, would be necessary to mediate between the human being and the inhuman divinity.

Job's scathingly sarcastic contempt for God's power and wisdom returns again in chapter 12 and is then turned in chapter 13 against the friends as well, "worthless physicians" who presume to plead the case for God. But then, again comes a new thought, now expressed in a paradox of hope and despair regarding his own righteousness and the possibility that it makes a difference to God.

> See, he will kill me; I have no hope;
> but I will defend my ways to his face.
> This will be my salvation,
> that the godless shall not come before him. (13:15–16)

Suddenly, now, Job speaks directly to God instead of to the friends (13:20—14:22), first begging for an audience unaccompanied by dread, then falling back once more to reflections on the transience of human existence. Even in the midst of this lament, however, Janzen perceives a moment of imaginative outreach absent in earlier speeches (Janzen, 108–9). Job imagines a life after death. Like a tree cut down that sprouts again, he imagines Sheol, the place of the dead, as a place where God might hide him protectively until such time as God longs for his presence again (14:13–15). His image of God has bifurcated: The same one who afflicts him without cause or measure might also someday long for him. Yet the imagination outstretched retreats again: Job knows only death as the human end.

The pattern of accusation, outreach, and withdrawal is repeated in his next speech in chapters 16 and 17, here with an affirmation of a mediator that he had denied in chapter 9: "Even now, in fact, my witness is in heaven,/ and he that vouches for me is on high" (16:19). Perhaps Job's trial with God can proceed after all. A culmination of sorts occurs in chapter 19, which again moves from accusation to imaginative outreach, this time without a retreat into despair. Job says, "I know that my Redeemer lives," and goes on with words usually translated as a statement of resurrection (19:25–27). Unfortunately, the exact meaning of this text, which is interpreted christologically in Handel's famous *Messiah,* is unclear. The term *redeemer* in the Hebrew Bible elsewhere refers to an avenger of blood, a kinsperson who would kill a relative's murderer. Does Job imagine the execution of God in return for his own death? Verses 26 and 27, moreover, are so broken in the Hebrew that no real sense can be made of them; they are hardly a clear affirmation of a resurrection belief, although that is one possible interpretation. What, then, is the meaning of these words of imaginative outreach? The reader is left with a puzzle once more. As if there is no more new to say, Job's final speeches largely return to his earlier defiance of God for the divine perpetuation of misery on the weak and innocent and the heaping of treasure on the wicked. Job's continued attachment to the theory of retribution is clear, even if it means castigation of God. His final speech of the dialogue proper (chaps. 26—27) contains a mass of contradiction, seeming to affirm God's power and just judgment at the same time that Job accuses him of injustice in his own case. This odd speech may contain remnants of the missing ones of Bildad and Zophar. As it stands, however, we might read here a combination of Job's bitter irony with respect to these conventional qualities of God and a deepened conviction of his own righteousness.

Chapters 28—31. Following what appears to be an originally independent poem on the inaccessibility of wisdom (chap. 28), Job makes a closing statement in his own defense. He reviews his own righteous past (chap. 29); he recounts the suffering that God has consigned him to (chap. 30); and finally, he takes a formal oath of innocence (chap. 31), ending with a challenge to his accuser to produce an indictment and come to trial with his equal.

> Surely I would carry it on my shoulder;
> I would bind it on me like a crown;
> I would give him an account of all my steps;
> like a prince I would approach him. (31:36–37)

The Voice from the Whirlwind and Job's Response (Job 38:1—42:6)

God finally speaks to Job, though not in terms we would expect. God neither refers to the question of the prologue, regarding the motivation for Job's faithful service, nor affirms Job's righteousness as Job had demanded. Nor does God address the larger question of innocent suffering. Interpreters have differed considerably not so much about what YHWH's speeches say as about what meaning they have in the context of the larger story. The divine presence is threatening, speaking from out of a whirlwind, and the words challenge Job rather than offering comfort or care.

> Who is this that darkens counsel by words without knowledge?
> Gird up your loins like a man,
> I will question you, and you shall declare [Jewish Publication
> Society, "inform"] to me. (38:2–3)

Although I have often heard students speak of God's "love" for Job, this sentiment is no easier to demonstrate in these speeches than it is in the prologue.

YHWH challenges Job's wisdom, and with it Job's power. Using rhetorical questions, God seems to demonstrate that Job knows nothing about the process of creation ("Where were you when I laid the foundation of the earth? / Tell me, if you have understanding" [38:4]) or its ongoing ways and means:

> Do you know when the mountain goats give birth?
> Do you observe the calving of the deer?
> Can you number the months that they fulfill,
> and do you know the time when they give birth? (39:1–2)

The process and maintenance of creation is portrayed as an ongoing struggle against forces of chaos. The surging waves of the sea must be barred behind doors, lest they overwhelm once more (38:8–11; compare Gen. 1:2, 6; 7:11), and the constellations must be tied and loosed on schedule. God also uses powerful metaphors of divine begetting and bearing:

> Has the rain a father,
> or who has begotten the drops of dew?
> From whose womb did the ice come forth,
> and who has given birth to the hoarfrost of heaven? (38:28–29)

Yet the natural world created by God does not always make sense. The ostrich lays eggs and then abandons them, dealing "cruelly with its young, as if they were not its own." Its labor is in vain, "yet it has no fear; because God has made it forget wisdom" (39:13–18).

Job's response to this first divine speech is ambiguous. He acknowledges that he is of small account, but refuses to go further (40:4–5). YHWH thus begins a second speech. It appears at first as if God might finally address the question of divine justice: "Will you even put me in the wrong? / Will you condemn me that you may be justified?" (40:8). This issue is quickly trumped, however, by divine power and glory and the fear it can produce in even the proudest humans (40:9–13). God raises the rhetorical ante once more with long descriptions about the horrific power of Behemoth and Leviathan, two personifications of the forces of chaos in nature, whom God controls with ease (40:15–41:26).

The divine speeches return us to the theological questions of the prologue, though they provide no satisfying answers. Did God appear to you before as a heartless being, engaged in macho competition with the satan? If so, the speeches in 38—41 offer no comfort! They can easily be seen as more of the same, a self-aggrandizing verbal pounding of the physically and spiritually beaten Job. Or did you read the prologue as proposing a test of Job's faith? This view now seems hard to reconcile with God's failure to refer to such a test, or whether Job passed it. Why would God not affirm Job's righteousness? At this point, is God satisfied with Job or not? (More on this in a moment.) And why no mention of the satan, who instigated the whole business in the first place? But perhaps the YHWH speeches change the terms of the prologue altogether. It is possible that the speeches are intended to shift Job's focus (and that of the reader) away from the theory of retribution as a way of relating to God. The powerful appeals to nature in all its splendor, danger, and incomprehensibility are often interpreted as demanding that frail humans, with their limited knowledge, simply bow to the power and mystery of the deity. It is hard to deny this effect. Yet, as we have seen, these are points that Job has made repeatedly throughout his protestations. YHWH, in fact, says nothing about the divine nature or power that Job has not already affirmed. And so the questions continue.

Job speaks one last time (42:1–6). But what does he say? Here lies one of the greatest puzzles of the book. Unfortunately, translators and interpreters often present the meaning of this text as much more self-evident than it is. Job begins by acknowledging, as he has many times before, that YHWH can do anything (42:2). He then affirms the limitations of his own wisdom (42:3); again, no startling new admission. He implies that he now has a knowledge of God that he did not have before (42:5), but what this is is not stated. The last verse of his speech, however, is the most difficult. The NRSV misleadingly translates the verse as a statement of humble repentance: "Therefore I despise myself, and repent in dust and ashes." Although timeworn, this translation is correctly disputed by recent scholars. The word "myself" does not appear in Hebrew, and the words for "despise" and "repent" have other possible meanings. Finally, the phrase "dust and ashes" appears elsewhere in the Bible as a metaphor for mortal humans (see Gen. 18:27; Job 30:19).

The odd syntax and vocabulary of the verse make it impossible to decide definitively on an alternative. Some scholars find here continued rebellion against God. John B. Curtis, for example, translates: "Therefore I feel loathing contempt and revulsion [implied: toward you, O God] and I am sorry for frail man" (Curtis, 510). Janzen reads something less cynical, but still sees Job standing up for himself: "Therefore I recant and change my mind concerning dust and ashes [i.e., mortal humans]" (Janzen, 251). What has Job changed his mind about? Janzen argues that Job now sees human frailty (our status as "dust and ashes") not as a source of abasement and separation from God, but as part of "the royal vocation of humanity…accepted and embraced with all its vulnerability to innocent suffering" (257–58). As elsewhere in the book of Job, the reader must take responsibility for interpreting this crucial but ambiguous verse.

The Prose Epilogue (Job 42:7–17)

The story now moves rapidly to a surprisingly "happy" ending. YHWH expresses anger at Eliphaz, Bildad, and Zophar (note Elihu's absence) for not speaking the truth about him, as his "servant Job" had done. God instructs Job to pray and sacrifice for the friends to avert God's wrath from them. This done, God restores Job's fortunes twofold. His brothers, sisters, and friends come to eat with him, offering gifts and comfort "for all the evil that YHWH had brought upon him" (42:11). He has seven more sons and three more daughters to replace those he lost; the three daughters, surprisingly, are named. Moreover, not only is their beauty applauded, but they are given an inheritance alongside their brothers. Job lives to the age of 140 and dies content.

What do you make of this ending? Some readers breathe a sigh of relief, feeling all's well that ends well—justice is restored in the end. Others find the ending frustrating, even maddening. How could life seem normal and content, after all Job had been through? How could "new" sons and daughters so easily replace the old? What happened to his concern for others who suffer and die at God's hand? How could Job be sure God would not "bring evil" on him again? And what was it that Job said about God that was "right"? These are questions that deserve your attention before you rest content.

The Book of Job in Comparison with Other Literature

The book of Job provides few if any clues to the date of its composition. It is possible that the prose prologue and epilogue are the remains of an older folktale whose easy assumption about the ultimate reward of the innocent sufferer was, literally, broken open by a later poet with more radical ideas. The high literary art of the final product, in a culture that was largely illiterate, certainly points to an author among the tiny educated scribal class. Some scholars suggest that the book was written during the Babylonian exile or in the early postexilic period, when Israelites would have been struggling with the question of why God had treated them so brutally. The lack of any historical indicators in a book whose focus is on a foreign individual offers no direct support to this hypothesis, however. Individuals have always suffered; a national crisis is not required to produce such literature, though it may contribute to it. Although the question of historical context remains—like so much about Job—unsettled, one can compare the book with other literature in and outside the Bible. Although the forcefulness of Job's theological challenges and the ambiguity of its answers may seem almost shocking, this book is not alone in addressing such issues.

Scholars usually consider Job, along with Proverbs and Ecclesiastes, as part of the biblical wisdom literature. Wisdom books focus on the knowledge humans can gain about life by observation of nature and society, rather than from direct divine revelation. Much of the book of Proverbs expresses conventional views of right and wrong behavior and the just consequences attached to each. Job argues with this understanding of life, but does so in a way that shows the poet's attachment to Proverbs' mode of retributive reasoning and its literary forms. There are many proverbial expressions in Job—for example, in 4:8 and 5:7. Can you find others? Even the book of Proverbs, however, admits that not everything can be explained (see, for instance, Prov. 16:1).

Ecclesiastes, like Job, challenges any complacent assurance that the meaning in life and relationship with God is easy to obtain. This book, too, argues with the conventional wisdom of Proverbs regarding the theory of retribution and the effectiveness of human effort in a world controlled by God. In contrast to Job, the emotional tone of Ecclesiastes is more detached and world weary. In Ecclesiastes, God is absent, rather than the enemy.

Biblical protest against the unfairness and sometimes torment of life is not limited to wisdom literature, however. Job's complaints about his pain and suffering resemble those of the psalms of lament (see, for instance, Ps. 22), where suffering is generally not explained but is often eased in the end, leading to rejoicing in God as savior. Thus, some have categorized the book of Job as an "answered lament." Not all laments are answered, however; see Psalms 44 and 88, as well as the book of Lamentations, for examples of unhealed suffering and unanswered questions about the "why." Elsewhere, Abraham, like Job, challenges God to act justly (Gen. 18:16–33).

As in the Bible, so also elsewhere in the ancient Near East. We find nothing exactly like Job, but we do find great questions about suffering posed in literary form (see Pritchard for the full texts of this literature and Crenshaw for detailed summaries). An Egyptian text, *The Dispute of a Man with His Soul,* ponders the desirability of death as release from life's woes, whereas *The Tale of the Eloquent Peasant* presents a wronged man making an impassioned argument for justice's demands. Mesopotamian culture addressed the problem of unjust suffering even more directly in texts such as *I Will Praise the Lord of Wisdom* and *A Babylonian Theodicy.* The latter work, like Job, presents a dialogue between an innocent sufferer and a less-than-helpful friend. The book of Job, then, although perhaps unique in its combination of literary power and interpretive ambiguity, shares its questions about human experience and the human-divine relationship with other persons of faith from the ancient times to the present.

Resources

James L. Crenshaw. *Old Testament Wisdom: An Introduction*. Atlanta: John Knox Press, 1981.

John Briggs Curtis. "On Job's Response to Yahweh." *Journal of Biblical Literature* 98 (1979): 497–511.

Norman Habel. *The Book of Job: A Commentary*. Old Testament Library. Philadelphia: Westminster Press, 1985.

J. Gerald Janzen. *Job*. Atlanta: John Knox Press, 1985.

David Penchansky. *The Betrayal of God: Ideological Conflict in the Book of Job*. Literary Currents in Biblical Interpretation. Louisville, Ky.: Westminster/John Knox Press, 1990.

James B. Pritchard, ed. *Ancient Near Eastern Texts Relating to the Old Testament*. 3d ed. with supplement. Princeton, N.J.: Princeton University Press, 1969.

15

Other Writings

LOWELL K. HANDY

This chapter discusses several relatively short books from the third division of the Jewish canon, the Writings. Four of these books come from a group called the Five Scrolls (*Megillot*), which includes the Song of Songs, Ruth, Lamentations, Ecclesiastes, and Esther. In Jewish tradition, each of these relatively short books is read in its entirety on a particular holy day. Ecclesiastes has already been discussed in chapter 13; the other four scrolls will be covered in this chapter. We will also consider the book of Daniel, which combines wisdom and short story traditions with apocalyptic visions.

Song of Songs

Rabbi Akiba (50?–132 C.E.) declared the Song of Songs (also known as the Song of Solomon and Canticles) to be the holy-of-holies in scripture, equating the book with the innermost room of the Jerusalem temple, the abode of God. This effectively ended a debate on whether a book should be considered sacred that never mentions God, deals in explicit sex, and presents behavior outside familial decorum. Until the end of the nineteenth century, the Song of Songs was interpreted by both Jews and Christians primarily as an allegory on the love of God for Israel, the love of God for the church, or the love of Jesus for the individual soul. Understood as an expression of divine love for Israel, it became the traditional liturgical reading for the eighth day of Passover. In the twentieth century, however, both Jewish and Christian scholars have read the book literally as divine sanction for human sexuality, and it has become a standard scripture for marriage services.

The Song of Songs is entirely poetic, though no consensus exists regarding whether the book consists of a single composition or is made up of several poems. The first verse ascribes the work to King Solomon, and a few scholars still argue for a Solomonic (900s B.C.E.) origin. However, most scholars suspect that the poetry was written by someone else at some other time. Theories about the poetry's origin are numerous, but four have been especially popular: that the poems are (1) marriage songs sung at weddings; (2) liturgical lyrics for sexual rituals in the temple; (3) hymns in praise of a fertility goddess; or (4) love poems written for loved ones. Parallels to Egyptian love poetry make the last theory most likely. These parallels include the motifs of lovers kept apart, singleness of desire for the loved one, calling the beloved "brother" or "sister" as terms of endearment, describing the loved one's physical attractiveness with metaphors from nature, and the overpowering longing for love causing breach of social norms.

The poetry itself revels in the delights of physical love between a woman and a man. Because much of the language is idiomatic, euphemistic, metaphoric, or bears multiple meanings, modern translations cannot replicate the numerous levels of meaning born by the Hebrew. Because most Bible translators intend their work to be readable, without embarrassment, from the pulpit, they provide fairly banal English text for this "sexy" book. Verse 5:4 provides a good illustration. Bearing in mind that "hand" and "foot" were standard ancient Near Eastern euphemisms for the penis, we read in the Hebrew text that "my lover extended his hand into the hole and my belly agitated within me" [author's translation, a variant text reads: "belly agitated for him"]. This often comes out in English as something like: "My beloved reached for the door latch and my heart yearned for him." Such translations continue to appear even though scholars almost universally agree that the verse is not about opening a gate but about sexual intercourse.

The poems are presented as speeches of a woman, a man, and a third group, the "daughters of Jerusalem." Some translations attempt to produce a drama with each character having his or her lines clearly denoted. Unfortunately, in a literal English translation the gender of the speaker is not conveyed, so the give and take of desire between lovers is lost. The Song of Songs is unique among biblical books in that the female figure is presented as the instigator of the activity and is presented as the equal of the man in matters of pursuing love. This is the more interesting in that the male is presented (1:12) in the person of King Solomon, whereas the woman appears to be a commoner (1:5–6) or at most a princess (7:1). Much exegetical skill has gone into determining the identity of the "Shulammite" (6:13). Does the term refer to (1) a female equivalent of Solomon, (2) a woman from a village called Shunem, or (3) a "peaceful one" as the title of a goddess (Anath, Ishtar, and Astarte all having been unconvincingly suggested)? We do not know.

The poems deal with several topics common in modern pop culture love lyrics. More text is used to describe the sexual attractiveness of the loved one than anything else. These descriptions can be literal or metaphorical, the latter including comparisons to animals, plants, architecture, and luxury goods. In addition, there are lines that explain the uniqueness of the loved one as more desirable than any other. There are descriptions of chance encounters that swell desire, as well as sections that reflect the familial displeasure with this infatuation. Characters daydream about lovemaking and attempt to sneak out of the house to rendezvous with their lovers. A few passages urge the lovers not to act on their desires too quickly (2:7; 3:5; 8:4); romantically inclined scholars argue that these are late insertions into the text. It may in the end be noted that neither lover is interested in the wisdom, piety, or commitment of the other, although these attributes are deemed attractive elsewhere in the Bible.

Ruth

Although Ruth follows Judges in most Christian Bibles, the Jewish Bible locates it among the Writings. The story deals with the manipulation of events by humans to bring about fair treatment by God, though it probably was accepted as canonical due to the final verses that connect the story to King David (4:17–22). Liturgically, it is the reading for the first day of *Shavuot,* the Feast of Weeks (Christians' Pentecost), which celebrates the gift of Torah by God to the Israelites at Sinai. Ruth is interpreted as demonstrating the graciousness of God toward anyone who lovingly accepts the gift of Torah as Ruth had accepted the God of her mother-in-law. In both Jewish and Christian tradition, the character of Ruth has stood as the paradigm of the sincere religious convert.

Although the short story is placed in the age of the Judges, the actual time of composition remains contested. The two favorite theories are (1) that Ruth was composed during the United Monarchy by court scribes wishing to produce an endearing tale of the origins of the Davidic lineage or to legitimate David's annexation of Moab, or (2) that Ruth was composed in the late 400s B.C.E. to counter legal proclamations by Ezra and Nehemiah requiring non-Judean wives to be divorced by Judean men. Neither theory has much to recommend it, but a postexilic date, perhaps even as late as the Ptolemaic Period (323–198 B.C.E.), appears more probable.

The central character of Ruth is Naomi. The narrative begins with her family, and she is the one who ends the story holding her (grand)son, who is her hope for her old age and for the future of her deceased husband Elimelech's lineage. The fictitious nature of the tale is by now well recognized among scholars. The names of the central characters are symbolic, with Naomi's sons' names the most obviously invented: Mahlon = "little sickly one" and Kilyon = "little destruction." The story follows Naomi as she leaves from and returns to Bethlehem, going out with a family of men and returning with a widowed daughter-in-law.

The status of widows in a patriarchal society sits at the center of the narrative. Both Naomi and Ruth represent powerlessness and poverty in the eyes of the culture in which the story is set. The story is partially about how such expectations are erroneous and partly about ethnic bigotry: Moabites were disparaged in biblical texts as both enemies and incompetent buffoons who were easily manipulated. In the end, widows, Moabites, and the ethnically tolerant secure Naomi's well-being and provide for the Davidic dynasty as well.

In leaving Judah with a husband and two sons, Naomi is in a socially enviable position: A husband means status, and sons mean future security. When all these men die in Moab, leaving three widows, Naomi's position is immediately reversed. Now she is a refugee responsible for two Moabite daughters-in-law. Orpah appears to be the more rational daughter-in-law, taking Naomi's good advice to return to her father's house. Ruth insists on going with Naomi as she returns to Judah, becoming a refugee herself in the process. Naomi leads the pair on their return. Greeted by her old acquaintances, Naomi insists she be called Mara, "Bitter," for everything has gone ill, yet she hopes for help from God who has treated her bitterly so far.

Help comes in a mundane manner: the Torah legislation. Deuteronomy 24:19 requires farmers to leave some standing grain and any grain dropped in harvesting for the poor and widows explicitly. Ruth sets out to glean this grain. The field in which she happens to work belongs to Boaz, a distant relative of Naomi's husband. Boaz takes one look at Ruth and instructs his help to make certain Ruth is well taken care of. They take care of her so well that she hauls a huge amount of grain, at least thirty pounds, back to Naomi. Naomi, seeing the reaction by Boaz, sets to work on a plan to take care of herself and her daughter-in-law. Here, we have the standard Judean/Israelite presentation of the clever Israelite and the manipulable Moabite (see Judg. 3:12–30). Making her way to the drunken Boaz at the threshing floor after the harvest festival, Ruth, as Naomi has instructed her, uncovers his "feet." He responds as predicted. As the wise and manipulative Naomi also seems to have foreseen, Boaz later takes steps to make Ruth his wife. However, a problem arises: There is a nearer kinsman who can take Elimelech's land

and is willing to do so, but if he takes the land he must also, apparently, take Ruth. He, it turns out, refuses to get involved with a Moabite. He forfeits the land to Boaz. Boaz marries Ruth and fathers a son, who is named by the women of Bethlehem and placed on Naomi's lap as her son. The book ends with a short genealogy leading to David, demonstrating the social consequences of such a *seemingly* mundane life.

Lamentations

The book of Lamentations consists of five anguished poems about the destruction of Jerusalem's temple. The book is solemnly recited on the ninth of Ab (a Jewish month overlapping July–August) in commemoration of the destructions of the temple, first by the Babylonians in 586 B.C.E. and then by the Romans in 70 C.E. The depiction of horror, despair, and loss ritually embodies the community's grief. For Christian liturgy the poems have traditionally been read on the afternoon and evening of Good Friday and for Holy Saturday services.

From rabbinic and patristic times, the authorship of Lamentations has been attributed to Jeremiah. It is for this reason that Christian Bibles tend to place the book immediately after Jeremiah, though some, such as the canon of Gregory the Theologian (329–389 C.E.), include the poems within Jeremiah. It is highly unlikely that Jeremiah wrote the poems. Although it is usually argued that the site of the destroyed temple continued to be used as a religious gathering place and that commemoration of the temple began with such assemblies (Jer. 41:5), it is not really likely that the poems were written immediately after the destruction as often proposed. People in Judah had more pressing issues. It is uncertain, in fact, how early the public grief for the temple's destruction began. The book of Lamentations appears to have been liturgical literature written for the Jewish memorial service now known as the Ninth of Ab. Therefore, it could have been composed anytime from 586 until the Rabbinic Period (10–425 C.E.), either as a unit or as individual poems.

Each of the five poems has its own structure and content. Together, they build from complete humiliation and despair to faint hope and desire for retribution. The first four poems are alphabetic acrostics built on the twenty-two letters of the Hebrew alphabet, and the final poem contains twenty-two verses. Each is a lament of the complaint type.

The first lament is divided into twenty-two sections, with each section having three lines. Only the first word of each section begins with the appropriate letter of the alphabet. Jerusalem is here presented as a widow whose husband has been slaughtered and whose children have been led away as prisoners (cities were regularly portrayed as women in the ancient

Near East). The poet describes Jerusalem as one who used to be admired and honored but has now been humiliated by those it used to lord over. This just punishment came about, the poet argues, because Jerusalem sinned against God by worshiping other deities. Jerusalem cried out to these other deities (lovers), but they could do nothing to counter the anger of God. The destruction of the city is described as impossible to bear, with God now far-removed from the town.

The second lament also has twenty-two sections of three lines with the first word of the first line bearing the acrostic letter. The text represents God as the enemy of Jerusalem. Again, Jerusalem is presented as having sinned against God. Here, the centrality of the city as the political, military, and religious capital of Judah/Israel is emphasized. It had been the source of security and bounty, but God found it evil and demolished it, even though it was God's chosen abode. Where there was plenty, now there is want; where food, now starvation; where motherly love, now mothers devouring children; where priest and prophet served, they now are slain; and the youth—future of the city—are killed. God does nothing to help. Hope is gone; despair remains. Never, claims the poet, has such a thorough destruction been delivered as God has made of Jerusalem.

The third lament's twenty-two sections have three lines, but here every line of each section begins with the appropriate letter of the alphabet. The poem is written as though by a single inhabitant of the ruined city. A short description of the despair of one caught in the siege and destruction of Jerusalem instigated by YHWH is conditioned by acknowledgment that God can have mercy if one has patience. It is acknowledged that the city had sinned, but the result is that the speaker lives not in Jerusalem but in Sheol, the pit beneath the earth where all the dead go. People, for no reason related directly to the speaker, have sought the poet's torment and death. Worse, the enemies of Jerusalem, and of God, now laugh and sneer. From this "life in death," the poem cries out to God to take revenge on these enemies.

The fourth lament has twenty-two sections of two lines each, with the first word of the first line bearing the acrostic letter. This poem is a description of the ruined city, focusing on the reversals in its fortune. The glorious city now is awful. Its beautiful inhabitants are now ugly; the wealthy are poor; and the satiated starve. Much of the poem appears to be standard material for describing a sacked city, but it should not be taken as exaggeration—war-ravaged lands suffer brutal horrors. Although there is no hope, the author pleads with God to do the same to Edom as was done to Jerusalem. This last is a recurring motif of the postexilic period. Edom, an off-again-on-again ally of Judah, had thrown its support to Babylonia in the siege of Jerusalem, and revenge is now demanded for this perceived betrayal.

The final lament consists of twenty-two lines but is not an acrostic. This is a plea for God to remember Jerusalem. God's prosperous city has been reduced to a community of orphans; free peoples have been enslaved; God's protected people are now conquered; women have been raped, men randomly murdered in broad daylight with no retribution, and the elderly abused. God does nothing. These conditions are, the poet insists, intolerable even if the people have sinned. Finally, at the very end of this last poem, there is the standard lament's conclusion, missing from the previous four in Lamentations: hope that God will yet restore the city.

Esther

The book of Esther's inclusion in the canon has been controversial. Gregory the Theologian left it off his list of scripture, and Martin Luther would have removed it were it not in the Jewish Bible. The major issue is the lack of reference to God in a work that does not lend itself to allegorical reading as the Song of Songs does. In addition, the annihilation of the enemies at the end of the text has not sat well with many commentators in both Jewish and Christian traditions. That Esther is the reading for the feast of Purim seems to have been the deciding factor in including the book, even though Purim is not one of the festivals required by Torah. This is one liturgical text where all the stops were pulled out, as it was usual not just to read Esther, but to act it out. Indeed, adding to the text to heighten the enjoyment of the presentation became required. Celebration of the victory of the Jews over their enemy's plot to exterminate them continues to be foundational to parties involving costumes, gifts, feasting, drinking, and theatrical skits.

The Hebrew text of Esther is so secular that someone copying the text early in the first century B.C.E. added sections to include God and piety for the central characters. It was this lengthened version that was adopted in Alexandrian Egypt and passed into Christian tradition. (For more about this expanded version of Esther, see pp. 252–53.) The Protestant reformers opted, however, to use the Hebrew version in the Jewish Bible.

Although there are several references to Persian governmental and cultural customs in the work, it appears to have been written in the Hellenistic Period (331 B.C.E. or later). King Ahasuerus, translated both as Xerxes and Artaxerxes, no doubt was intended to represent King Xerxes I of Persia (486–465) in his winter palace at Susa. Although the action takes place in Persia at its greatest extent, the text actually is commentary on life in the Hellenistic diaspora, where Jewish identity was threatened by dispersal in another culture to which Jews held allegiance but in which they sought to have dual loyalty rather than to disappear through assimilation.

Persia figures as an ambiguous power, capable of both great destruction and great protection. The book of Esther centers particularly on the standing of the ethnic Jews within Persia: their problems, their salvation, and their revenge on enemies new and traditional. Identity, hidden identity, and loss of identity permeate the narrative. Reversals of position and status are central plot devices: The high are brought low as the villains become victims partially through their own flawed schemes and partially through the wisdom of Esther. All this takes place against the exotic backdrop of the lavish palace life of the Persian king.

The story's structure is fairly simple. The introduction presents the basic situation: Persia is ruled by Ahasuerus, who is totally manipulable by those around him, here at an exaggerated drinking party. Commands of the ruler once posted cannot be retracted—even if the king did not know what he was doing—and we see that many commands ultimately come not from the ruler but from those around him. Therefore, this man is dangerous, not because he is evil, but because he caves in to advisors.

Following the introduction, the text assumes a chiastic structure, with paired motifs on either side of a central event:

A—the rise of Haman, an evil advisor (2:21—3:6)
   B—Haman sets out to destroy the Jews (3:7—4:17)
      C—Haman plots to bring destruction (5:1—6:9)
         D—Ahasuerus approves Haman's plan for honors—but
            with Mordecai as the honoree (6:10)
      C—Esther plots to thwart destruction (6:11—8:6)
   B—Esther sets out to save the Jews (8:7—9:32)
A—the rise of Mordecai, a good advisor (10:1–3)

The figures of Esther and Mordecai are stock characters. Esther is unbelievably beautiful, exiled, orphaned, and a woman—all possible handicaps in the story's world—but she also is wise and brave. Being Jewish is the immediate danger in the story, but Esther's willingness to declare her Jewishness and outwit Haman's decree saves the Jews. Mordecai is a wise courtier, exiled, having some authority, but less than the villain. Although Mordecai is the object of Haman's wrath against the Jews, it is Esther who does the planning, takes the overt risks, and brings about the ultimate reversal. Ahasuerus is a Great Ruler of the World figure, wielding power over the known world but at a loss with what to do with it. Haman represents self-consumed evil. Descended from the Agagites, traditional enemies of the Benjaminites (see 1 Sam. 15), he is the foil to the Benjaminites Mordecai and Esther. Vashti, Ahasuerus' first queen, is displaced because she stands up for proper decorum, refusing to be made a sexual show-and-tell presentation. Vashti's removal leads to the choice of Esther as queen, based solely on her sexual appearance, but Esther turns out to be as determined as Vashti, so that Vashti's figure foreshadows Esther herself.

The festival of Purim has unknown origins. The name is Akkadian, for "lots." In the story, Haman casts lots to determine a propitious date for the genocide of the Jews. The chosen date ironically turns out to be propitious for the Jews rather than for Haman.

Daniel

In Jewish scripture, Daniel is among the less-important Writings. However, Daniel was considered a prophet by early Christians, so he appears in Christian Bibles as a fourth major prophet, following Ezekiel. The book has two parts: a series of short stories (chaps. 1—6) and a succession of visions concerning empires that are then explained by angelic commentators (7—12). Both parts deal with world empires, YHWH's cosmic rule, and the need for Jews to retain their identity and religion in the face of cultural threats.

The origins of the book are varied. The central figure derives his name from a legendary character, Danil (mentioned in Ezek. 14:14, 20), who appears in the tale of Aqhat on tablets discovered at the ancient city of Ugarit (destroyed in the 1200s B.C.E.). This character is a pious king to whom bad events happen. To this name were attached standard character traits from the biblical short story tradition: wisdom, piety, Judean exile, courtier. The Great Rulers of the World in Daniel 1—6 are an interesting lot. Nebuchadnezzar (Dan. 1—4) is a compilation of three Neo-Babylonian rulers and their reigns: Nabopolassar, Nebuchadnezzar II, and Nabonidus. The historical Belshazzar (Dan. 5) was the heir apparent to Nabonidus but was never king in Babylon, though he did get to play the role while his father lived for ten years in Arabia. Darius the Mede (Dan. 6) is an invented figure combining a Persian royal name with the realm of Media; he plays the parts of both Cyrus the Great and a Greek ruler named Antiochus IV (about whom we shall learn more later).

Although all the book's chapters are nominally set in the Babylonian and Persian/Median courts, the real-life background for some of the stories and all the visions is the reign of Antiochus IV, who attempted to destroy Judaism within Judah (167 B.C.E.). Interestingly, part of the book (2:4—7:28) is in Aramaic and the rest in Hebrew, suggesting that Daniel had more than one author. The Greek edition of Daniel includes two additional stories (chapters 13 and 14), as well as expanded versions of the Aramaic short stories. (For more on these additions, see pp. 255–57.)

The six short stories in chapters 1 to 6 probably were composed as separate tales, but now form a continuous narrative. Jewish exiles are selected by Nebuchadnezzar on the basis of their appearance to stand around in his palace and look impressive. Daniel and his three companions quickly demonstrate the superiority of Judean culture to Babylonian culture and are promoted. Central to the recognition of Daniel by the king is Daniel's divinely given wisdom, ten times greater than all the wisdom of the Babylonian empire. Because Daniel places this wisdom at the service of Nebuchadnezzar, Daniel rises swiftly in the administration. Slowly, Nebuchadnezzar comes to realize that the Judeans' God is in fact the true God and the true ruler of the universe. This happens in three stages. First, God reveals to Daniel the dream of the king, showing that this deity knows secrets, but the king worships *Daniel*. Second, God protects the three friends from death in the furnace, showing that their God is powerful, whereas the king's idol is not, but the king merely treats their God as the replacement for his idol. Third, God dramatically demonstrates that Nebuchadnezzar is king only because and as long as God allows it; the king then understands that God is God and the true universal ruler.

The Belshazzar story (Dan. 5) reveals what happens when the following king, who knows about God but does not believe, refuses to recognize what his father had learned. God removes the kingdom from him and gives it to another. Finally (Dan. 6), the jealousy of others against Daniel's promotions, brought about by Daniel's trust in God, leads them to attempt to destroy Daniel by the proclamation of King Darius the Mede. Darius trusts Daniel but allows himself to be talked into declaring himself the sole divinity. God saves Daniel, and the conspirators are slain in his stead. This last story reflects a situation in which human rulers took for themselves divine status. It almost certainly derives from the Hellenistic Period, probably referring to a ruler named Antiochus IV, who called himself Epiphanes ("[god] manifest").

The revelations to Daniel that appear in chapters 7 to 12 all deal with two topics. First, they describe the succession of human empires. The sole Aramaic vision (Dan. 7) deals with the progression of four empires in the guise of wondrous beasts: Babylonian (lionlike), Median (bearlike), Persian (leopardlike), and Alexander/Ptolemaic (like nothing else). The conquest of Alexander the Great over the Persians is then elaborated in Daniel 8's vision of a ram (Persians and Medes) being destroyed by a goat (Alexander). Finally, Daniel 9—12 presents an extensive symbolic description of the world from Babylonian times to the destruction of Antiochus IV. These predictions are presented in such great detail that the conflict between Ptolemaic and Seleucid rulers (the rulers who inherited the Egyptian and

Syrian parts of Alexander's empire, respectively) can be followed down to 164 B.C.E., just before the death of Antiochus IV, whose demise was different from the one presented in the "visions," suggesting that they were composed just before his death.

The second central motif in these visions is the revealing of God's absolute control over all empires, culminating in a vision of a coming kingdom ruled by God (the "Ancient of Days") and not by humans. (God's coming is foreshadowed in Nebuchadnezzar's first dream, with its image of the stone carved by no hand [2:34].) According to all these visions, the breaking in of God's kingdom will be immediately preceded by terrible suffering for those who remain true to God's Torah. This alludes to events during the reign of Antiochus IV. The visions suggest that the earthly conflict corresponds to a divine battle in which Michael, the protective "angel" of Israel, will prevail.

The purposefully ambiguous numbers presented in the visions for dating coming events have elicited, and continue to elicit, no end of interpretations. The author of Daniel used the seventy years in Jeremiah 25:11–12 and 29:10 as part of the numbering system for the visions, setting precedent for attempts, which began immediately on the appearance of the book of Daniel, to determine the empire correlations of the numbers. Apocalyptic literature in the early church, including the New Testament, rests heavily on these "prophecies" of Daniel.

Resources

John J. Collins. *Daniel with an Introduction to Apocalyptic Literature.* Grand Rapids, Mich.: Eerdmans, 1984.

Marcia Faulk. *Love Lyrics from the Bible: A Translation and Literary Study of The Song of Songs.* Sheffield, U.K.: Almond, 1982.

Michael V. Fox. *Character and Ideology in the Book of Esther.* Columbia: University of South Carolina, 1991.

———. *The Song of Songs and the Ancient Egyptian Love Songs.* Madison: University of Wisconsin, 1985.

Delbert R. Hillers. *Lamentations.* 2d, rev. edition. New York: Doubleday, 1992.

Ellen van Wolde. *Ruth and Naomi.* London: SCM Press, 1997.

16

The Apocrypha

WALTER HARRELSON

Introduction

The collection of books that make up the Christian Bible varies among Christian communities. The thirty-nine books that in time came to comprise the Jewish Bible are *canonical*—that is, accepted as authoritative scripture—for all Christian churches.

But the Septuagint—the Greek translation of the Jewish Scriptures made in Alexandria before the beginning of Christianity—included other Jewish writings. The Jewish community eventually excluded these books from its scriptures, whereas they were retained by most early Christian bodies. These books came to be called *deuterocanonical* ("belonging to the second canon"), by which was meant that they were accepted as authoritative scripture later than the other books of the Old Testament. (See also the Canon Arrangements table, p. 7.)

Protestant reformers of the sixteenth century found some of the teaching of these deuterocanonical writings questionable and removed them from their collection of canonical scripture, although the books were often retained as an appendix to the Bible. Protestants refer to these books as the *Apocrypha* ("hidden writings") and consider them useful for edification, but not authoritative.

The Roman Catholic Church accepted the following books, arranged in the *New Revised Standard Version* of the Bible as follows: Tobit, Judith, the Additions to Esther, Wisdom of Solomon, Ecclesiasticus (also called Sirach or Ben Sira), Baruch, The Letter of Jeremiah (called Baruch 6 in some listings), the Additions to the Book of Daniel (three books: The Prayer of Azariah and the Song of the Three Jews, Susanna, and Bel and the

Dragon), 1 Maccabees, and 2 Maccabees. In an appendix to the Vulgate were placed three other books: 1 Esdras, 2 Esdras, and the Prayer of Manasseh. These three books are found in the Greek and Slavonic Bibles as deuterocanonical, along with Psalm 151 and 3 Maccabees. In an appendix to the Greek Bible is found 4 Maccabees. These eighteen writings make up the texts accepted by some Christian churches as deuterocanonical and therefore authoritative. None of them is scripture for the Jewish community or for Reformed Christian churches.

There were many other Jewish writings known to the Jewish and Christian communities at the time the final collection of scripture was being made. Some of those writings were preserved in the Coptic, Syriac, Armenian, and Ethiopic Bibles, and others were preserved by particular churches as well. Those additional books are referred to today as the Old Testament *Pseudepigrapha* ("writings done under false names"), because many of them were attributed falsely to early biblical personalities (Enoch, Adam, Moses, etc.) as authors.

Many of the deuterocanonical writings and Pseudepigrapha have been discovered, usually in fragmentary form, among the Dead Sea Scrolls. Clearly, a good deal of time passed before the Jewish and the various Christian communities decided exactly which of these later writings, if any, belonged in the Bible. All the writings listed in our Apocrypha are authoritative for some Christians, with the possible exception of 4 Maccabees. These writings are also widely studied and used among many Protestant churches today and are, of course, valuable for all students of the Bible.

Types of Literature

Most of the apocryphal writings date from the years 200 B.C.E. to 100 C.E., a time of great literary activity among various Jewish communities. The original documents of the Dead Sea community were all written during this period, as were the New Testament and the works of the Jewish historian Josephus and the Jewish philosopher Philo. Here is a list of the types of literature found in the collection:

Histories: *1 Maccabees, 2 Maccabees, 1 Esdras*

Short stories and legends: *Tobit, Judith, Additions to Esther, Susanna, Bel and the Dragon, 3 Maccabees, the Letter of Jeremiah (plus the story of the three pages in 1 Esdras)*

Wisdom collections: *Sirach, Wisdom of Solomon, Baruch (in part)*

Apocalypses (visions of the end of the world): *2 Esdras 11—12; 13*

Poems and Prayers: *Baruch (in part), Prayer of Azariah and the Song of the Three Jews, Psalm 151, Prayer of Manasseh*

Philosophical and Theological Reflection: *2 Esdras 3—10 and 4 Maccabees*

In its variety, this collection closely parallels the Hebrew Bible. This should not be surprising, because the stream of literary activity that produced the Old Testament did not, of course, cease to flow when the latest writing found in the Hebrew Bible, the book of Daniel, was completed (about 165 B.C.E.).

Individual Apocryphal Writings

The Book of Tobit

In this romantic account, a wealthy and pious Jew, Tobit, living in Assyrian exile, loses his fortune and his eyesight and regains both through the assistance of his faithful son Tobias and an angel. The book incorporates popular folk themes: rewards for acts of piety extended to the dead, entertaining angels unawares, exorcisms of demons, and perilous journeys that turn out well. It includes a rich collection of folk wisdom and moral guidance (chap. 4), and marvelous prayers for divine aid. In it, God guides the course of history and brings help in crises, but God also counts on human imagination, initiative, and readiness to face dangers and trials.

The book highly praises the virtue of giving alms. This teaching may have prompted Protestant reformers to remove the book from their canon, because the church practice of collecting alms was condemned by the reformers.

The book was written in Hebrew or Aramaic during the second century B.C.E. Fragments of the work were found among the Dead Sea Scrolls, and manuscripts of the book are widespread over the entire early Christian world.

The Book of Judith

Judith is a folk narrative that tells how a pious and wealthy widow named Judith risks her life and honor to save Israel's people and temple from a massive Assyrian army. The author sets the scene near the old city of Shechem (Greek Neapolis, today Nablus), where the town of Bethulia (a fictitious name) and its inhabitants are besieged by the Assyrian general Holofernes (also a fictitious name) as they attempt to block passage of the army on its way to Jerusalem.

The author, a Jewish writer of the early 100s B.C.E., describes the Assyrian army as an invincible force moving westward and then southwest, conquering all before it. Palestine and Transjordan quickly submit and pay tribute. Achior, an Ammonite ally of Assyria, then counsels the Assyrians on how to conquer Israel: They should watch for evidence that the Israelites have betrayed the covenant with their God. Only if the people fall into idolatry or otherwise fail their God will they fall prey to Assyria. But even though it is plain to foreign neighbors that God will protect a faithful Israel, the community's own leaders seem unwilling to believe God's promises of protection and deliverance.

Judith, however, does believe. She attempts to rally Israel's religious and political leaders. When that effort fails, she prepares to bring about the defeat of the enemy herself. Judith is not, like Esther, encouraged by a male to take her stand. She alone in all Bethulia is ready to place her life in God's hands and risk all to save Israel. The story shows what God can and will do through one faithful Jew (Judith's name means "Jewish woman").

Judith enters the camp of Holofernes at the foot of the mountain, while Israel's leaders hide behind Bethulia's walls. Judith leaves the initiative to Holofernes, who is avid to take her into his tent. She emerges with his head in her bag, returns, and displays the head from the walls of the besieged city. The Assyrian forces panic and bolt, only to be cut down by pursuing Israelites. Judith claims no reward for her acts; she has, after all, simply done what a faithful child of the covenant should do.

The story is carefully put together, with a long and detailed beginning and speeches in the manner of boastful Hellenistic oratory. Jerusalem and its temple, at some distance from the battle, loom as the motivation for Judith's bravery. One Jewish woman cares about the land, the city, the temple, the promise. And one faithful woman, in God's service, suffices.

Additions to Esther

The title of the book should read "Greek Esther," because the Greek work is its own story, differing from the Hebrew original at many minor points throughout the text. The additions, however, are Greek Esther's most striking contribution to the tradition. In contrast to the Hebrew book of Esther, which subtly keeps Israel's God in the background and emphasizes the responsibility of human actors for preserving the Jewish community, the Greek book emphasizes that its characters are deeply pious Jews who devoutly trust the God of Israel. In good Hellenistic Greek literary style, Greek Esther presents a heroine who will, like Judith, risk all to uphold God's Torah and ward off danger to the people of the covenant.

In the Hebrew book of Esther, King Ahasuerus of Persia is persuaded by his evil counselor, Haman, to destroy all Jews because, Haman charges, they follow their own laws and are not ready to bow down to the Persian king or his representatives. Meanwhile, Esther has been selected to replace the rebellious Queen Vashti in the Persian court. Her uncle, Mordecai, who has reared Esther, appeals to Esther to intervene with Ahasuerus on behalf of the Jewish people. Esther, with fear and trembling, does so, and the king relents. Mordecai and his people are spared and are permitted to take vengeance on their enemies on the thirteenth and fourteenth days of the month of Adar each year. The name given to this Jewish festival, not found in the laws of Moses, is Purim.

Greek Esther adds background and detail to the Hebrew account. Addition A relates a dream of Mordecai that points to trouble ahead for the Jewish exiles. This addition also gives detail about Mordecai's part in saving the Persian king (here called Artaxerxes the Great) from a palace plot. The event is duly recorded in the Persian annals and will in time save Mordecai's life when he is attacked by his enemy Haman.

The other additions fill out the story, including marvelous prayers of Mordecai and Esther and the proclamations of Ahasuerus concerning the Jews. Addition F brings the Greek story to an end, referring back to and interpreting Mordecai's dream of the two dragons, reported in Addition A. The entire Greek Esther needs to be read as a distinct document, not merely as the Hebrew Esther with some additions.

The Wisdom of Solomon

This Greek document deals with the theme of God's gift of Wisdom (also discussed in Prov. 8 and the apocryphal book of Sirach). According to Proverbs 8, Wisdom was present with God at the creation, looking on and perhaps assisting in the creation. According to Sirach 24, Wisdom, indeed, was a kind of mist that spread out over the entire creation and was identical with God's Torah (law, teaching), the first five books of the Bible. In the Wisdom of Solomon, a first-century B.C.E. author presents Wisdom as "breath of the power of God, /and a pure emanation of the glory of the Almighty" (Wis. 7:25a). This document had an enormous influence on the early Christian community.

According to the author of the Wisdom of Solomon, this quasi-divine gift to the human community has taken residence within the life and history of the Jewish people. The writing traces Israelite history from this vantage point, showing how Wisdom has guided all God's dealings with Israel throughout the centuries until this day.

The Wisdom of Solomon shows the extent to which some Jewish thinking had been influenced by Greek thought. Although thoroughly Jewish, the book makes use of Greek views of the immortality of the soul and uses a number of Greek literary devices. It supplies a bridge between Judaism and the Greek and Roman world, in association with which both Christianity and Judaism develop. The work is quoted or alluded to often in the writings of the New Testament.

Sirach

Also called Ecclesiasticus, The Wisdom of Jesus Son of Sirach, or Ben Sira, this important book from the 100s B.C.E. gives us the lecture notes of a Judean master teacher, preserved and translated by his grandson for the Greek-speaking community of Alexandria. Some of the work exists also in Medieval Hebrew, and portions of it in Hebrew have been found among the Dead Sea Scrolls.

For Sirach, Wisdom was an active, dynamic, female presence with God at the creation, touching the whole of the creation but conferred by God on the people Israel as God's Torah (see Sir. 1; 24). No one but God knows fully the depths of Wisdom's glory. Wisdom is at once hidden to all but God (as in Job 28) and fully available to mortals as God's Torah. The inexhaustible riches of Torah bring wonder to her students.

Sirach's fifty-one chapters are clearly modeled on the book of Proverbs. The "praises of famous men" (no women receive praise) in chapters 44 to 50 is a summary of the heroes of faith like that found in Hebrews 11 in the New Testament. The most notable person praised is the high priest Simon (chap. 50), officiating at the sacrificial altar in Jerusalem with "a garland of priests" surrounding him.

Baruch

The book of Baruch is a composite writing of unknown date, attributed to Jeremiah's scribe Baruch (see Jer. 36). It is therefore a pseudepigraph—that is, a writing falsely attributed to a biblical personality as its author. Whereas Jeremiah 43 places both Jeremiah and Baruch in Egypt, the apocryphal book claims to have been written in Babylon.

The writing has three distinct parts, the first prose and the second two poetic. The prose section (1:1—3:8) contains a lengthy confession of sin, similar to that in Daniel 9, along with instructions for the prayer to be read aloud in Jerusalem at the site of the ruined temple. The second section (3:9—4:4) is a poem on wisdom, similar to Job 28 but identifying wisdom with the Torah. Wisdom is both hidden, inexhaustible in its depths, and utterly explicit, written down for all to see and follow. The third part is a set of prayers to, for, and by Jerusalem/Zion, in the style of texts from Isaiah 40—66, rich, sonorous, and full of hope. The whole work suggests a community under the political control of a foreign power, with some freedom to observe its own laws and customs and hoping for restoration of life and worship in the Holy Land.

However much Israel has sinned against God and brought destruction and exile upon itself, the three parts of Baruch insist, God has not abandoned Israel but is ready to respond to prayers of repentance and a change of heart and life. There is yet a future for God's people, but as they await the day of redemption, they may rightly pray for their foreign rulers. The advice echoes Jeremiah 29, which counsels exiles to build houses, plant vineyards, marry and bear children, and pray for the welfare of the land in which they dwell. The three parts of Baruch were all written in Hebrew, probably during the 100s B.C.E.

The Letter of Jeremiah

This writing, attributed to Jeremiah, picks up a theme found in the early sermons of the prophet Jeremiah: Israel has forsaken the true and living God, the "fountain of living waters," and turned to the worship of idols that are no more than "cracked cisterns that can hold no water" (Jer. 2:13). It does so, however, in a manner reminiscent of one of the later parts of the book of Jeremiah, 10:1–16, a mocking poem on the foolishness of those who worship gods made of human hands. The theme is widespread in the literature of psalms and prophets (see especially Ps. 115; 135; Isa. 44) and is forcefully laid down in Deuteronomy 4, where Moses reminds the community that even at the mountain of revelation they "saw no form" of God. Rather, they heard God's clear and commanding word. Torah provides their guidance; the invisible God shines through its words, its teaching.

No specific date can be determined for the letter. It probably was composed in Hebrew and became a part of the Greek translation of the Jewish Scriptures in the 200s or 100s B.C.E.

Additions to Daniel

The Greek book of Daniel differs strikingly from the Hebrew book, just as Greek Esther differs markedly from Hebrew Esther. Three large additions are found in Greek manuscripts of the book, the first placed in the middle of Daniel 3 and the other two added either at the end of the book of Daniel or in locations that seemed to preserve the chronology of the stories.

The first addition's title, the Prayer of Azariah and the Song of the Three Jews, suggests its contents. It contains Azariah's prayer to God in the fiery furnace into which Nebuchadnezzar has thrown the three Jewish youths for refusing to worship a golden statue. It also reports a song sung by the three young men as they recognize that God has delivered them from the fire through an angelic presence.

Both parts are similar to prayers and praises found elsewhere in the Hebrew Bible and among the Dead Sea Scrolls, and both appear among the Odes that follow the Book of Psalms in many Greek manuscripts of the Old Testament. (These Odes repeat prayers and praises—for instance, prayers from Isaiah 12 and 38—found in other biblical locations.) Azariah's prayer is a lament of a suffering community that cries out for God's help and mercy, acknowledging the community's sin and failings but counting on God once again to deliver them from the enemy's hands. The song of praise and thanksgiving of the three youths has found a continuing place in the liturgical life of the church.

The book of Susanna is a marvelous prose narrative set in Babylonian exile, with its characters drawn from the wealthy section of the Jewish community there. A rich man marries a beautiful and morally upright girl named Susanna. The husband's home is the center of much of the community's public activities, serving as the court of justice, and Susanna is clearly the center of attention there because of her grace and beauty. Two unnamed elders (identified by tradition with the false prophets Ahab and Zedekiah, mentioned in Jer. 29:21–23) render judgment at Susanna's home and secretly lust after the young woman. On one occasion the two of them hide in a household garden where Susanna often rests in the afternoon. They demand that Susanna lie with them; if she refuses, they will say that they found her with a young man. Susanna, trapped, still refuses them. She cries out, alarming the household. The elders tell their lies. On the next day, the elders repeat their false testimony in court. Susanna is condemned to death and led off for execution.

But God "stirred up the holy spirit" of Daniel, here presented as a young man with no official standing. Daniel denounces the community for accepting the testimony of the elders without making inquiries. He separates the elders, finds contradictions in their stories, and exposes their guilt. The elders then suffer the fate that they had planned for Susanna.

Like Esther and Judith, Susanna is both beautiful and virtuous. She is also courageous, faithful to Torah at the risk of her own life and reputation. She denounces the corruption of the judicial process, claims her innocence, and awaits God's help. Daniel is God's instrument in bringing the help, but only in response to Susanna's prior faith and courage.

The young Daniel's skill in discovering the truth has been influential in the development of police and court procedures. Daniel is a prototype as well of the detective hero who makes the imperfect judicial system render justice.

Daniel's detective investigations continue in Bel and the Dragon. The story draws on themes from the Babylonian creation story and, like the Letter of Jeremiah, shows the folly of idol worship. As in the book of Judith, the historical references seem to be deliberately falsified: Cyrus of Persia is the king with whom Daniel deals, but the people and the religious practices are Babylonian.

Three episodes appear in the story. First, Daniel devises a plan to show the king that the huge amounts of food and drink provided daily for the statue of the god Bel are actually eaten by the priests and their families. Daniel spreads ashes on the floor of the temple in the evening. The next day, the footprints of the priests and their families are plain to see.

Next, Daniel destroys a great serpent revered by the people. He feeds it a mixture of pitch, fat, and hair, which causes it to explode. This act, however, is too much for the people. They have Daniel thrown into a den of voracious lions, but Daniel is protected, as in chapter 6 of the Hebrew book of Daniel. The lions do no harm, and Daniel is miraculously fed by the prophet Habakkuk, who is transported from Judea, with food, by an angel. The angel returns Habakkuk to his home, and on the seventh day the king releases Daniel and feeds his enemies to the lions.

All three parts of the story involve food and may have been created for telling at public banquets. They add to the tradition of Daniel as an ingenious and wise servant of God and savior of God's people in exile.

First Maccabees

First Maccabees is a historical work of great importance for the study of the Bible. It was originally written in Hebrew toward the end of the 100s B.C.E. The author copies the style of Samuel and Kings to tell how the Jewish state was restored in the Hasmonean Kingdom, which stemmed from the Maccabean revolt in 168 B.C.E. and endured from 142 to 63 B.C.E. Several of its rulers combined the offices of Ethnarch and high priest, exercising, at least formally, independence of the Seleucid kingdom (formed in the area north and east of Palestine during the breakup of Alexander's empire). This period of independence from foreign rule brought high hopes to many within the Jewish community, although some privileged and favored families no doubt were more comfortable under the occasionally benevolent rule of foreigners. (Jeremiah's advice had been sound: Settling down among foreigners and even praying for the welfare of their rulers had not always been a disaster.)

The spread of Hellenistic culture throughout the entire Middle East following the campaigns of Alexander the Great (332–323 B.C.E.) had brought new literary and cultural riches to the Jewish community but also great temptations. First Maccabees speaks of those temptations: adopting Greek dress, language, and culture; joining in the public sports events; and abandoning the Jewish dietary laws and other requirements of Jewish life.

When the Seleucid ruler Antiochus IV came to the throne in 175 B.C.E., he required worship of state deities and veneration of the ruler. Before long, the temple was profaned; practice of Jewish law was forbidden; and those found with copies of the Torah were put to death. In the town of Modein, Mattathias and his five sons refused to make the required offering to state deities, instead attacking and killing a Seleucid officer. They took to the hills, rallied the people to guerrilla warfare, and won victory after victory. By 165 B.C.E., one of the sons, Judas, was able to reclaim Jerusalem, cleanse the temple, and restore the practice of Judaism. A new festival was added to the Jewish year, Hanukkah, commemorating the rededication of the temple.

First Maccabees ends with John Hyrcanus I, the son of Simon, the last surviving son of Mattathias, firmly established as Ethnarch and high priest of the Jewish state and with fair relations existing between the Jewish people and the Greek kingdom to the north. However, stormy days lay ahead for the independent Jewish state. By 63 B.C.E., Roman forces would exercise political control over the entire area.

Second Maccabees

Second Maccabees covers a shorter period than 1 Maccabees and has a different purpose. The author of 2 Maccabees abridges and recasts an existent historical work written by Jason of Cyrene to demonstrate the value of individual acts of courage and devotion to God. In Greek style, the author addresses readers directly and also has characters deliver long speeches. The narrative vividly details the piety, bravery, and battle skills of Judas and the extraordinary courage of a widow and her seven sons, tortured to death because they will not renounce their faith. The martyr stories from 2 Maccabees 7 were of immense influence in Christian history, literature, and art.

First and Second Maccabees complement each other very well. First Maccabees tells the historical story from the end of the reign of Alexander the Great (323 B.C.E.) until the beginning of the rule of John Hyrcanus I (134 B.C.E.), following biblical literary models. Second Maccabees concentrates on the period of 180–161 B.C.E., providing much detail about the wars of Judas Maccabeus and his final victory, using models of Greek history writing. Both are highly effective in accomplishing their purposes. Our knowledge of the two centuries preceding the birth of Christianity would be much leaner without these writings.

First Esdras

First Esdras probably originated as an alternative version of the canonical book of Ezra, to which were appended some sections from 2 Chronicles (35:1—36:23), Nehemiah (7:38—8:12), and one document not found in the Bible. First Esdras is valuable for textual studies of Ezra and Nehemiah, but its chief literary importance stems from that nonbiblical document—a story of three bodyguards or pages in the court of King Darius of Persia

(521—485 B.C.E.). After a great banquet given by the king, the three pages decide to entertain the king and win honor for themselves by each writing out an answer to the question, What one thing is the strongest in all the world? The three answers are slipped under the pillow of the sleeping king.

The king awakes, has the contest explained to him, and summons all the leaders of Persia and Media to hold court and have the three pages explain their answers publicly. Such a form of entertainment is well known from ancient societies. The distinctive feature of this one is found in the answer of the third page. The first page claims that wine is the strongest thing in the world, a leveler that erases the difference between even the king and the least of his subjects. The second, more diplomatically, argues that the king is the strongest, having at his command all the other strengths of the community. The third contends that women are stronger, for even the king submits to the desires of women. But the third page also affirms that "truth is great, and stronger than all things" (4:35b). Only truth stands untainted in all the earth; all other things are marked by failure, unrighteousness, and lack of integrity. The page closes with the affirmation, "Blessed be the God of truth!" (4:40d).

The story has claimed a place for itself for obvious reasons. The Latin quotation "*magna est veritas, et praevalet*" nicely sums up the message: "Great is truth, and it will prevail." The Hebrew term '*emet*, referring to faithfulness, integrity, and trustworthiness, probably underlies the Greek term used for "truth" in 1 Esdras.

The document cannot be dated with any precision. Because the first-century C.E. historian Josephus quotes from this work rather than from the book of Ezra, we know the writing existed in his time; it may be considerably older.

The Prayer of Manasseh

According to Chronicles, the evil king Manasseh was taken to Babylonia, acknowledged his evil ways, repented, and was then restored to kingship by God. The "prayer of Manasseh" presents itself as the text mentioned in 2 Chronicles 33:18–20, but it was more likely written in the first century B.C.E., in Greek, following the pattern of penitential prayers in the book of Psalms and elsewhere. Some Greek manuscripts include it as one of the Odes (a collection of biblical prayers placed just after the book of Psalms). It is not considered canonical by Roman Catholic and Protestant Christians but is accepted as deuterocanonical by the Greek Orthodox Church. It reflects the picture of God in Exodus 34:6–7: merciful, compassionate, and ready to forgive the people's sins to "the thousandth generation." The Prayer of Manasseh beautifully articulates the hope that such a God of mercy and love will demonstrate that love. The attribution implies that if God was willing to forgive so legendary an evildoer as King Manasseh, later penitents have good reason to hope for the same divine compassion.

Psalm 151

Psalm 151 is a brief poem attributed to King David. It tells of his being chosen over his taller and stronger brothers, of his musical skills, and of his defeat of the giant Goliath. Some Greek manuscripts include it in the book of Psalms. A somewhat longer version that lacks the reference to Goliath appears in Hebrew in a Psalms manuscript among the Dead Sea Scrolls, followed by a fragment of another psalm that does mention David's victory over Goliath. Originally, then, there were two psalms, one telling of David's choice by God over his brothers and of his musical skill and theological wisdom, and the second recounting his victory over the giant. Psalm 151 is deuterocanonical only for the Greek and Slavonic churches, not for Roman Catholic or Protestant Christianity.

Third Maccabees

Despite its title, 3 Maccabees has nothing to do with the Maccabean brothers or their times. It is set in Egypt in the late 200s B.C.E. The Jewish community has enjoyed legal protections for many years. Then the Egyptian king tries to enter the Jerusalem temple. He is prevented from doing so, but he subsequently sets out to destroy the Jewish community, canceling its protected status and trying to annihilate its customs. (Here we can see the associations that prompted the title.) The document then tells of the miraculous sparing of the Jewish community, the king's repentance, and his becoming the guarantor of the safety of Jews in all Egypt.

In the neoclassical style of Greek literature of the Hellenistic period, 3 Maccabees "quotes" many speeches in full. Some, such as the high priest Simon's prayer for God to protect the Jerusalem temple from desecration (2:2–20), are beautifully eloquent. In other places the style is wordy and tedious. The book offers a vivid account of elephants, frenzied by spice-mixed wine, that are ready to trample the Jews to death. But when God's angels confront them, the animals turn back on the Egyptian tormenters (6:16–21).

Third Maccabees dates from the first century B.C.E. Rome was becoming the dominant force in the whole of the eastern Mediterranean world during this time, and the large Jewish community in Egypt was surely imperiled by Roman policy and actions. The book offers encouragement amid unrest and danger, showing God's readiness to intervene on behalf of those who call on the deity in confidence and trust. It suggests that God's angels will protect a faithful people from injustice and violent acts. Although 3 Maccabees appears in many early manuscripts of the Greek Bible, Saint Jerome did not include it in his Latin translation of the Bible. It is, however, deuterocanonical for the Greek and Slavonic churches.

Second Esdras

Several documents in the Bible and the Apocrypha bear the name of Ezra or Esdras, and in the Greek and Latin Bibles there is no uniformity in the names given to works attributed to Ezra. This chapter uses the terminology normally applied when the Apocrypha are published as a separate collection: Ezra is the canonical Ezra; 1 Esdras is the apocryphal Ezra consisting of canonical Ezra and portions of 2 Chronicles and Nehemiah, plus the story of the three pages; 2 Esdras is the work here being discussed.

Second Esdras contains materials from the first, second, and third centuries C.E. The central chapters, 3 to 14, were written in Hebrew (or possibly Aramaic) by a Palestinian Jew toward the end of the first century (this makes them roughly contemporary with the New Testament). Chapters 1 and 2 come from the second century and were written in Greek by an unknown Christian. Chapters 15 and 16 also were written in Greek by an unknown Christian, probably in the third century. Chapters 1 and 2 and 15 and 16 are not found in the Oriental versions of 2 Esdras (Syriac, Armenian, Ethiopic, Arabic).

Chapters 3 to 14 contain four distinct documents, now woven together as a series of seven visions. The first four visions (chaps. 3—10) are a dialogue between Ezra and the interpreting angel Uriel. The last three (chaps. 11—14) are a kind of literature called apocalypse, in which signs are revealed showing that the last days, when all God's purposes will be fulfilled, are at hand. These last three visions involve no interpreting angel; Ezra speaks directly to God, in the manner of Moses, and is answered by God (see chap. 14 in particular).

The last three visions (chaps. 11—14) probably date to the same period from which the first four visions come—near the end of the first century C.E. Chapters 3 to 10, however, have a distinct and powerful purpose, strikingly different from the other visions. Ezra and the angel discuss the pervasive presence of sin and evil in the world and what can be done, if anything, to give sinners another opportunity to repent before eternal damnation becomes their fate. These remarkable chapters present Ezra as a friend of sinners and an intermediary on behalf of sinful Israel.

Chapters 3 to 10 contain eloquent and forceful pleas from Ezra for God to help human beings understand God's dealings with sinners. Surely, the author insists, God does not find it just and right for most of the population of earth to perish for their sins. Could not a better way have been found than for Adam to have sinned and thereby doomed most of his descendants to eternal death? The writing is an eloquent effort at theodicy—that is, a justification of God's ways with humankind. Like Job, the writing leaves the justification in the hands and care of a God whose ways remain a cosmic mystery. But also like Job, 2 Esdras 3—10 offers a hint at how a merciful and forgiving God might prove to be a friend of sinners.

The solution to the question of the fate of evildoers is found in chapters 9 and 10, where Ezra has a vision of a transformed Jerusalem (Zion, "mother of us all" [9:7a]) with massive foundations, in the process of being built, whose extent remains God's own mystery. The author draws on the vision of Zechariah in Zechariah 2:1–12 (2:6–16 in Hebrew), where a man is directed to measure the length and breadth of Jerusalem, only to be called back and the order canceled. Who can know, save God alone, the acreage needed for those whom God will settle in the restored city, the very center of the universe? Isaiah 35 also shows Zion welcoming all the wounded and weary of earth to their true home.

The apocalypses in chapters 11 and 12 and in chapter 13 are directed against the Roman empire for its mistreatment of Israel. They promise that soon God will step in and rescue the embattled people. Ezra's revelations assure the people that God is in firm control of world history. These revelations, however, are intended for the wise; they should not be shared too widely, for the message may elude ordinary folk.

This same distinction between public literature and hidden literature appears in chapter 14, the seventh vision. Here, Ezra's role as the new Moses is underscored. In the exile, we learn, God's revelation through scripture is in danger of complete loss. Ezra prays that God dictate the Torah (here, the entire Hebrew Bible) to him so that he can preserve it for all time. God agrees, sets aside forty days for the revelation, and instructs Ezra to secure scribes and writing tablets. Then God presents a cup of liquid for Ezra to drink, and Ezra dictates, without interruption, ninety-two books. Twenty-two of these are the Hebrew Bible (counted in most Bibles today as thirty-nine books); the others are to be reserved for the wise among the people.

Early Jewish interpretations varied concerning which writings were sacred scriptures and which were not. Writings believed to have been written later than the time of Ezra were finally excluded. The legend in 2 Esdras 14 is probably the source of this understanding.

It may surprise Christians that Ezra appears here as the friend of sinners, because the books of Ezra and Nehemiah portray him as a strict upholder of the letter of the law. However, the two perspectives are compatible. One who really cares about God's demands must care equally about those who fail to measure up to those demands, for God's demands arise out of divine love and mercy and aim to spread love and mercy among all peoples.

Fourth Maccabees

Fourth Maccabees appears in many manuscripts of the Septuagint (the Greek Old Testament) and was probably quite popular in Eastern churches for centuries. It is still valued among Orthodox congregations, who include it today as an appendix to the Greek Bible.

The book, written in Greek at some time between the end of the Hasmonean Period (63 B.C.E.) and the destruction of Jerusalem in 66–70 C.E., is a diatribe—a long, discursive treatment of a subject. The subject? Israel's Torah as the gift through which human beings bring their passions under the sway of inspired reason. The Jewish author has been greatly influenced by Greek philosophy and expresses a basically Stoic outlook. What qualities in the human self are the controlling and dominant ones? Does intellect control, or do the baser emotions control? For the Greek philosophers, of course, a divinely inspired reason (Greek *nous*) must govern. Our author agrees, but that divinely inspired reason is nothing other than the revealed Torah, God's own reason, which can and should govern all human actions.

The author takes from 2 Maccabees the extreme example of the widow and her seven sons, all of whom steadfastly held to their faith despite extreme torture by the Hellenistic enemy. Also included is the story of Eleasar, an elderly and widely respected man (4 Maccabees 5—6) who accepted torture and death rather than give honor to the Seleucid ruler Antiochus IV. The author of 4 Maccabees thus encourages all readers to recognize that passionate commitment to God is itself the product of inspired reason. The Torah is not a set of demands forced on human beings; Torah is a living reality, commanding the union of heart and mind and soul. Thought and piety are partners, for both are inspired by devotion to God's gift of Torah. The author also holds that God accepted the sacrifice of the martyrs as atonement for Israel's sins.

Important Themes in the Apocrypha

The wisdom texts of the Apocrypha contain a theme of critical importance for later Jewish and Christian communities: the place of Wisdom in relation to God. Wisdom embodies the familiar connotations of skill, intelligence, and artistry, but appears more significantly as divine Wisdom, sometimes spoken of as hidden, sometimes as present in the whole of creation, and sometimes as entrusted to Israel in the form of God's gift of

Torah. In Sirach 24, Wisdom is a mist, present at the beginning so that nothing God creates escapes her touch. That theme is elaborated in the Wisdom of Solomon 7: Wisdom is a pure emanation of the divine selfhood that pervades and lives on in all things. Sirach 24 and Baruch 4 identify that same Wisdom with the revealed Word of God, the Torah. Jewish and Christian thinkers will develop this line of thought, relating Wisdom, Word, and Spirit into classical Jewish and Christian theology. Both the Hebrew and Greek terms for wisdom (*hokma* and *sophia*) will also be greatly expanded in meaning in mystical and speculative texts of the Jewish and Christian communities.

Wisdom is not the only important feminine figure in the Apocrypha. These writings also present us with memorable portraits of human women in positions of critical importance for the life of the Jewish community: Esther, Judith, Tobit's wife Anna (falsely accused of theft and more by her husband), Sarah (the bride of Tobit's son Tobias), the martyred widow of 2 Maccabees, and Susanna.

Scattered like gems through the Apocrypha are eloquent prayers and praises. Mordecai's and Esther's prayers in Greek Esther are classics, as is Judith's prayer before she ventures into the camp of Holofernes (Jdt. 9). In the book of Tobit, his son Tobias and Tobias' bride Sarah spend their bridal night in prayer, asking for protection from the demon. An eloquent prayer closes the book of Sirach (chap. 51), and 2 Esdras is full of searching prayers to God on behalf of a sinful world. The prayer of the three young men (in the Additions to Daniel) occupies a prominent place in daily Roman Catholic liturgy.

Some special texts need also to be mentioned. The first occurrence of the assertion that God created the world out of nothing is found in the speech of the martyred widow of 2 Maccabees 7:28. The efficacy of prayers for the dead was affirmed by 2 Maccabees 12:43–45, it seemed. (This text may have led the Protestant reformers to exclude the Apocrypha from their biblical canon.) The immortality of the soul is strongly affirmed in the Wisdom of Solomon 3:1–9, a text often included in liturgical offices for the dead. Tobit's counsel to his son Tobias as the latter prepares to go on a long journey to retrieve funds on deposit with Tobit's kinsman are a remarkably fine summary of Jewish morals and piety.

Both the Jewish and the Christian communities have much to gain by a study of the literature of the Apocrypha. It is fortunate indeed that other Jewish writings are also available today to augment the study of Jewish life, literature, and faith during the period from 200 B.C.E. to 100 C.E. The Old Testament Pseudepigrapha are available in English translation, and so is the literature of the Dead Sea Scrolls.

Resources

James H. Charlesworth. *The Old Testament Pseudepigrapha*. 2 Vols. New York: Doubleday, 1983, 1985.

Florentino Garcia Martinez. *The Dead Sea Scrolls Translated*. Grand Rapids, Mich.: Eerdmans, 1996.

Bruce M. Metzger, *An Introduction to the Apocrypha*. New York: Oxford, 1957.

Bruce M. Metzger and Roland E. Murphy, eds. *The New Oxford Study Bible*. NRSV ed. New York: Oxford University Press, 1991.

George W. E. Nickelsburg. *Jewish Literature between the Bible and the Mishnah*. Philadelphia: Fortress Press, 1981.

Geza Vermes. *The Dead Sea Scrolls in English*. 3d ed. London: Penguin, 1990.

Glossary

Ammon—A small kingdom located east of the Jordan River, in what is today Jordan.

Apocalypse—Greek for "revelation." A literary form, typically using very vivid imagery, that reports a vision or angelic message concerning the impending end of history (see Apocalyptic). The book of Revelation is sometimes referred to as the Apocalypse.

Apocalyptic—A theological worldview, associated with the literary genre of apocalypse, that sees present history as hopelessly evil and looks forward to a radical intervention in which God will punish evildoers, reward the faithful, and recreate earth in a way conforming to God's will.

Apocrypha—Greek for "hidden things." A Protestant term for the deuterocanonical books of the Roman Catholic and Orthodox canons (see pp. 7 and 249–50).

Aram—A small kingdom located north of Israel in the approximate region of modern-day Syria.

B.C.E.—"Before the Common Era," a commonly used alternative for B.C. (see p. 10).

Book of the Twelve—A term for the Minor Prophets as a unit.

Canaan—The geographical region lying between the Jordan River, the Dead Sea, and the Mediterranean Sea.

Canonical—Belonging to a particular religious community's authoritative body of scripture. (See also Deuterocanonical and pp. 249–50.)

Canonical criticism—A form of biblical scholarship that attempts to understand specific texts in the larger context of the biblical canon. One school of canon criticism, associated especially with Brevard S. Childs, emphasizes the final form of the canon. Another, associated especially with James A. Sanders, focuses on the interactions between traditions as the canon developed.

C.E.—"Common Era," a commonly used alternative for A.D. (see p. 10).

Dead Sea Scrolls—Ancient Jewish copies of biblical books and other documents (copied or written between the last part of the third century B.C.E. and the mid-first century C.E.) found in caves near Qumran on the Dead Sea.

Decalogue—Greek for "ten words," a term for the Ten Commandments.

Deuterocanonical—Describes books that belong to a particular Christian community's authoritative Old Testament but are not part of the Jewish Bible (see pp. 249–50).

Deutero-Isaiah—Isaiah 40—55, thought by most critical scholars to have been written around the time of Cyrus of Persia (sometime around 538 B.C.E.). Also called Second Isaiah.

Deuteronomistic History—A historical work comprised of Joshua, Judges, 1 and 2 Samuel, and 1 and 2 Kings (equivalent in scope to the Former Prophets), showing how the principles enunciated in Deuteronomy worked out in the period from the tribes' entry into Canaan to the Babylonian exile (see pp. 79–80 and 97–98).

Diaspora—Greek for "scattering." The spread of Jewish communities into countries outside of Judea, or, collectively, the Jews living in such communities.

Divided Monarchy—The period from Solomon's death to the fall of Samaria in 721 B.C.E..

Edom—A small kingdom located south of Moab, east of the valley that runs between the Gulf of Aqaba and the Dead Sea, in what is today Jordan.

Exile—The period from the deportations of elite Judeans to Babylon in 597 and 587–586 B.C.E. to Cyrus's proclamation in 538, which permitted them to return to Jerusalem.

First Isaiah—Isaiah 1—39 or, more specifically, the parts thereof that are attributed to Isaiah of Jerusalem.

First Temple Period—The time from Solomon's reign to the fall of Jerusalem in 586 B.C.E.

Former Prophets—A Jewish canonical subdivision containing the books of Joshua, Judges, 1 and 2 Samuel, and 1 and 2 Kings. (The Jewish canon places Ruth among the writings.)

Hellenistic Period—The period following Alexander the Great's appropriation of Judea in 331 B.C.E. Some writers end the period when Judea becomes independent under the Hasmoneans in 167 B.C.E.; some end it when Roman rule begins in 37 B.C.E.; and some stress the continuation of Hellenistic (cosmopolitan Greek) influence even under Roman rule.

Hyksos—An Asiatic people who conquered and ruled Egypt in the 1600s and 1500s B.C.E.

Judah, Judea—The territory governed from Jerusalem in the post-Solomonic First Temple Period and Hellenistic Period, respectively.

Latter Prophets—A Jewish canonical subdivision containing Isaiah, Jeremiah, Ezekiel, and the Minor Prophets. (The Jewish canon places Daniel among the Writings.)

LXX—see Septuagint.

Masoretic Text (MT)—A Hebrew Bible text produced early in the Middle Ages by Jewish scholars who consulted differing manuscripts in the process of compiling an authoritative text for each book.

Minor Prophets—The twelve short prophetic books from Hosea through Malachi.

Moab—A small kingdom located east of the Dead Sea, in what is today Jordan.

MT—see Masoretic Text.

Nubia—A kingdom located just south of ancient Egypt in what is now southernmost Egypt and northern Sudan.

Parallelism—The pairing of lines and elements in biblical poetry, especially when the paired elements have similar meanings, but also used to describe contrasting and complementary line structures.

Pentateuch—Latin for "five books." A scholarly term for the first five books of the Bible, Genesis through Deuteronomy.

Persian Period—The period in which Judah was incorporated into the Persian Empire, 539–331 B.C.E.

Philistines—Sea Peoples who settled the southern Mediterranean coast of Palestine in the 1100s B.C.E.

Phoenicia—A group of trading cities on the eastern Mediterranean coast between Israel and Aram, famous for sea-faring skills, economic power, and production of a brilliant purple dye.

Psalter—A collection of psalms. The biblical book of Psalms is often referred to as the Psalter.

Pseudepigrapha—Greek for "writings under false names." A general term for ancient Jewish and Christian religious writings, many attributed to ancient biblical personalities, which were revered and have been preserved but are not canonical.

Reader response criticism—A form of biblical scholarship that focuses on understanding texts from the point of view of how a reader in a particular cultural context would understand the words, rather than emphasizing the author's intentions.

Redaction criticism—A form of biblical scholarship that focuses on the editing ("redaction") various biblical books are thought to have undergone.

Satan—A Hebrew word meaning "adversary." The First Testament normally speaks of "the satan," suggesting that the term is a title or description rather than a name (see pp. 224–26).

Sea Peoples—Aegean peoples who attacked the Hittite Empire, Syria, Palestine, and Egypt beginning in the 1200s B.C.E. The Philistines were descended from the Sea Peoples.

Second Isaiah—See Deutero-Isaiah.

Second Temple Period—The period from the Second Temple's dedication in 515 B.C.E. to its destruction by the Romans in 70 C.E. Sometimes, more loosely, the whole period from Cyrus' edict in 539 B.C.E. to the destruction of the Second Temple.

Septuagint (LXX)—An ancient Greek translation of the Hebrew Bible. In some cases, it seems to preserve editions of Hebrew Bible books that are older or different from those represented in the Masoretic Text. In addition to the books of the Hebrew Bible, LXX collections often included additional Jewish writings (the Apocrypha, discussed in chap. 16). This enlarged collection became the Old Testament of the early Christian church.

Sheol—The Hebrew term for an underworld. It was not a place of punishment or "life after death," but simply a location where dead souls languished. Psalms often uses "Sheol" as a synonym for death or the grave.

Superscription—Latin for "written above." A heading or title inserted in the biblical text by ancient editors at the top of a psalm, book, or section.

Third Isaiah—Isaiah 56—66, understood as coming from the Second Temple Period.

Torah—A Hebrew word meaning "teaching" or "instruction," although it is more commonly translated "law." Usually refers to the Pentateuch but can also refer to God's teaching in a larger sense.

Ugarit—An ancient city in Syria that was destroyed by the Sea Peoples, important to biblical studies because of the many religious texts found in its ruins.

United Monarchy—The period in which Judah and Israel were united, first under Saul's rule, then under David and Solomon.

Writing Prophets—see Latter Prophets.

Writings—The third division of the Jewish canon, containing Psalms, Proverbs, Job, the Song of Solomon, Ruth, Lamentations, Ecclesiastes, Esther, Daniel, Ezra–Nehemiah, and 1 and 2 Chronicles.

Yehud—Name of the district governed from Jerusalem in the Persian Period.

YHWH—The consonants of God's proper name, often rendered in English translation as "the LORD" (see pp. 11–12).

Index of Topics

LaVergne, TN USA
15 February 2010
173071LV00004BA/2/P